Hangover

to

Jesus

By Gerald J. Zgabay Jr.

Acknowledgments

First and foremost, I want to dedicate this book to my wife, Tabby. Without her grace, unconditional love and commitment, I would not be the man I am today.

I would like to honor my parents, Gerald Sr. and Karen, for the hard, loving, and selfless decisions and sacrifices they had to make as they guided our family to a place of faith and love. Thank you both for all you have done for me and our family. I am forever grateful. I love you both very much.

Also, I would like to honor my in-laws Bruce and Kathryn who taught me how to follow my God-given dreams. Thank you for encouraging my faith journey and showing me who Christ is through unconditional love. I love you both.

Finally, I want thank Janice Jackson for her unconditional, graceful discipleship in my life as she led by setting an example of how to live out faith. Cliff Wilson for giving one "hell" of a message and sharing the truth of Jesus Christ not only in word but by his obedience. And Melodee, who listened to God when he told her to pick up a strange hitchhiker in Del Rio; by simply giving me a ride you put me on a path to my salvation.

Prologue

The early morning air is thick with mist hitting my face as I drive down the rural farm-to-market road with my windows down, hanging my head out periodically, trying to stay awake after a long night of partying. Lighting a cigarette, I take the curves by cutting across the lanes out of laziness and impatience, trying to make my trip quicker. As I approach the street leading to my house, I throw my truck into neutral attempting to diminish the sound of my engine by coasting into my driveway. With extreme concentration I open my truck door and close it without making a sound. Now that is talent, I think to myself with pride! I secure my key for the house door so that I do not have to fumble through clanging keys.

When I open the door to the kitchen, I am welcomed by the aroma of coffee brewing; that means it is at least 4:30 a.m. Dad always starts his coffee early and lies down for a few more minutes before heading out to work. I know now that I am busted. To make matters worse, as I round the dinner table to go to my bedroom, I am welcomed by praying Jesus. This is a picture of Jesus praying on a rock, staring up at a light shining down on him. Jesus, of course, is a perfectly groomed white man with long, flowing hair. There is nothing Middle Eastern looking, or anything that would point to living in the wilderness like a nomad about this praying Jesus who has been through so much with me.

1

Many families have knickknacks throughout their homes that have some sort of significance to someone in the family — you know, like a snow globe on a shelf to remind them of a great vacation spot, or a figurine that belongs to a special loved one. Whatever it might be, the purpose of these items is to remind the family, or a member of the family, of times of joy, love, happiness, or even pain and sorrow they have experienced. My family is no different. I can, even now, picture in my head the same old shelf filled with knickknacks from our family's past, including a few newer pieces as grandchildren have been born and add to the family legacy. The praying Jesus picture has traveled with Mom and Dad, through several moves, for over thirty years! If you saw the picture, you would think, *"Why do they keep it?"* The truth is that anything with a story tied to it, no matter what it is, serves as an important part of history and is in some cases very valuable. These items are commonly referred to as family heirlooms. These are often coveted because of what they represent — family wealth, history, or memories.

My mom, always looking for a deal, strolled into the local Walmart with her money-saving coupons. She probably went in to get a few household items but walked out with a basketful, including a portrait of praying Jesus. Who would have thought that my mom's ability to find a bargain at Walmart would create a family heirloom, worth nothing of monetary value but having symbolic value that speaks through generations? In 1980 my parents were living in Rockdale, a small central Texas town. This was the place where restoration began, and I believe that restoration began with my mom's purchase of the cheap praying Jesus picture that hung over the dinner table for years to come. What she didn't realize was that this picture would become a cornerstone in every home we would live in.

Praying Jesus served as a continual reminder. When I was a child, and throughout my teenage years, it served as a reminder of a judgment that was constantly upon me. This feeling or belief concerning the Jesus portrait was born out of a poor spiritual upbringing that included a mixture of Catholic religion, conflicting teachings, and contradicting leadership from family and friends. I would not discover the true meaning behind this picture until later in my life.

To know a person— to truly know a person — you must know where they have been. Why a person struggles, succeeds or fails can, in most cases, be directed back to where they have been. What was their family life like? Did they have a family, and if so, what were the parents' patterns and practices? What were the beliefs of the family? Was there some type of abuse whether verbal, physical, or emotional? Were there challenges that shaped determination, passion, or addictions? To know me is to know about the praying Jesus picture and the influence that this simple image has had throughout my life. It tells a story through its constant presence, hanging on walls during happy times, sad times and angry times.

My earliest childhood memories are of sitting next to my sister beneath a dining room table hiding from the yelling and arguing. When I was around six years old, my dad was a raging alcoholic with a temper accompanied by yelling and anger. On the other hand, he has always been a hardworking man who did whatever he could to supply the essentials and to support the family financially. We never went without anything because of my dad's strong work ethic. He has been in the oil business for over thirty-five years, starting when he was a young teenager. He exhibits professional traits such as great pride in, dedication to, and respect for his work that are sadly dwindling in the "microwave" society that we have all grown accustomed to. I remember riding on my dad's lap while he drove workover rigs to and from oil locations. Sitting with my dad, I was drawn to the level of respect and admiration he was given, wanting to work alongside him because of the respect he gave people who worked hard. To this day, I still like to stand with my dad because he demands respect in a way that draws you into his presence.

However, a shadow also accompanies him: his addictive personality. His past is covered with heartache and pain from a childhood in which his parents passed away too early. My dad was two years old when his mother was hospitalized with leukemia; she passed away when he was nine. Even though he never got to know her, the pain of losing his mother cut deep. His father passed away when he was eighteen years old without their ever really getting to know each other. My dad says it was because their lives always seemed to be torn apart by pain.

He has a great deal of pride because he has made his own way through hard work and determination, not taking handouts. However, when these traits are not properly managed, it results in privately dealing with heartache or pain in the same ways he was shown by his father.

My mom is the definition of a praying woman. Even though we were not active churchgoers—and we didn't have an intimate relationship with God—Mom knew of God. She was baptized on the same day as her father, Ernest. Eventually a nasty split in the same church in which they dedicated their lives to God wounded her and her family's opinion of the church, but her experience of seeing her father being baptized alongside her would stay with her. She knew there was a power and importance to God. My mom was in and out of the workforce, really only working when needed to help support the family. She attempted to shelter us from the evil of the world — the same evil that she had experienced firsthand through molestation and rape in her formative years. She had an incredible self-appointed duty of protecting her children. During our childhood, it was Mom who would defend, protect and do whatever it took to alleviate the fear, anger or sadness from my dad's rages. When most would have given up, she remained dedicated to my dad. Even through the thick of his struggles she stood right by his side. Mom's dedication to my dad came from a past sprinkled with men in her life who had failed her. Dad was the strong man she needed. Even through the tough times in their marriage, they loved each other-and were destined to be together. One lost motherly compassion all too early in life, and the other was hurt badly by the men in her life. They needed each other. Even with all the baggage of emotions, pain and anger they remain married to this day, for over thirty years.

If you were to meet my parents today you would not believe the stories of struggle and pain caused by addiction, but that is where the praying Jesus picture comes into play. To many, this is an outdated picture, and concerning Jesus' skin color, I'm sure it is. It can be seen in many Catholic families' homes, but this praying Jesus picture, this reminder, serves as a sign of where we have come from as a family and who is responsible for the restoration of our family. All my mom's prayers and crying out to the Lord to help my dad and protect her children were all lifted up to Jesus. The praying Jesus picture reveals the truth that a man with much pride still needs a savior. Praying Jesus represents the love that God has for His children.

In Ephesians 2, Paul disregards any of our own abilities to earn God's love. He reiterates that God's love is a free gift and is gracefully given in His faithfulness to the covenant promises made to Abraham, Isaac, and to Jacob (Deut. 6:10, 7:7–8, The Message). My dad had to get to a point where he gave up his own abilities to free himself from the bondage of addiction. My mom had already given up trying to fix the situation herself. She was giving it all to God. Even to this day, I can still remember her cries and sobs coming from behind closed doors. Then she would present herself as strong and in control, consoling her children with watery eyes and dried tear tracks on her face. My dad would conclude that he was going to lose everything if he did not overcome his addictions. This conclusion would come by way of a night spent in jail and several nights where my mom made tough decisions to take us out of a potentially dangerous situation. These hard moments in their marriage would start the restoration process, but it would not be an overnight fix.

Like many alcoholic or drug-afflicted families, we attended family counseling. I do not remember much, but I do remember that we went as a family and some extremely compassionate people were there. All through my childhood, teens, and part of my adult life I believed that this family counseling was what healed our family. While it definitely played a part, it was not until my dad made the decision to change, to experience *real change*, that true healing and restoration began to happen. My dad's moment of real change came to him in the way of God delivering a message, but before he received this message, he was in a place of total brokenness. That message would come on October 8, 1985, following a failed suicide attempt. After an eighteen-year battle with alcohol, my dad reached his bottom. Realizing the pain that he was inflicting on his family, the same pain that he had experienced throughout his life, he made a choice that would alter our family's legacy forever. This particular night he was at home alone, drinking whiskey. He loaded a .32-caliber pistol with one bullet. While crying out to the Lord, he stuck the pistol in his mouth and pulled the trigger until he passed out. When he woke up the next morning he realized something was different. He opened the chamber of the pistol to find the bullet with an indention in the center of it; it had misfired. At that moment, my dad recalls, "It's like the Lord was saying: 'I'm not through with you yet, and you finally reached the place in your life I want you to be.'" That place is a reckless abandonment that leaves us screaming out to God and not leaning on ourselves or the idols in our world. From that moment on, he quit drinking and began to start the restoration process with his family. He still has that bullet to this day, and I keep the .32-caliber pistol to serve as a reminder of the choice my dad made. It reveals how far a man has to fall to be totally broken, to realize that God demands obedience and how one choice can change the course of a family for generations.

To know the importance of one's convictions, passions, and desires, you must know where they have been and what they have gone through. The portrait of Jesus hanging over my family's dinner table, the bullet my dad holds close to him, the .32-caliber pistol I now keep in my home, these things signify the presence of Jesus Christ in my life.

These simple items play an important role, just as the stones in Joshua chapter 4 did. Joshua was Moses' successor and was assigned the daunting task of leading the team of priests over the Jordan River while carrying the Ark of the Covenant. The Ark of the Covenant plays a prominent role in Joshua's life, not to mention Israel's journey as a people. It signifies the presence of God, His covenant with His people, His commitment to His promises and the consequent obligation of Israel (Josh. 3:3). When Joshua escorted the group of priests carrying the Ark of the Covenant, I am sure it was a life-changing moment for all present. When the priests arrived at the Jordan River and dipped their toes in the water's edge, the river stopped flowing from upstream; the water rose up like a dam (Josh. 3:14–16). This had to be a wild moment. Yes, Joshua was told this would happen, but how many times are we caught off guard or surprised when God *actually* shows up? It is an amazing, scary, and awe-inspiring moment. God knows that one huge flaw of humans is that we quickly forget His promises and how he operates in our lives whether we acknowledge it or not. This was the reason God directed Joshua to gather stones (Josh. 4). Even though the people of Israel had been brought through the wilderness by God, had been supplied with everything they needed, and had been disciplined and blessed in difficult moments, they still needed a reminder (Deut. 8:1–20). These stones, these insignificant rocks, were placed as a sign. Joshua says when your children ask what these stones mean, you will tell them the Lord showed up and created a way.

To this day, my parents hang that portrait of Jesus kneeling on that rock in every house they have moved to. The difference is that now I know why Jesus is kneeling. He was there in the desert of our family history, disciplining us with trials and providing blessings. See, praying Jesus is not just some corny, stereotypical American portrait of Jesus—it is a sign, a point of reference. It reveals that a family was held together only by the grace of God and the power of prayer. The bullet my dad has tucked away reveals a decision to step up and lead his family. The pistol displays the ripple effect of a praying woman who trusted God, even to the point of almost losing her husband to save him. When my son sees that picture of praying Jesus, I pray that he will know that his life is still being impacted by the choice my dad made to put that pistol in his mouth in an act of disobedience and desperation, only to be radically changed by the one true God, so that generations would be forced to look to the cross and understand that God changed a man's heart through his desperation.

2

For most of my childhood, we lived in a small town of around five hundred people about forty miles west of Bryan–College Station, which is of course home of the Fightin' Texas Aggies. For all of you who just yelled out, "Whoop," you have just proven the cult-like status of this iconic institution and the reason our family rooted for the hated Texas Longhorns in Austin. My dad is not the biggest football fan, but even he hated those stinking Ags and would always watch the Lone Star Showdown between the rivals. My sister chose to be the "black sheep" and would consistently request anything with a Texas A&M logo on it every Christmas. My parents would reluctantly purchase these items, all in the name of love! The good thing was that my sister would lose all creditability concerning football when she started asking for Miami Dolphin stuff. I remember a time when I quickly scorned her for her misguided ways concerning football and that she could not even name any of the Miami Dolphins. I quickly realized that it was not the football she was interested in; it was actually the love of dolphins. I am still not sure where the whole Aggie thing came from, but I am sure it was her way of rebelling at an early age. Prayers would be answered later in life, and my brother-in-law would set her straight. I am proud to say she is part of a happy Texas Longhorn fan base, but with the good came bad: my brother-in-law is a stinking Texas Rangers fan!

Not only did we back the Texas Longhorns, but my mom's side of the family were raging Houston Oilers fans. When I say raging, I mean every adjective possible to define intense, raging fan. My initial exposure to Houston Oilers football was walking up to my aunt's house, hearing the screaming and obscenities bellowing out from their home. If you had been a passerby at the time, you would have thought that some major domestic violence was taking place maybe even a showdown of rival gangs. But it was just a house full of my relatives screaming at Warren Moon to complete a _ _ pass! My grandpa was the biggest Houston Oilers fan. When I saw him, with his permanent injury from his time serving in the military, lift himself up to scream passionately at the team he loved, it somehow caused me to want to experience that same passion. This exposure would shape my entire sports perspective. I would start to emulate the players of the Oilers. Trying to throw like Warren Moon, catch the ball while my toes would slide to stay inbounds like Haywood Jeffires, imitating the bone-crushing hits Drew Hill would welcome just to have the chance to bounce up as if they didn't even phase him, and, of course, trying to practice the oh-so-important touchdown celebration by Ernest Givins—the electric slide. By the way, I was good at the electric slide, but, sadly, not a lot of people witnessed this because of a lack of actual in-game touchdowns!

My earlier exposure to this intense interaction with football would shape my dedication to those teams. When I was seven or eight years old I really did not care either way, but being exposed to the passion and the emotional roller coaster of Houston Oilers football resulted in my being a Houston fan for life. Even when the team sold and moved to Tennessee, I would still hold out hope for a team to return to Houston. Where does this type of dedication come from? Is it really about the team or the game of football? Why do fans pile into stadiums rain or shine, dragging their children close at hand? Why do people completely rearrange their schedules to accommodate a football game and insist that everyone pile into a room or bar to watch? Everyone's level of exposure is different. These die-hard fans are born out of an exposure that they received from a father, brother, grandfather, or anyone they respect that revealed a passion, a sense of purpose, or a level of acceptance. When I started to wear the colors of the teams my family supported, I felt a level of acceptance; I would request team-logoed items just to feel that level of acceptance. It worked both ways, especially living in an Aggie suburb and rooting for the hated Longhorns. I liked the attention I received when I walked into a place that was 90 percent Aggie fans because, in my mind, I was a part of something special and unique. Not just following what was socially acceptable or safe.

Exposure is the state of being in contact with something. My exposure limits would not remain as trivial as sports team alliances but instead would evolve because of a simple choice to look. When I was around eleven or twelve years old, I caught my first glance at a fully nude woman in a magazine known worldwide, called *Hustler*. My friend at the time, who we will call Wayne, had an awesome pad. His parents were considerably older than mine and I remember thinking at one point that his parents were actually his grandparents. They may have been his parents, but they treated him like a stereotyped set of grandparents would treat their grandchildren. He had everything! He was an only child and had a couple of rooms in his house dedicated just to stuff that kept him busy. The coolest part of this setup was that his dad owned and operated a mechanic shop and junkyard. We were both big fans of the Michael J. Fox *Back to the Future* movie series, and we retrofitted an old, wrecked Winnebago into a time machine. We were always in character, too. I was Marty McFly because I had brown hair and no lab coat. Wayne was always the wide-eyed scientist Emmett Brown, or "Doc," as he was better known, because he had a lab coat and was very fair-skinned with blond hair that was almost white. He also had a scientist kit with beakers and Bunsen burners, and he technically owned the Winnebago! Wayne would even use the famous movie quote, "Great Scott!" as he ran around in a crazy fashion when a problem would arise on one of our time-traveling adventures. We even constructed the all-important flux capacitor. The Winnebago became our little escape from the world. Wayne struggled in his relationship with his parents in many ways due to the drastic age difference. He took advantage of their being naïve about current events and the overall pop culture growing around them. His parents had an old-school, *Leave It to Beaver*-type mentality toward parenting and life. He was also kind of an outcast in school, and I felt like an outcast emotionally; we were very much like the characters we played out. The friendship didn't make sense to anyone else but us.

One particular day, we ran across his dad's secret stash of *Hustler* magazines. *Hustler* magazine is a hardcore pornography magazine that was world renowned for crusades of pictorial hardcore porn in the early 1970s. Larry Flynt, the creator of *Hustler*, would singlehandedly revolutionize the porn industry with his powerful push for the evolution of porn. When Wayne and I found these magazines, that moment would create a desire that was not there before. I can almost remember his look when he was exposed to the images on the pages, and I am sure that I had a similar look. The only way to describe this moment is that our eyes were opened, and we knew something was different (Gen. 3:7, Holman Christian Standard Bible (HCSB)). It was as if we had picked an apple right off the tree in the Garden of Eden. When I was exposed to that *Hustler* magazine, something changed.

All sorts of chemical reactions occur through a neurochemical called dopamine, which is created by the brain to help control how the brain works. The ventral tegmental area of the brain sends out a continual dose of dopamine to the nucleus accumbens, prefrontal cortex, and amygdala (Gross, C. and Luff, S. *Pure Eyes*, Baker, 2010). In sum, emotions, surroundings, atmosphere, and even textures create a curiosity and desire. The images we were exposed to were bad, and we knew it. It was taking a bit of forbidden fruit. It was wrong but tasted so good. We were both told by our parents at some point that this was bad, and when our parents would cover our eyes or direct us to turn away during certain parts of movies, we knew they didn't want us to see, but why? Why was it okay for them to see but not me? When Eve was approached in Genesis 3:2 (HCSB) and asked by the serpent, "Did God actually say you shall not eat of any tree in the garden?" the seed of doubt was planted. I can remember a brief moment when I met Wayne's eyes as we looked at the *Hustler* magazine. I would like to think that we both knew this was a game changer, but the reality was that we knew it was wrong[7] and we liked it. When I saw these images of nude women strategically placed on the fully colored pages as if they were looking right at me, inviting me into something that I had no understanding of, I felt an intense, euphoric rush that made me want more. It was as if the earth stopped spinning and it was all about me. The serpent for Eve was Satan, who did nothing but emphasize God's prohibition and not His provision, reminding her of all that God had said not to do instead of all that God had provided her. Satan reduced God's commands to a question, casting doubt upon God's sincerity, defaming His motives and denying the truthfulness of His threat of death. In Genesis 3:3 (HCSB), her statement is like the statement I said to myself in that moment of battling with what was prohibited and what was allowed. Eve reiterates to herself, as if she is questioning, "But God said 'You shall not eat of the fruit of the tree that is in the midst of the garden neither shall you touch it, or you will die?'" In that moment of looking at those provocative images, I was seeing my mother's hand over my eyes, thinking to myself, this is wrong. In that moment, however, it did not feel wrong. Eve was told by Satan that "you will not die" because God knows the truth will be revealed to you that will make you like God; I was approached with the same state of mind. It suddenly made sense to me why the men in my life would do double-takes and stare at women with certain physical features that were deemed attractive by the masses. In reality, this just set the example of how attraction can be corrupted when driven only by sexual lust.

In my mind it was as if my mother did not want me to enjoy this knowledge, so I took a big bite of this "fruit." What Wayne and I didn't realize is that our innocent world of *Back to the Future* adventures was over, and our consciences would condemn us into a destructive cycle where we would assert our own autonomy.

This isn't some modern-day problem brought on by the growing accessibility to pornography or the growing media channels or an overly obsessed sexually acceptant culture. The root problem is countless men disengaged and drifting; men are so caught up in their own allures of a dark, seductive culture that they in fact have led their own selves and their families recklessly. My father is a good man, and he instilled great moral and character traits by exhibiting an example of good ethics, respect, and hard work. His struggles with his own addictions and relationship with God would overflow into my life.

Now, don't misunderstand me as saying that my faults fall solely on my father. I am simply laying out the groundwork for how generational sins are created. My dad inherited much more than a last name from his father. Along with the hardworking, respectful mentality that he was taught, he also inherited the bondage of his father's sins. The lack of unconditional love, a love that doesn't have to be earned or tallied, is ground zero, or the cornerstone, of what men in my family yearned for the most, yet never received. This is something that has been taught and exhibited by each man in each generation. We measured results in ourselves by seeking our father's love and reciting the phrase, "Dad will love me if. …" This is a dangerous phrase and mentality to adopt, one that ultimately results in feeling that we as children are unable to earn our father's love because, unbeknownst to the father, he has yoked his children with a heavy burden of earning acceptance. This heavy yoke of earning acceptance is equated to God's love because the father is the example and source of leadership and authority for children. If the father is always absent, then children will feel as if God is never there. If the father measures by results, then children can never be good enough for God. If the father always corrects, criticizes, or points out the wrongs in their children, then they will feel unaccepted because God is always pointing out the wrongs. The list goes on and on. Personally, when I ran across images of a beautiful woman on the pages of *Hustler* in a mechanic's garage, she was very accepting and inviting, and it was as if the serpent whispered in my ear, telling me the lies that I would never measure up to my parents' expectations, teacher's expectations, or the expectations of anyone. Of course, at twelve years old, I was processing thoughts in an immature state of mind, but the Bible never clarifies how old Adam and Eve were. Jesus repeats several times throughout his ministry to have faith as a child. Well, for me, there is a flip side. We always equate faith with God, but we can also have faith in Satan and his promises of immediate, gratifying relief from the hurt and pain of the world. However, any relief found in this way is ultimately followed by more areas of hurt and pain. Satan promises one thing, but in the end fills our lives with shame, frustration, and anger so that we become unable to be vulnerable and experience love. This deceiver entices and invites us to pursue what we were not created for. That day at Wayne's house, in his dad's garage, I decided to have more faith in Satan because I was hurting, and I wanted to feel accepted. Those eyes on the pages of *Hustler* accepted me for who I was; pornography would become my bible. That Winnebago that was used for innocent reenactments of Marty's and Doc's adventures would become a temple of worship that would strengthen the sin of lust in our lives—making idol worship.

One commandment is sometimes overlooked or just plain chalked up as not relevant for modern times, but it remains true more than ever in the midst of struggle. It is in Exodus 20, and it is commandment number 4: "Do not make an idol for yourself, whether in the shape of anything in the heavens above or on the earth below or in the waves under the earth." One very important part of that commandment is the word *idol*. An idol is an image or representation of a god used as an object of worship. Worship is something or someone that you give extravagant respect, admiration, or devotion to. There is a second part of Exodus 20:4–5 that doesn't always come out when speaking about the commandments: "I the Lord your God am a jealous God, punishing the children for the father's sin to the third and fourth generations of those who hate me" (Exodus 20:5). My father's idol of addiction and man's approval would be passed on to me. People might read that and think that God is vindictive, but, no, he is just simply disciplining. God finishes up the fourth commandment with this last phrase: "But showing faithful love to a thousand generations of those who love Me and keep my commandments." God is love, but God is also just. Generations can be destroyed by the bondage of sin inherited from fathers, or generations can be restored with the inheritance of a real, intimate, mature relationship with God that is learned only through living examples by fathers.

The lack of Christian leadership in my life would result in my being easily lured into a world of addiction and a burning desire to be accepted. I devoted time to images of women in various sexual poses and positions, making them my idol and the object of my affection. It was a "god" that fed me immediately, easily, and secretly. Is this my father's fault? No. However, his struggles would become mine. My mom and dad did lay the groundwork for revival in our family by making some very difficult decisions to make drastic changes in their own lives in regard to marriage, socializing, and their environment. What God is pointing out in Scripture is this simple fact: if you look to the world for your purpose, affection, and acceptance, then your children will, too. They will struggle, just as you have, until someone breaks the cycle and looks to God for their purpose, affection, and acceptance. Even though my parents had made some conscious, selfless decisions, the damage had been done because of what I had been exposed to and the lack of exposure to a living God. Jesus wasn't real to me and I didn't have an understanding of what it meant to look to Him in my time of need or place my faith in him. My example of faith was people who attended church every once in a while, who had crosses as knickknacks, or Bibles as memorabilia in their house. No one ever explained to me what it meant to have salvation and grace. Jesus was nothing more than a glorified Santa Claus to me. He was the praying Jesus picture hanging above my parents' dinner table, but that didn't make Him real in my life. It certainly didn't release me from the consequences of the self-indulgent path I was about to encounter faster than eighty-eight miles per hour! Side note for those non–*Back to the Future* fans: eighty-eight miles per hour is what initiates the flux capacitor.

My exposure to those screaming family members over something as trivial as the end score of a football game would lead me to seek a level of acceptance by putting on the colors of those teams. Still to this day, I think of my grandfather pushing himself out of the chair to display his agreement or disagreement with his Houston Oilers. When I was exposed to these dedicated fans of football, I immediately started to act out those players on TV and yearn for that attention. Idolizing sports is no different than creating an idol of sex; both create a displacement of our love and affection. Is the festival in Exodus 32 that the people demanded because they needed a God to follow that much different than our modern-day worship synagogues referred to as stadiums? Rising early, fighting traffic, offering the burnt offerings in the form of barbecue, while indulging in food and drink. Not so much different when we take our justification off the situation and place it under the covering of the Bible. My point is that our exposure, both negative and positive, impacts us deeply. Some exposure takes us to places of boldness, courage, and finding our identity in Christ; some exposure takes us to places of shame, anger, frustration, and looking to others for our identity. When Eve and Adam ate the fruit together, the fruit that God knew was not good for them, they immediately felt shame. Genesis 3:7 says their eyes were opened. It's not that their eyes were physically shut, then forced open, but that their innocence had died, and their eyes were opened to the world of sin. It is interesting that the first thing they became aware of was their nakedness, as this is the symbol of truly robbing innocence by shaming our bodies. It happens every day. It happened to me and Wayne. XXXchurch.com reports that the median age for first-time pornography use is eleven to thirteen years old for boys. Wayne and I where twelve when we took a bite out of the fruit of lust, taking our innocent adventures of freedom and joy in our imagination and corrupting them into a twisted, deprived journey into a world we had no understanding of or maturity in. With our lack of exposure to the acceptance of Jesus Christ, would we turn to the shame of Satan to guide our paths? My life would be forever changed with one decision. This one decision would be the bedrock of each shameful act for the next twenty years.

3

During my middle school years my family and I lived in a house that was simply amazing. It wasn't a house of great value or filled with lots of amenities, but it was atop a hill, on three hundred acres, about twenty miles out of town, down a windy, hilly country road. On this land were woods, tanks (or ponds, for you city folk) and the endless adventure of exploring.

This land was a fully functioning farm at one time but had been limited to a small cattle operation by the time we arrived. My parents didn't own this beautiful property but rented it from an elderly couple who were well into their eighties when we met them. Facing the combination of advancing age and children moving away, they could no longer keep up with the daily demands and schedule of the farm or continue to chance living so far from medical treatment. We all had an immediate bond with each other because we all met a need that each one was missing.

Pete and Tracy Owens became grandparent figures for me and my sister because we didn't have a close relationship with our grandmother from my mother's side. My mom's dad and both my dad's parents had already passed away. Pete and Tracy also became parental figures to my dad because he had lost his parents at such a young age, and my mom was drawn to Tracy because of the distance that had grown between her and her own mother. The relationship was two-sided, though. Pete and Tracy were instantly drawn to my parents because of the strained relationship they had with their own children who had all moved away, leaving them to become managers of their own affairs instead of being involved in their lives. It was the perfect storm and the perfect place for a young boy searching for his manhood.

At this time my father worked for an oil company that allowed him to have a flexible schedule. My parents' willing spirits and love for this couple would result in our becoming the caretakers of this amazing property. The agreement was a $300 monthly rent and the perks of the land while caring for the three hundred head of cattle, hay production, and any property maintenance. Of course, this led me to some amazing life-training skills that I still carry with me to this day. Learning how to work and learning how to be trusted with job duties that would be considered insane in today's times of an overbearing, overprotective nanny state. My sister and I had the opportunity to learn how to care for newborn calves, raise chickens, fish, feed cattle, slop hogs, garden, and perform all the other chores that come with running a small farm. My dad also had the opportunity to go back to the roots of his childhood, when he had worked on ranches and farms. In the midst of his troubled childhood, the happy moments had come during an honest day's work with hardworking men while earning their respect. My mom served the Owens as if they were her own parents. She drove into town, checking on them throughout the week and taking a real interest in their lives. Pete and Tracy gave us something that we didn't know we needed: loving people of peace who loved us unconditionally. We would grow very close to Pete and Tracy; we were treated as family, even being invited over for Christmas and other holidays. Since the relationship with our own family on both sides was distant and most of the time strained, this relationship with the Owenses was what the small tribe of four wanderers needed.

Our family was still reeling from the aftermath of pain left in the wake of an alcoholic father. Dad and Mom were reconciling their relationship and doing the same with us. Our distance from our immediate family was really the result of my parents' protecting themselves. Unfortunately, when addicts are working through sobriety, they must make hard decisions to simply not be exposed to those things that triggered the addiction in the first place. Even at a young age, I somewhat had a concept of this and could feel the tension and awkwardness at family events.

This house on the hill became our sanctuary. I loved seeing my mom's tender heart as she served with the genuineness of a daughter, unconditionally loving Pete and Tracy as she served them with basic needs. We would have suppers, sometimes weekly, at their house, enjoying what became one of my favorite dishes: sausage, sauerkraut, and boiled potatoes—a typical German dish, which symbolized their heritage. They taught us the game of 42 as a family. A domino game that, in all honesty, I still do not really understand. When we were working at chores on the small farm we had revived as a family, I would look back many times and see my mom just staring at my sister and me with a smile on her face as we bottle-fed calves or worked the garden. At least, she was smiling as long as no wasps were flying around; they seem to always pick her out of a crowd. But that was fun for us because we would then watch Dad take his cap off and attempt to swat the wasp out of midair. My dad would take walks with us to the tanks to fish or walk down the dirt road that wound its way through the thick forest of mature trees and free-running wildlife. I didn't know Scripture then, but I remember the peace and acceptance I felt when I was walking those woods. A comfort came with being out in the middle of nowhere with nothing but the wind moving through the trees, a calming chime of leaves working together in harmony. An eerie closeness comes from being completely vulnerable to the elements of the world without the distractions of modern culture.

When I was allowed to walk those woods alone, it served as my escape. My escape was simply an act of slipping away from the pursuit of my guilt and shame that had begun to grow as my mind was slowly warped by sexual immorality. Sometimes, in my mind's eye, I visually try to see Adam and Eve running around after they disobeyed God's one commandment. God looks for both Adam and Eve as they are running around, hiding behind trees (Genesis 3:8–9, HCSB). Their response is that of fear because of what they had been exposed to after having their eyes opened through their disobedience. I still remember being a young, middle-school boy trying to process the newfound thoughts, feelings, and sensations I had discovered. When I went out in the woods, I felt at peace and not clouded with the wants and desires of my mind. God meets Adam and Eve in the forest as they try to hide and talks with them (Genesis 3:10–24, HCSB). He explains to them what has happened and what the consequences are for their actions. As Adam squirms and attempts to push fault off on Eve he is reminded that his own choice put him in this situation. Being a middle-school-aged child, walking in those woods, I battled with thoughts and desires that I had no idea how to deal with, because there was certainly no knowledge of Jesus or an open line of communication that that would allow me to share with my parents about something as embarrassing as sexual impurity.

As I have mentioned several times my parents made some tough decisions, but they didn't have an open, obedient, intentional relationship with Jesus that overflowed into my life. I was allowed to watch pretty much any television show or movie I wanted. Their assumption was that television and movies were just entertainment, but to a young boy who had tasted the desire of pornography, it was like stockpiling images to be reproduced by my imagination during my shameful acts.

The examples of sexual purity that I received early in my life weren't exactly a biblical model. The men in my life displayed more of a real-world example. Look but don't touch was my initial sexual-purity stance. The idea that our lustful attitude would enter through our eyes and that our adulterous actions would come by way of the hand never occurred to any of the men who were influencing me at the time. Matthew 5:27–30 (HCSB) had no bearing on my life, and it certainly wasn't being modeled in any of the men around me. It would be years before I would come to grips with the severity of the demand in Matthew 5:29 (HCSB) that illustrates the radical nature of Jesus' ethics and my radical need for a relationship with Him.

When I walked those woods, I felt acceptance; however, I am not entirely sure if I ever did feel truly accepted. My interaction with God was minimal at best. Since the beginning, when Adam's and Eve's sin alienated them from God and introduced strife into human relationships, we as humans have experienced a deep need to belong. The Owenses' place was that place of belonging and acceptance for me. I had adopted my parents' point of views of churches, which, unbeknownst to me, alienated me further from God.

Going to Catholic Church as a middle-school/junior-high-aged kid is challenging. In my experience, the Catholic Church typically isn't the best at providing opportunities for legitimate Christian fellowship and discipleship for its members. Church for me was a very distant and cold place, a place where I saw people who during the rest of the week did the very things that were spoken against at services. I remember feeling more distant from God in the church and around those so-called Christians. There were definitely some great cooks in our church, but no one who really modeled to me what the gargantuan statue of the man nailed to a cross above our altar supposedly died for.

In my mind, they also seemed to stare at me the whole service. I was already in an identity crisis and had a negative self-image because of my struggle with a poor sense of worth, so all those eyes made me extremely uncomfortable. My parents had good intentions when they would attempt to stroke my ego and give me the "you can do whatever you want" speech, but my lifestyle was already forming habits that would eventually become my needs. I can now say, as a male in my early forties, looking back, that this was where my addiction started. In the depths of shame and guilt, not really even understanding why I felt so much shame and guilt. I did, however, figure out very quickly what made the shame and guilt go away even if for a short time.

One thing that is highly misconstrued in our world is the phrase "boys will be boys." There is some truth to the saying, as can be seen in the natural ability of a young boy to pick a stick up and use it for a weapon of some sort, or just throw it as far as he can. Working with my hands and getting dirty from a day of working in the garden, hay field, or with the animals we raised were my moments of becoming a man. The day my dad allowed me to operate a tractor to shred a field is one that I will never forget. My dad entrusting me with the responsibility of running the John Deere tractor with a shredder on the back, making ridiculous amounts of noise from the engine, the smell of diesel, freshly cut grass and the sound of weeds and grass being mutilated was amazing. Every boy needs to know that he is powerful. Like it or not, there is something fierce in the heart of a boy. We all want to be heroes, and we all want to battle. Not every boy's battle sense is the same. Some are drawn to guns and swords, some to the principles and causes, but each boy wants to battle. Sadly, in our current culture, there is a type of *disarming* of boys because of the lack of male guidance. With more boys left to be raised in single-parent households with, in most cases, the mother, a portion of manhood is left for the boy to learn on his own. With the proper male guidance to train a young boy in how to embrace his adventurous nature he will grow to respect that which is deemed dangerous and stay away from that which is corrupt. My dad was an excellent mentor and guide who taught me fishing, gardening, chopping wood, caring for animals, firearms, respect for fellow men and elders, and a little hunting. My mom taught me the other half—cooking, sewing, cleaning, compassion, and respect for women. My sister and I were extremely blessed to have both our parents active in our lives. However, as I mentioned a few sentences earlier, proper guidance and mentoring will train us to recognize what is dangerous and corrupt to our well-being. My battle of feeling shame and guilt was a misplaced understanding of my sexual nature. I was feeling deep shame and guilt for my exposure to and now a desire for sexual gratification because Jesus was not presented to me. Yes, you may say at the fault of my parents, but my parents were in the middle of their own spiritual journey. Without a clear direction of my identity in Jesus Christ, my identity became my shame and guilt and eventually grew to include anger.

In middle school, one boy and his older brother used to ride me pretty hard with insults and one-liners each day when I got on the school bus. Middle school is a tough time in a lot of people's lives, and for me it was the time that I was bullied. Having a spirit of shame and guilt left me feeling weak and helpless; therefore, I needed to feel strong or in control. One particular day I made a decision that I was going to feel strong and in control. As my sister and I waited for the bus in front of our house, I said to myself, "If Jeff says anything to me, I am going to say something back." I was so pumped up and wired that when I got on the bus, I looked for him. He always sat one row from the back because his brother sat in the back row. When I entered the bus and started to walk down the aisle, he made a sexual remark to my sister, and I snapped. I jumped over the seat and lunged at him. Grabbing a handful of his hair and using it as a handle, I began to ram his head into the side window. This moment of rage was a blur. All the frustration of my shame and guilt was coming out in that very moment. It was exhilarating, terrifying, and refreshing to know that this one kid would not continue his reign of bullying in my life, and how I reacted scared me. This is when I would learn the defensive tactic of generating fear in others to make myself seem more powerful or in control. Nobody is more twisted than people who attempt to be in control, establishing themselves by trying to manipulate people and situations in life. When this occurs, we essentially are trying to play God. God doesn't call us to be in control of people, environments, or circumstances, he calls us to self-control (Galatians 5:23, HCSB).

Genesis 4 (NIV) recounts the story of Cain and Abel, sons of Adam and Eve. Cain was a very angry young man. His failure in worship and his subsequent angry response were basic to his unethical behavior. This was his identity, and it was a corrupted view. God questions Cain to clarify what he should be doing in verse 7 of Genesis 4 but makes him aware that if he doesn't change and do the right thing, a threatening demon will be awaiting him at the door. Most of us know what happens. Cain gives in to the angry response and kills his brother, Abel. I embraced my identity in the world around me as Cain did. My worship was distorted, and the anger from my shame and guilt had led to a serpent lying in wait for me at the door.

My identity was that of a confused, fearful, and angry boy who was also responsible, loving, and compassionate. My identity was like that of a boy who grew up in a single-parent household, getting an unbalanced view of life. A child raised by a single parent will instinctively search out that which is missing, regardless of whether it is a negative or positive impact on their life. For example, inner-city males are often drawn to gangs, in part because, statistically speaking, most inner-city children have no active father figure in their life. So, they search for a father figure in an attempt to fill that void. When I compare myself to a child from a single-parent home, I am referring to my lack of relationship with God, my heavenly Father, at the time. My parents taught me so much about life. This is the reason why my sister and I are hardworking and respectable people; however, the lack of spiritual guidance in being properly guided through the Gospel resulted in our seeking identity.

Toward the end of my middle-school years, I was really getting into music. My parents were also into music. My mom's choice of tunes were the eighties, and my dad was into the likes of Janis Joplin, Jimi Hendrix, and Bob Dylan. Therefore, I grew to appreciate the emotion and meaning behind music, especially that born in the movements of the sixties and seventies. My era of music was the nineties, and I was drawn to the early bands such as Nirvana, Pearl Jam and Bush. I got into the harder genres in high school and my early twenties, such as Korn, Marilyn Manson, and Tool. Of course, I would also have Dr. Dre's *The Chronic* albums in my collection. Pearl Jam released a song in 1993 called "Elderly Woman Behind the Counter in a Small Town"; it was one of my favorite songs from Pearl Jam and remains so today. A lyric in that song would make me secretly wonder if it was describing me. The lyric was: "I changed by not changing at all, small town predicts my fate."

My dad had a reputation among our small community. He was known to party hard and was also a very violent man; some would say he was unstable. My dad's presence alone created a lot of fear among people in the community when he was young and running the streets. As I started to get out in the community and hang out with friends, I would be known as Gerald's boy. As a side note, I haven't mentioned it yet, but I am a junior, and, yes, I did go by Junior. Only those who knew me by Junior can call me that! Everyone else, please call me Gerald.

People who knew my dad would tell stories about the adventures that they were a part of with him or had heard about. These stories began to create my identity. When I would hear that lyric in Pearl Jam's song, I would think to myself that everyone already had a prediction for how my life would go. The life that my dad lived before he decided to change his path was being predicted for me by the people of this small town. It was so glorifying and motivating to know that I could be as popular as my dad was. I was changing by not changing at all. I would not disappoint my crowd of onlookers in my community. By the time I arrived for my freshmen year in high school I was embracing the identity that was being defined and predicted by everyone else around me.

This three- to four-year window, from the ages of nine to thirteen, was a critical time in my life. It was not coincidence that we as a family ended up living on an old, nonfunctional farm. I believe it was divinely appointed that we ended up there. As we worked together to restore this farm and add life to it, the same was happening in our family. Our love for each other as a family is deeply rooted in those days spent on that farm working, playing, and just loving each other. When we moved from that farm into a new home that my parents had built, and as my sister and I entered high school, we would return to that deep-rooted love for each other to weather the storms. Without those years spent as a boy walking the trails in those woods, always wondering what was around the corner and what I would find, I don't think I would be here today. I didn't get to walk those trails as much as I would have liked to, but the times I did left an indelible impression in my mind. Even without really knowing God, my Heavenly Father was stirring me, preparing me for my own trail, the one he made just for me. I would embark on this trail when I entered high school, carrying my baggage of anger, shame, guilt, impurities, and misconceptions of Jesus. Overall, innocence was lost, and I had grown an appetite for the forbidden fruit.

4

My interest in basketball was generated in 1992. Lying on my living room floor that year, watching the NCAA Tournament, I witnessed how, with his buzzer beater, Christian Laettner and the Duke Blue Devils destroyed Kentucky's dreams of advancing to the next round. My interest in basketball was stirred by the fact that one shot, one play, one choice can totally alter a basketball game, no matter how good or bad the team is. But it was a cocky, angry, little-known player for the New York Knicks by the name of John Starks who created a passion for the sport that remains with me today.

John Starks and the New York Knicks never got past the Chicago Bulls in the nineties during the Eastern Conference Finals while Michael Jordan was leading the latter team, which won six world championships in eight years. Needless to say, they the Knicks were always the underdog in every match, even on their home court—Madison Square Garden. They were considered second best each year compared to Jordan and his Bulls teams. However, in the 1993 Eastern Conference Finals, during the final quarter of Game 2, with fifty seconds remaining, Starks and the Knicks were attempting to hang on to go up 2-0 in the series. Starks proceeded to bring the ball down court, dribbling on the right as Patrick Ewing rushed over to set a screen intended to spring Starks into the middle of the court to run out the clock. Instead of using the screen, Starks briefly hesitated before exploding the opposite way of the pick and hurtling into the lane. Horace Grant (the Chicago Bulls forward) stepped up to meet him, and time seemed to slow down. As I began to stand up on the bed from a lying position,

I watched as Starks leapt into the air—and into NBA history—before reaching the paint (the area under the basketball goal). Jordan would hurry to help on defense, but he was too late. Starks would throw down what came to be known as the Dunk, a monster left-handed jam that sent Madison Square Garden into hysteria, and with Jordan on the receiving end of that demoralizing dunk. At that moment, nothing and everything made sense. Starks was up, and Jordan was down. The moment still stays with me. I was an instant New York Knicks fan, and Starks was the main reason. He led this team of ruthless underdogs consisting of Ewing, the most intimidating center in the league during the nineties; Charles Oakley, who seemed to have everyone's back as long as he could throw a punch; Anthony Mason, who played with a chip on his shoulder every game; Derek Harper, who was a former member of the league doormat Dallas Mavericks and wanted to prove he belonged in every game; and, of course, Starks.

Starks gave the average person hope because of his background and path to the NBA. After playing only one year of basketball at Tulsa Central High School, he bounced around several colleges, being expelled from one and spending a week in jail for robbery during his transfer to another college. He would finish up his collegiate career with Oklahoma State. Starks was a troubled young man, but he was an extremely hard worker. In 1986 he worked at a supermarket. He was a man who fans seemed to connect with.

Starks played as if his life depended on it and I was drawn to that because he wasn't playing a part. The same fierce tenacity, desire to win, and heart would show all throughout his life whether sitting in jail, working at a supermarket, or playing in the NBA; he was transparent. He would take on the biggest names in basketball and make it his personal mission to destroy them during the game both physically and mentally. By the time players finished playing against Starks they would question their own abilities. Almost instantly, I was asking for a basketball goal and shoes and had my family all out shooting hoops. My dad had strategically installed a basketball goal on the front of the barn, and my mom would take me to buy a pair of Patrick Ewing shoes known simply as "Ewings." Even in writing this about these men of basketball, I realize it reflects my struggle to find identity, but I was drawn to those alter egos that I wanted to be like.

The year 1993 was when I really begin to grow into an awkward young man. I had grown to my adult height by the end of my eighth-grade year and had a vicious case of acne. This made me a target for some bullying but nothing too extreme. The bullying only went so far because, I think, most kids knew that my patience had a limit. My awkwardness and clumsiness resulted in my being a 6-feet-tall, 170-pound offensive lineman on my junior high football team. I was on the B team. In junior high football no one gets cut, so there are different teams formed to allow every kid a shot at playing time. The coaching staff and parents make them sound special, but in reality we all knew what they meant.

Like the incident on the bus with Jeff, I also had an incident while practicing on the junior high football team that simmered down the bullying. While practicing, a couple of kids would just ride me pretty hard with their onslaught of slang, derogatory remarks such as faggot, queer, and numerous references to the female genitalia. This reached a limit after one play in which I had received the brunt of the blame. As we went to line up and run the play again, one particular aggressor on my team said something. I'm not even sure what it was, but I remember the look in his eye when he said it. That look he gave me of wanting to demoralize me and embarrass me resulted in my wanting to inflict the same pain on him. In a brief moment I took my helmet off and slammed it across his facemask. The jolt caused him to stumble, and I took the opportunity to jump on him and straddle him. I began to do whatever I could to hurt him. His friend ran to his rescue and jumped on my back, which resulted in my flipping him off my back and flat on his. The whole moment is still a blur. Coaches soon stepped in and I was stuck standing by myself as they helped the other two kids up. The whole violent moment left me standing on an island, with the whole team and coaches staring at me in shock and disgust. This may have just been the way I felt and not their actual feeling. My parents remained loving and were very protective of my sister and me; heck, to this day, they still attempt to protect us as adults from the world. My dad's job was more flexible, so he came up to the school and defended his son. Come to think of it, my mom and dad have always protected me from any type of punishment that wasn't by their hand. Therefore, if I was upset or angry about my day, it didn't matter, because I knew I had loving parents. There was a sense of safety in the reassurance of having parents who would protect their children.

Now, I didn't just skate free through life without getting punished for anything, not by any stretch of the imagination. To teach respect, parents must be diligent in corrective discipline. If I was defending myself, my sister, or my family, or standing up for something worthy of a fight for what was right, it was discipline on how to properly and respectfully approach those situations. My issue was that I was getting one message from my parents, a different one from the school, and then an entirely different one from the culture. I would try to suppress my anger and frustrations as a child. This would begin a trait of angry outburst and rants at the slightest issue. I was just so confused about who I was, what I was, and what I was supposed to do.

When I think about why my outbursts were so violent, I am taken back to a time when death became a reality. Death was a frequent occurrence for a season in our family, starting with my grandfather—my mom's dad—and going through several other funerals that included members of my father's family. My dad and I served as altar boys for most of these funerals, excluding my grandfather's, because the rest were held in Catholic churches. My dad was always asked to serve alongside me in an altar boy role for each funeral as far back as I can remember. For those who are not up on the Catholic hierarchy, an altar boy is an individual who was chosen or strongly encouraged to serve the priest during services. This would include the all-embarrassing and overwhelming act for a socially awkward teenager of lighting candles. What I remember was holding a seemingly massive pole with a little flame on the end, attempting to light a twelve-foot candle. Now I am aware that my perception was not to scale, but when you are walking in front of a crowded church with the one thought of not to screw up, the pressure increases the intensity of the moment. During funerals, we would be the two people standing on each side of the priest while he walked around the coffin and read at both the church and gravesite. Yes, this was in front of hundreds of people as well.

During each funeral I served at, I went through the same thought process. Is this really what life is all about? This is the ending to life, lying in a custom-designed box, while, really, the occupants of the first couple of rows of the church were the only people with a real, vested interest in the life that just ended, either financially or emotionally. I would look around the church or funeral home and start to examine their relationship with the recently deceased, wondering why some people were so distraught over the death of a person they barely knew or didn't even like. I am aware of the shallowness of the judgment that I was assigning, but there was a sliver of truth in it. I would conclude that most people are distraught because of the fear of their own mortality. Then I would just sit there with a sinking feeling about death, just the thought of dying and being placed in a box. Then I would think of the embalming process and how the eyes and lips are sewn shut. Sure, I would be touched emotionally because of losing a loved one, but I would be overwhelmed by the fact that everyone I know, including myself, would end up in the ground to rot for all eternity.

I would wake up in the middle of the night with a deep hurt in my stomach because my fear would entrap me even in my sleep. It really hit an unhealthy point when I was crying in the tub, sitting and holding my knees close to my chest, just full of fear and emotions, knowing that my parents, my sister, and I would all die. This feeling, this unhealthy view about death would haunt me well into my twenties.

These moments of panic in my preteen and teenage years would result in my mom setting up meetings with Father Folk, our priest at St. Mary's. Now that I am a father, I can't even imagine the pain she felt on my behalf. My parents both had relationships with God and, as long as I can remember, have always been very open and direct about death. The only issue was that I had a distorted view of who God was and where Jesus tied into everything. This distorted view would ultimately result in my own journey, but not after visiting Father Folk's house for a couple of counseling sessions.

Father Folk smoked, drank liquor, and drove a Mercedes. He was the first person I had ever met who ordered his steak rare! Right off the bat, my view of church leaders was that they were hypocrites, because from my viewpoint he was supposed to stand out from what was culturally the norm. Smoking, drinking and using money for selfish gain were all attributes of the people whom my parents steered away from; therefore, I had a prejudgment that I attached on Father Folk. This distorted view of the church and its leaders was a huge barrier that would prevent me from totally committing to God or His church for many years.

Father Folk's house was perfectly positioned right across from the church building. It was a somewhat modest home, but I had heard enough conversation about how the church's finances funded his lifestyle. When I heard these conversations, they had a sense of ownership tied to them, like the people who tithed to the church owned the preacher. Therefore, I adopted this "you work for me" mindset, which, sadly, is the distorted view of so many self-proclaimed, shallow Christians missing the whole point of the Gospel and who really owns whom. As I walked into Father Folk's house the first time, there were books everywhere, crucifixes everywhere, and pictures of different saints. The house smelled like an old building. It reminded me of the smell of a musky, wrecked RV; the one that Wayne and I played in at his dad's junkyard. He never was rude or pushy about anything. He talked a lot about faith, but I would somehow get him off subject to talk about exorcisms or other extreme, glamorous war stories and interactions with evil. I was intrigued by the stories of Father Folk's battle with the devil. In some weird and twisted way, this helped me grow an amazement for the spirit world, but I wouldn't call it faith.

In 2 Corinthians 5:7 (HCSB), Paul states, "For we walk by faith, not by sight." Not me; I wanted to see. While my parents had just embarked on their own spiritual journey and restoration within their own lives and I knew, deep down, something amazing had happened, I wasn't sure if it was God, Jesus, or just human willpower. We were taught the basics because my parents didn't know how to articulate the power of God to us. This is referred to as spiritual milk by Peter in 1 Peter 2:2 (HCSB). Our family was drinking spiritual milk and didn't even know there was "T-bone steaks" of knowledge for the taking. We were taught to believe in God, love one another, respect elders, value ethics, and work hard, but my questions of *why* would overwhelm my mind.

In the book of Judges, in the Old Testament, Joshua passes away after a long life of seeing some pretty intense events. I mean, he walked with Moses and was chosen as Moses's predecessor. Joshua, as a child, was a part of Moses's parting of the Red Sea, following a pillar of fire and getting water from a rock. He would see another Red Sea miracle while bringing over the Ark of the Covenant as an adult, then go on to be a tool for God to do more miracles. The problem was that a generation of people who experienced all those amazing miracles apparently didn't explain to their children the significance of those events. The book of Judges is basically about the lack of leadership in this period that failed to point the people to a sole relationship with the one, true God, Yahweh. Israel worshipped other gods alongside Yahweh, God, and thus failed to keep the covenant. The ignorance, pride, and lack of understanding led them down destructive paths for the people and generations after them (Judges 2:11–19, HCSB). I have no doubt that my family tree was filled with God-fearing, obedient people devoted to God's will at some point, but somewhere, the message had gotten distorted. My parents would be the two people who would start the process of cleaning up the distorted heritage in the perspective of who God is, what God is, and how God works through the actions that played out in front of my eyes through their own faith journey.

Foundations are important. I've sat in my office, which overlooks downtown Houston, and watched an entire twenty-five-floor building be built from the ground up. Before building even starts, they clean off the lot and make a beautiful, level, open canvas without any blemishes. They proceed to drill hundreds of feet of holes that are filled with concrete, iron, and whatever else would support the massive structure that is going on top. Foundations are important.

Paul wrote his letter to the Corinthian church, a church that he had established, because he had received word that the church, basically, had turned into a sideshow of misfits. He wrote this band of recently converted pagans turned Christian a letter of foundational truths. Early in the letter he writes, "For no one can lay a foundation other than that which is laid, which is Jesus Christ," meaning this group of people were struggling with disunity, immorality, and lawsuits, among other things because they had built their faith on a foundation that had been tested by fire and had been consumed by the fire (1 Corinthians 3:12–14, HCSB).

I would get pieces of a severely distorted foundation of faith, God, and Jesus from movies and music. A major piece of my foundation, one that my parents didn't realize would open up Pandora's box, would come by way of a film that was released in May 1994—*The Crow*. This movie would become an idol for me. *The Crow* hit the box office even after the lead actor was killed while filming one of the brutal scenes that involved heavy gunfire, because of an improperly prepared prop gun. Though the Brandon Lee's death was ruled due to accidental negligence, speculation still surrounds it today. The movie was full of violence, sex, drugs, and one of the hardest soundtracks led by some up-and-coming hard rock bands. The film was an instant cult classic. In between all the guns, drugs, and rock 'n' roll was the story of a man and his fiancée who were brutally murdered over an unpaid debt. The couple is painted in a picture of true love, almost like a cultural, distorted, updated version of Romeo and Juliet. One year after their brutal murders, the character Eric Draven returns from the afterlife to avenge his own death and that of his fiancée. The way he returns is that a crow that becomes his source of strength has somehow spiritually invoked him. The movie drew me in because of the revenge plot and the dark attire accompanied by face paint that created an eerie but attractive demeanor. There were references to a god in the film, but I am sure it was not the one true God. This is where invoking and spiritual curiosity enticed me. The movie would be almost a mantra that I would look to in times of difficulty. The famous line that Eric Draven says to Tin Tin (one of his murderers) right before Draven ends his life is, "Victims—aren't we all?" You better believe that I had the full movie posters in my room, having another distorted view of God presented to me in the name of art. Granted, the movie had some great moments, but 99 percent of it pointed to a man's own power invoked by the spirit world with a heavy dose of revenge against those who had hurt him or done him wrong. Not exactly the message a fourteen- or fifteen-year-old should be receiving, this was the type of message that no longer pointed to God, but to self. The movie ends with Eric Draven returning to the grave to rest with his slain fiancée after killing all the people who had anything to do with their murders. Hardly a true picture of Jesus and the Gospels of the Bible.

God is real. That's all I really had a handle on coming out of my eighth-grade year and entering into my freshman year of high school. The *whys* would overwhelm me. I would lay awake at night, going through so many scenarios that would go something like this: "God made me, my parents, the trees, the world, the planets, the stars; who made God? There is no God!" At that point, I would either run to my parents' room, looking for comfort from my mom, who could always calm me down, or lie awake worried, crying, and fearful of the grave. I was literally a prisoner in my mind, a prison of thoughts, and prisoners need recreation time to break away from the cell. My recreation time was gardening.

I was a little bit of an oddball among my peers because not too many teenagers were looking forward to gardening. My dad loved to garden as well. It was his escape from misplaced feelings, reeling from his parents' untimely death and financial pressures of raising a family. Also, he was a recovering alcoholic, and as any addict of anything knows, you are always recovering. The triggers that led an addict to addiction have to be handled. For my dad, gardening was a peaceful reminder of the glory of God. He never said it, but it was the reason that I just wanted to be by his side. Now, there were times of frustration that we had to deal with, like when the tiller that we used to prepare gardens three times more than it was made for over a course of several years just wouldn't go any more. After an onslaught of f-bombs from my dad, the poor little tiller caught fire. Mom and my sister Roxanne freaked out, then burst into laughter from the porch. Gardening calmed me. It gave me moments of freedom from my thoughts. Gardening helped me process my thoughts. It was my personal psychologist. Even through some of my darkest times, I would garden. My dad never realized the gift of gardening and the importance it played on my foundation of faith. Gardening kept me going when I wanted to just give up on life.

Faith really depends on its object, and when you really take a step back and examine the difference between Christian faith and non-Christian faith, the only difference is the object of that faith. The most critical issue in life is what you believe and whom you believe in. My mother's faith is so deeply seated in God that it is virtually unshakable; however, when she would tell me that I just had to have faith, it made no sense to me because I had no understanding of faith and I couldn't have faith in faith. None of it made sense; however, we pass over railroad crossings each day, faithfully believing that the blinking lights and crossbar will come down to prevent us from becoming devoured by a several-ton machine moving sixty miles per hour down the tracks. I was once riding with my boss and noticed that he stopped at every railroad crossing, even on highways! This particular day, he must have noticed that I was impatiently riding in the passenger seat of his truck while it took forever for us to get back to the office. He turned and said, "I stop at every railroad crossing." I responded, "Yeah, noticed that; why?" I sometimes regret asking that question because I think of his response almost every time I cross a railroad track. He said, "My daughter was killed by a train while crossing a track where the signal had malfunctioned." As I sat there, slack jawed, trying to not act shocked, he then followed up with, "I heard the accident and drove to it...to find that it was my own daughter." All I could say was I was sorry to hear that. Here was a man who had lost all his faith in the railroad warning system because of the death of his daughter. Faith in God is like this. We take for granted each day the knowledge we have of God when, in reality, we don't know the truths of who God really is.

At a railroad crossing, there is so much that we don't know concerning the details of the railroad system. The signal might not work, the sensors on the tracks that signal the lights to flash and bar to go down might falter—there are probably a hundred things that could go wrong. My point is that the average person does not have a working knowledge of the railroad safety systems. Faith is like that. Our problem with faith in God is not because the object of our faith has failed us or that it is insufficient. It's because we don't have a true knowledge of God and His ways. Paul says in Romans 10:17 (HCSB) that faith comes from what is heard and what is heard comes through the message about Christ.

I was looking to follow any man who would have me, whether my father, John Starks or a fictional character like Eric Draven. I would trust and have faith in what I considered reality. I would believe in the people around me because it was truth, all the while unconsciously turning from God because of my lack of knowledge of God. As I got into the full swing of my high school career, my growing interest in basketball, music, sex, and evil, accompanied by my frustration with God, would start to mix together into a dangerous cocktail. Unbeknownst to me at the time, a group of guys in Bakersfield, California, were forming a band that was taking the underground, heavy metal scene to a whole other level with their intense, twisted lyrics and unique sound that would capture my feelings in music.

Starks was an average, frustrated, "himself against the world" basketball player who went right at the elites of basketball with an aggressiveness and swagger that symbolized an "I don't care what you think" attitude. This fed right into my growing frustration with God, the church, and the so-called Christians of the church. As soon as Jonathan Davis screamed, "ARE YOU READY?" on Korn's self-titled album, I was ready but didn't really fully understand what I was ready for, or what I was truly accepting with my ignorant, anger-filled, and fearful response of yes.

5

My parents built a custom home in my dad's hometown of Deanville, Texas, shortly after they decided that they wanted to own a home. When I say custom home, some automatically assume a luxurious, spacious home with all of the amenities. While this was a nice home, it was built more for raising a family than luxury.

They built on property that my mom's mother and father lived on until my grandfather passed away and my grandmother moved in with my aunt. This piece of property was about an acre that was heavily overgrown because it had sat vacant for so long. Once again we, as a family, worked together to rejuvenate a this property while making the occasional exploration to find relics left behind by my grandfather in an old storage shed. These items were left as trash, but in my family nothing is trash, and everything is kept because you never know when you might need a six-foot piece of steel cable or if the fifty-year old medicine bottles could be worth some money in the future. I'm being sarcastic, but I must admit that I have inherited this same mentality toward my own little hidden treasures that I find.

Once we were settled into the house after a long, drawn-out building process (that is a whole story in itself because of the rain, sewage issues, and using a bucket for an outhouse), Mom and Dad started the enhancing process. Every place my parents have lived in, they have enhanced with either extended back porches, swimming pools, or outdoor kitchens—anything to add value or curb appeal. In this particular house my parents had decided to convert our back porch into a family room. It was a great room to hang out in, whether for a special occasion or just to chill and watch a movie. One particular night, as I was surfing the channels, I ran across late-night Cinemax, HBO, and Showtime. Cinemax was often referred to as "skin-a-max" because of the softcore porn it showed during the late night hours. What my parents never intended was for this family room to become my temple of idol worship.

Before I get too far, I want to clarify something. Sex is good. Don't misinterpret my intentions when I call pornography and any type of sexual action outside marriage a form of idol worship. Sex was designed for a man and a woman to enjoy under the umbrella of marriage. God's original intent for sex was that a man leaves his father and mother and embraces his wife. They become one flesh by sexually committing themselves to each other and lying naked in no shame (Genesis 2:24, HCSB). When Paul speaks to the Corinthians, in 1 Corinthians 6, about sexual matters, he tells them what man has made God's gift of sex into, encouraging us to flee from sexual immorality.

Every other sin a person commits is outside the body, but the sexually immoral person sins against his own body (1 Corinthians 6:18 HCSB). Any type of sexual action outside marriage is immoral and will bring problems. The physical union involving sexual immorality has special consequences because it interferes with our Christian identity as people who have been united with Christ through the Holy Spirit (1 Corinthians 6:18, Reformation Study Bible). Just like food, God gave sex for our pleasure, but under his parameters and certainly not to become our object of worship. This is a sticky subject with most non-Christians and, for the most part, self-proclaiming Christians. People from both sides don't like to admit that their sexual actions and what they participate in is idol worship outside the sanctity of marriage.

Just as our earthly fathers give us gifts for pleasure, God gives us gifts for our pleasure. The problem is that the gift is intended to point us back to the father, not to ourselves, or it can become our death. Take the example of a car given by your father. He has rules, such as drive the speed limit, no drinking and driving, and be home by curfew. But what happens to this gift meant for our pleasure when we don't follow our father's directions? We get in trouble or get ourselves in bad situations, or the car ends up causing injury or even death. Why? Because the car became the focus of our affection, not our father. We just got selfish with the gift from our father, and instead of its being for pleasure, it became the object of our affection.

When I discovered this world of softcore porn that played late at night, I took to a new level what had been looking at nude women in magazines and provocative ads in catalogs. Previously, I had listened and watched the older men around me stare while commenting on features of women. Now I was seeing this live on TV. In the book *Pure Eyes: A Man's Guide to Sexual Integrity* (Baker Books, 2010), authors Craig Gross and Steven Luff interview Dr. Ralph Koek, a clinical professor in the Department of Psychiatry and Behavioral Sciences at the David Geffen School of Medicine at UCLA. He has extensive experience treating patients with all sorts of addictions. Additionally, his focus is research in brain-behavior relationships in mental illness. In the interview, he discusses scientific studies on humans with drug addictions, comparing and finding similarity between behavior found in a chemical addiction (alcohol, heroin, cocaine, nicotine, and so on) and pornography addiction. In *Pure Eyes*, he concludes:

> What we now understand from careful study with modern neuroimaging methods in human brains as well as from animal studies is that the normal reward system starts with a subcortical connection between a center in the midbrain called the ventral tegmental area where dopamine is synthesized and from which it is released with a projection or a transmission or a sending of the dopamine from that area to three major limbic reward system nuclei.

Without getting too caught up in all of these psychological terms, we can see that Dr. Koek is pointing out that our brain is literally rewired by these shots of dopamine that create a need or desire that is not necessarily tied to the actual object of dopamine, but the feeling that dopamine creates. When I was feeling stressed, upset, or unhappy, I would turn to pornography because of the euphoric rush I would get from the dopamine. This vicious circle creates the same feelings of frustration, shame, and failure that had led me to seek it out in the first place. Therefore, I used pornography to cope with my feelings, as a way to hide those inner thoughts. The pictures and magazines had started to lose their effect on me, no longer providing the feeling I was seeking. I was like a junkie who had a taste of a gateway drug. Movies, magazines, and provocative ads were my gateway drug. My tolerance had already started to build, meaning that I needed more. People don't just wake up one day and snort heroin, because their bodies would shut down, but several months of alcohol and marijuana use will build a tolerance.

When I was a sophomore in high school, I applied for a job at a local convenience store. One of my friends helped me get in, though later he was fired for watching football during working hours. We laugh about it now, but when it happened, there was no laughing. I have always worked. My parents instilled that trait in me early on. Even when I entered my freshman year and tried out for football, I quickly realized that my time could be spent more productively than getting beaten around as a six-foot-one, 175-pound offensive lineman. I really wanted to play basketball; however, those dreams came crashing down when I started to look at collegiate players and didn't find six-foot-one-inch-tall centers. Needless to say, my attitude was that if sports weren't going to get me anywhere and I could work, make money, and get a vehicle, sports would have to take a back seat. I do regret not playing basketball and truly wish that I had participated in it, but in all honesty, my attitude had started to grow pretty careless. I wanted to fit in. I didn't want to get picked on throughout high school, and I surely didn't want to miss out on anything.

When I started working at the convenience store, the person training me was a senior at school. He revealed a secret to me one Monday night that later would change my status among my peers and ensure that I would be a part of the in crowd.

The first time I heard this little secret, I thought it was outlandish and foolish. He would say it so nonchalantly, as if breaking the law was no big deal, as if this convenience store had its own set of rules and laws that superseded those of the owners. "Hey, if you ever need beer, cigarettes, or snuff, just let me know," he said, as if this was no big deal. I responded with, "No, I am good," not realizing the power and game-changing ability this kind of access could add to my life.

Shortly after I got my first vehicle, a friend of and I were riding around town, and in the process, we made it a point to talk to some girls. We stopped, started up a conversation, and before I knew it, I had started dating one of the girls we met that day. The relationship was pretty innocent until several months later, when I heard her mother mention marriage and my name in the same sentence. I was officially freaked out. Sure, I had given her a promise ring, but the purpose behind this had a totally different meaning to me than to her. My girlfriend and her family saw it as a promise of marriage! I sure wish I had understood that tidbit of knowledge before I gave the ring to her! I had also told her that I loved her, but I had no idea of the power this declaration carried for a teenage girl.

The promise ring really didn't have any meaning to me. I simply gave it because, for some odd reason, guys were giving girls promise rings in high school, and, for me, it seemed the logical next step along the way to sex. This relationship, as you can imagine, was getting a bit out of control for a sophomore in high school. Not sexually, just emotionally, and I wanted out. I was certainly not ready to marry anyone or even ready to think about marriage, but I had no idea how to end the relationship. Sure, I could have talked to her about my feelings, but an overwhelming fear of her father and older brother kept me hanging on for several more months until I had the perfect plan. The plan was not all of my own making; the guys I was hanging out with provided excellent guidance with all of their in-depth knowledge of relationships. At the end of school, her freshman year, she went on a family vacation for a week. I was invited but graciously declined because I had to work. The first night she was out of town, I initiated the plan.

Phase one: find other girls to be seen with. This fell right into place when two girls moved into town from some big city like New Orleans or Dallas. These girls were unlike any of the girls we had ever hung out with. My friend Cedric and I were the first to meet them, and not by accident; we actually followed them as they walked from their house after we saw them moving in. We pulled over and started to talk. These girls spoke grown, as we call it. They dressed cool and had hairstyles from magazines, and they were talking to us! After our first visit, we invited them to a nonexistent party. They agreed to go and told us to pick them up. This would be Cedric's and my first experience with planning a party. We drove around town, went to people's houses, and invited them to a party on property next to Cedric's parents' house. At the time, I fought off the peer pressure to drink, even though Cedric was a drinker, and even in his immaturity, he respected my decision. For almost the entire week we hung out with these girls, Dee and Christi, all the while creating speculation and rumors. Phase one complete.

Phase two was tricky and a little dangerous. Ride around town with another girl in my truck and let the rumors grow. Over the course of the week, these two newcomers to our country town hung out with us every night, it seemed. My parents, either feeling sorry for me or not knowing how to handle my newfound freedom, allowed me to stay out late. I would ride around with the girls, sometimes with the windows down and always around a lot of people. I know this was a jerky way to handle it, but in my mind, this seemed like a great idea. At least, that is, until my girlfriend got back in town. I was being distant and didn't even go see her when she returned. I called and broke up with her the day after she got back from her vacation; it was a Friday night. What followed this breakup was good for my social agenda but would set me back for years to come.

Shortly after, with my rebellious spirit in full bloom, I picked up Dee and we went riding around town. Later, as we were parked at the courthouse square, sitting in my truck and talking, my now ex-girlfriend and her sister skidded up beside us. She and her sister got out of the car and began to punch my truck and windows, while an onslaught of phrases that are better left unsaid were directed at Dee and me. Dee quickly exited the vehicle and jumped in her car and sped off. I remained, a hostage in my own truck, with one extremely angry sister defending her sister's honor and one highly emotional ex-girlfriend screaming, "Why?"

How I wish I had chosen my words and handled the situation differently. Let's just say the words that came out of my mouth in this moment were crude, disgusting, and degrading.

That short moment of screaming profanities directed at a brokenhearted, teenage girl, her sister, and her entire family would ignite a level of hate in her violent brother Jon for the next several months. I should mention that he had already graduated from high school and most of his band of brothers were living with their parents and unemployed. These guys had plenty of time on their hands. They did have a few members of their posse who were still in high school, most of them younger brothers of the older members. I didn't do the best job of handling or helping this situation. I badly ended my relationship with a girl from a very tight-knit family. A family loosely managed as depicted in *The Godfather*. Disrespect one of the family members and you have disrespected the entire family. As innocently as I entered into the relationship with this girl and her family, I ended it as a jerk. It was a mistake getting involved with a girl whom I never intended to stay with. The bottom line is that this whole situation started with words.

Uncontrolled speech is likened to a fire that rages out of control. James says, in James 3:5 (MSG), that a great forest is set ablaze by such a small fire; that small fire is the part of the body that puts thoughts into action by words, the tongue. James described the result of our words as staining the whole body and setting on fire the entire course of life. He ends chapter 3 of his letter saying our tongues are set on fire by hell, no humans can tame the tongue, and the most powerful description of our words is "It is a restless evil, full of deadly poison" (Reformation Study Bible).

Think about speech. We are the biggest hypocrites in our words, because the same mouth we use to love, bless, and encourage is also the mouth we use to curse, ridicule, or hurt others. The words I chose to use this particular day were a torch thrown into a cavern of gasoline, setting ablaze relationships with girls, friends, parents, and God. The deadly poison would slowly seep into every part of my soul, slowly killing me from the inside out.

After the breakup, the rumors and story had gotten around like an out-of-control forest fire. Cedric and I had quickly grown a reputation that was garnering the attention of upperclassmen. Being sixteen years old and staying out all hours of the night gave us the ability to associate ourselves with older teenagers and those older guys who seemed cool, but in the back of our minds we thought we were a little weird for hanging out with high school kids (think Wooderson from *Dazed and Confused* here). At the local hangout spot, Sonic Drive-In, Cedric and I ordered our food. As we sat and ate, Lane walked up to the truck. He was an upperclassman, so I was nervous about what was about to happen. He was fairly popular and one of those guys who had living a dual lifestyle down to an art. Parents and teachers saw him as a great kid without blemish or fault; we would find out very soon that Lane had a whole other talent of beer bongs and keg stands. When he got to Cedric's window he invited us to a party, and, of course, we accepted. For a kid who had dealt with confidence issues and depression, this was an invitation to be part of the in crowd. My anxiety grew in that moment because I knew that I would have to make some major decisions and fight one of my biggest battles with peer pressure ever. Between accepting the invitation and the actual party, I became an angry, frustrated, nervous wreck. This would prime me for my first public profession of my new idol of substance abuse.

Saturday night was approaching, and I had been invited to my first official party with gambling, kegs, and rumors of drugs. I was extremely scared and nervous. I had never been to a party like this one, held for the sole purpose of indulging in all that was prohibited for a teenager. I had never drunk alcohol or smoked cigarettes. My stance, up to this point, was that I never wanted to go down the same road my father went down. Seeing the direct results of alcoholism and its effect on my family always kept me from giving into peer pressure. That would all change. This night was different.

When Moses lays out the endless laws and rules in the book of Exodus, there is a verse tucked away in chapter 23, in a section about social justice. Exodus 23:2 (HCSB) states to not fall in with the many to do evil; this cautions us to not pervert our judgment by allowing the might of the multitude to go against our own consciences in giving judgment. Remember, this is a verse on social justice. I had made a decision, under the influence of fear, that was driven by an identity crisis. Wanting to be accepted, I took the opportunity to go to this party.

Later that night, I met up with Lane and another upperclassman. Cedric and I jumped into a car to ride with a couple of guys whom neither of us knew all that well, other than by their reputation. All I knew was that I felt accepted and popular because these guys had invited me. This was just another party for them, but for me, this was a life-changing event. Up to this point, I had just dealt with my emotional disconnect by self-medicating with late-night HBO and Cinemax in my parents' back room, alone and private. When I arrived at this party, I was somewhat still white-knuckling my stance that I wouldn't drink. I had already fought a lot of battles about not drinking alcohol, smoking cigarettes, or doing drugs with the guys I had grown up around, but this was different. Cedric had already been drinking and smoking for about a year. We also watched pornography and had a growing desire that was only heightened and amplified when we started to indulge in alcohol.

I can remember my first sip of beer. As I took the cup poured from the keg and looked around, I believe God gave me a glance of what I was going to become. As I looked at the cup of beer, I thought of those moments under the table as a child as my dad struggled with alcohol. I thought about my mom and my sister and me, who were hurt by those moments. What I also realized was that there were teenagers and adults at this party who claimed to be Christians and were indulging in the activities. As the first sip of beer went down my throat, I knew that I had made a decision, and as people cheered and embraced me because I was drinking, it felt somewhat right. Not the feeling of right like "my parents are sure going to be proud," but the feeling of right that the Corinthians had with their defective view of the resurrection after they were corrupted by bad company (1 Corinthians 15:33, HCSB). This was a modern-day group of Corinthians with a defective view of Christianity, and I would allow them to corrupt my already damaged faith.

Pinpointing where things took a vicious turn in my life is hard to single out, with all of the choices and decisions I made. Events, conversations, and relationships run together. As murky as it sometimes is, I know that the decision to accept this invite was the start of something different. The night I started to drink was when I discovered that there were teenagers just like me, with all the same feelings and emotions. All the same twisted beliefs and a very distorted view of God and faith. I would discover this whole other world of secrets and deception after breaking up with my first girlfriend and going all in at this party.

Still to this day, I have no idea how I was able to get home. It would be the first of many nights behind the wheel, heavily intoxicated. In one night, I started drinking and smoking and tried pot (marijuana). Things escalated after this particular night. It seemed, almost instantly, that Cedric and I were getting invited to parties and late-night debauchery regularly. I stopped going to the Catholic Church I had been attending on Wednesday nights after I looked around and realized that most of the people in the room were at the parties, having sex or overall just deceitful to their parents. If these were the people in church, I could just stop wasting my time there and pick up an extra night of work at the convenience store. That's what I thought, and that's what I did.

I was at a point in my immature rationalization to finally approach the senior who was training me at the convenience store about that little secret he had mentioned. He taught me the trick of getting beer and cigarettes out of the store. Basically, I would buy the beer or cigarettes while on my shift, and when I would stock the coolers I would put what I had purchased in one of the empty boxes to disguise it as trash. As I would take the trash out I would place the boxes or bag behind the dumpster, which I always conveniently parked next to. On my way out for the night, I would nonchalantly throw my purchases in the back of my truck and be ready for the night's adventures.

When I got promoted to cashier and could work the store by myself, I took things to another level. I started to take the empty boxes from twelve packs of soda and replace them with beer, so that now I was buying beer at a discounted price. I was doing all of this in secret; no one knew of my schemes. I had developed a private, classified sector of my mind that was just for me. It was my own little sick game that fed a continuous need to feel wanted, needed, and desired. Some of my biggest regrets in life are how I took advantage of a trusting family who owned this business.

This convenience store became my own little secretive supplier of goods to be sold or consumed. I had gone as far as to overcharge each customer five to ten cents for different items. I would get them distracted by having a conversation with them to avoid getting caught. If I did, I would play it off as if I had made a mistake. I would tally the pennies that I overcharged people and would make an extra twenty to forty dollars a night, depending on the flow of business. Not my proudest or most honorable moment, but this is what I came up with to feed my growing addiction.

As I closed out my junior year of high school, I started to date one of my ex-girlfriend's friends. This was an extremely volatile situation, and thinking back, I cannot even remember why I was attracted to Maggie. Maybe it was the whole drama of dating a girl after breaking up with her friend. I do not know. However, I do know that it was a crazy situation. At this point in my life I had grown some in popularity, and it was being fueled by my ability to consume large amounts of alcohol, my "don't care" attitude and my extreme outbursts that were violently charged by rants of profane phrases. These were usually directed at someone whom I was really, deep down, scared of, and I knew that if push came to shove, I would most likely get my rear kicked. I was officially a smoker and drank consistently. Cedric and I still had late curfews that allowed us to hang out with all sorts of people. I had, and still have, the ability to talk, communicate, or hang out with anyone from any walk of life.

The nights I would work, I would shoot over to Maggie's house till about eleven; then I would either go home or meet up with Cedric. He and I would usually just ride around, drinking and talking. We would actually have some pretty deep conversations, often centered on our own demise and our personal points of view concerning God. Cedric lived with his mom and stepdad but saw his dad occasionally. Like any son, he had a deep love for his father. During our freshman year, his dad had died a lonely and painful death. He had drunk until passing out, flat on his back in the living room floor, and drowned in his own vomit. Making this even more horrible was the fact that he remained there for several days before being found. He was known for disappearing and going on drinking binges, so no one thought anything of it when he was gone for a couple of days. This rocked Cedric's world and we were the perfect storm, creating a toxic, destructive partnership that would take us on many drunken adventures. The problem was that Cedric and I had our own demons to deal with after the night was over and we had made it back to our homes, usually drunk or heavily buzzed. I think that is why we spent so much time together; we were both dealing with issues, and it helped to have someone to relate to. However, when no one was looking, we were dealing with our issues in very dangerous, deceitful, and isolated ways.

My dirty little secret started with the mindless surfing of stations in my parents' family room, which became the start of a continuous abuse against my own body for years to come. Paul says it this way in 1 Corinthians 6:18 (HCSB): "The person who is sexually immoral sins against his own body." My parents led with lots of grace, which is not bad, but without truth, all that grace resulted in my wandering into dangerous places and absorbing harmful influences. The church I was associated with, and people who claimed to be Christians, delivered heavy-handed truth that was legalistic and produced a spirit of rebellion in me. Pornography was on all my friends' minds in some form or fashion. We cracked jokes, made snide remarks, and were, overall, disgusting with our verbiage. My level of interest in pornography was different and was heightened by drugs and alcohol. When no one was looking, I was using pornography as a coping mechanism, essentially a way to hide. Hide from what, though? Hiding from the weighing truth and grace of Jesus (John 1:14, HCSB), and running from the challenge to be different and set apart. Hiding from an already intentional God pressing His will on my life and attempting to reveal purpose. Obviously, this was neither clear nor noticeable to me at the time, but I certainly felt it on some level.

Our purpose or destination is somewhere we are headed, but I felt that I had no purpose in life. This feeling of having no purpose resulted in my turning to pornography, because that was where I felt needed and wanted. The eyes of the participants staring back me from the pages or screens in my dirty secret gave me a good feeling followed by self-punishment. The flip side was that I wanted to feel pain, because I felt the need to punish myself by abusing my body that God had created. The ultimate punishment, in my mind, against a God that gave me no purpose was to destroy the one thing he created for good.

6

Don't talk to strangers. We have probably all been taught this by parents, teachers, or police officers at some point in our lives. It's a universal command spoken to just about every child around the globe in essentially the same context. The "don't talk to strangers" campaign taught generations of children to fear strangers. On top of this, I think we are ingrained with a natural sense of fear or discernment that subconsciously tells us when we are encountering a person whom we don't know well enough to trust. An interesting statistic, though, is that 90 percent of abductions are not committed by strangers at all, according to research by the Kids Foundation. It is astonishing to me that abducted children know their abductor most of the time.

A problem with the campaign to teach children not to talk to strangers arises when, in the very next breath, we also demand them to respect their elders. To a child, everyone is an elder. It becomes confusing, wanting to respect elders but also not wanting to talk to strangers. Are you to honor your parents by following the rule of not talking to strangers, or do you run the risk of disrespecting an elder only to possibly be punished for it later? A very confusing moment indeed!

With the 90 percent, those who knew their abductors, what do you tell them? The abductor could be a trusted friend of the family, an uncle or aunt, and in some cases, one of the parents. We teach our children this very confusing lesson and then wonder why so much confusion sets in as a child matures into a teenager and adulthood. This is the seed of the confusion – who are the strangers?

This is the biggest paradox of confusion for all believers of any faith-based organization. Whether it be Christianity, Islam, Satanism, or even atheism, we find hypocrisy and inconsistency in all faiths. And, yes, atheism is a faith, but we will get to that later. Here's the reality: We are all looking to follow something or someone. To believe in something bigger than ourselves, creating a sense of purpose. Strangers step into those moments and manipulate them for their own sick, twisted entertainment. As kids, we are always put on guard concerning strangers, but as we grow older, do these strangers we are warned about simply stop being a threat, or are the dangers of strangers always present?

There was a young man by the name of Timothy who was mentored by his spiritual father, the apostle Paul (Philippians 2:22, HCSB). Timothy was a young believer in Lystra, a Roman colony in the province of Galatia. Paul's and Timothy's paths crossed during Paul's second mission trip. Timothy joined Paul for the remainder of his second mission and on his third mission trip. These two guys truly had a father-son relationship. Paul refers to Timothy in 1 Corinthians 4:17 (NIV) as his beloved and faithful child in the Lord. Timothy's family was similar to many American families that we see today. Not much is known about his father, but his mother and grandmother were believers in Christ as the result of one of Paul's mission trips. Essentially, these women were single mothers. With no male guidance in the household, Timothy searched out male leadership, as all boys do who grow up without fathers.

On one of the mission trips, Paul decided to leave Timothy in Ephesus, one of Paul's church plants. He needed someone on the ground to fight the presence of false teachers. Timothy had walked with Paul many miles and interacted with many types of people. Paul realized the disastrous effect of false teachers on people and the church. These false teachers are characterized as not genuine, not true, and teaching to fool or deceive the people. They were deliberately teaching that which was untrue to gain control of the church, so is the threat of dangerous strangers always present? Yes! Paul writes Timothy as a concerned and proactive father warning his son of dangers. In 1 Timothy 1:3 (Reformation Study Bible), Paul tells Timothy to stay on track and warns him of those introducing fantasy stories.

A stranger is defined as a foreigner, newcomer, outsider, one who is unaccustomed to or unacquainted with something specified, a person not legally party to an act, proceeding, etc. There are strangers whom we don't know and need to seek out for relationships. That is not what I am referring to and not what Paul is telling Timothy. It's the strangers who are false teachers, who are out there digressing us into weak-minded individuals, resulting in weak-minded judgment that resembles that of sheep following each other to slaughter. The same objective as that of a stranger luring a small child into their world for their own twisted doctrine that ends in hopelessness, pain, and confusion is exactly what Paul instructs Timothy to fight against. Whether we like to admit it or not, we have allowed people to bait us into their world of irresponsibility that defies authority, overriding God's law for life, sex, and truth. I have allowed plenty of strangers to lure me into their world, feeding me plenty of false teachings. When do strangers come to lure? When you are at your most vulnerable.

One of the loneliest moments in my life was when I was in a gymnasium full of people during my high school graduation. I sat in the second to the last chair because my cousin and I were the only two students with last names starting with Z. And his first initial was an L, which was obviously after my first initial of G. Honestly, I couldn't tell you what words were said or who said them. I do remember the sinking feeling as names were called out of those graduating. I was secretly hoping that something would happen like a fire or bombing in that gym to prevent the graduation from continuing. For most, this was an exciting moment, but for me it was terrifying. I have always been a deep thinker and have been labeled as a forward thinker, but I often kept these thoughts to myself because it isn't good party etiquette to talk about what tomorrow might bring as a result of today. While waiting for my name to be called, I could read the writing on the wall. I had no plans, no ambition, seemingly no purpose—I was officially lost. Not physically but mentally. Looking up and around at all the people in my class, supposed friends and family, I was overwhelmed with the fear of what my future would bring. Like looking into a mirror, I could see all of those who had sat in these seats at my high school at past graduations repeating the same cycle, whether good or bad, of their family and peers.

One of the definitions of insanity is doing the same action repeatedly but expecting different results each time. In the book of Daniel, King Belshazzar brings Daniel into his chambers after some really freaky writing on his wall is written by a hand that appears (Daniel 5:5-6, HCSB). The king is unable to interpret it and brings Daniel in because of his reputation as a wise man and interpreter of visions and dreams. The interpretation is not good: in Aramaic, *mene*, *mene*, *tekel*, *parsin*. Daniel tells him that the words mean that the king's days are numbered because he has failed to measure up to God's standards of righteousness (Daniel 5:24-28, HCSB).

At graduation, I did not measure myself to God's standards, but I knew I had fallen short of whatever standard I had created for myself. I used to say all the time that I wouldn't live to see thirty. I would say this in a joking manner, but in the privacy of my mind I believed it. The writing on the wall that I read in the gymnasium, as my name was called to walk across the stage, was similar to a longtime prison inmate getting the call for parole. What was I supposed to do now? I was somebody on the inside but was now being released into a world with no status or direction. For twelve years, I had been told where to go, what to do, and how to do it. I'll admit though, that even in the structure school had provided, I found strangers who enticed me with pleasures, and those strangers were quickly becoming part of the family.

That summer after my graduation, Cedric and I took a trip to Galveston Island. It was our summer vacation. We didn't tell a lot of people we were going, because we didn't want anyone else going. I was going to meet Cedric's stepbrother, who was into drugs and who partied hard. We had all smoked weed, even Maggie, but it was mostly full of fillers and stems—bad weed. Our purpose that summer after graduation was to find better weed.

We rolled into Texas City, just north of Galveston Island, to meet up with Cedric's stepbrother Trent at a hotel where we had reserved a room for the night. When I met Trent, he was what I would think a playboy would look and act like. He sold drugs, went to Houston nightclubs, and had stories of sexual encounters with all sorts of women. At the time, I was in awe, and Trent was a stranger whom I allowed to invite me into his world. Instead of being lured in by candy, I was lured in by laced weed. We were sitting at the small two-chair table in our room when Trent brought up his backpack, or what he referred to as his candy bag. He took out two long, cigar-looking joints. The baggy had humidity in it as if they were warm when placed in it, and he called them blunts. I had never seen these in person, only heard of them in rap songs.

It took a while to get it to light because it was damp. As Cedric took the first hit, Trent explained to us that it was laced. I didn't know what that meant, so I took my hit, and we smoked about half, then started to feel the effects. What happened from that point was a blur. What I do remember is seeing what seemed to be a large insect on the ceiling. It looked like a spider but gradually got bigger and bigger. Time slowed, talking was difficult, and I could not understand anyone and felt like I was hearing underwater. I grabbed the bed and hung on all night. I was filled with fear and anxiety but also had an incredible euphoric feeling like I was free from my thoughts, failures, and the consistent reminder of what I wasn't. When we woke the next morning, we had slamming headaches and realized that we didn't even leave the room all night. Trent had left us because we were rolling (or extremely high) way too hard to even leave the room. When we returned home, we brought back our newfound sedative but the same old vision—keep the party going. Really, we just could not face the reality that we had low expectations placed on our lives by family, friends, and peers. Graduating high school was one of the milestones that we were at least supposed to obtain. I found that life was easy when I had low goals. Problem was, the goals were so low that I had no purpose, because after graduation, my goal was to get a job. I had held a job almost my entire high school career. What now? That summer, I went into a spiral of questions and fears. I was eighteen years old, graduated, working at a convenience store, and drowning in self-hatred, anger, and depression. The experience in Texas City was my first official crossover from the socially acceptable usage of weed and alcohol, and I loved it.

It is recorded in Matthew 6 that Jesus said "If your eye is bad, your whole body will be full of darkness" (Matt. 6:23, MSG). How I started to love the darkness! Still to this day, I can listen to bands and artists like Korn, Marilyn Manson, Slipknot, and Nine Inch Nails among many others and totally understand the feelings and emotions trapped behind their lyrics. I had a friend named Mike who was the only one who would listen to this type of music with me because we shared a common struggle—seeking purpose and the need for unconditional love. Both of us would fall head over heels with the first girl who would show us any interest, and if she would have sex with us, then she would own us. A secret of mine was that I would sometimes take the country back roads home and stop somewhere along the way where no one would hear me and just blast the music; just scream and curse. Why? I did not know how else to handle it. My eye had become bad. The drinking, smoking, and partying were just byproducts of my growing addiction to pornography. My whole body was paying the price for what Marilyn Manson calls "our 15 minutes of shame." Just as Jesus tells us in Matthew 6, you will love the darkness if your eyes are corrupted with evil.

From 1997 to the end of 1999, alcohol was a staple in my diet. I can almost count on my hands the days I went without drinking. I had sunk into a dark place, and Maggie was the perfect person to have a relationship with in these dark moments. She had her own issues and absolutely no direction, just like me. Maggie and I had created an unintentional, loveless, passionless relationship that was built on lies, deception, and depravity. Our relationship was built on a cornerstone of sex. Both of us struggled with similar things that made us a combustible couple, like fire and gasoline meeting. I can remember very few moments that were drama-free, positive, and encouraging interactions between us.

After dating for a couple of months, we decided to have sex. We would have sex at her parents' trailer before a party while her dad was working and her mom was out with friends. My first real sexual experience was with Maggie while Cedric, and Maggie's friend Sam waited in the living room, drinking. I believed that Maggie kept Sam around as a friend because

Sam was somewhat the innocent one of the bunch. She was one of the only friends I remember who really respected Maggie and was there for her. Cedric always wanted to have sex with Sam, but she would never have anything to do with him. He had grown into somewhat of a tolerable pervert with some pretty graphic sexual escapades under his belt. Not too many respectable girls would give him a chance because of his track record.

Maggie had a lot of issues with her parents and family, and she was looking for an escape. She came from a family of heavy drinkers, and when we first started going to parties I was impressed by her ability to drink so much. She would hang with the best of them. What started to happen was that, like all of us, Maggie grew a tolerance and wanted more. She started to smoke and drink hard liquor pretty regularly before she was out of high school. She was two years behind me in school, so she naturally hung out with slightly older people and was invited to parties that most high school students were not at.

Maggie, Cedric, and I hung out a lot over the next couple of years, moving from one party to the next. They really weren't even parties, because it was rarely a special event. It was something that I did, like brushing my teeth. I didn't smoke weed or do any other type of drugs too often because I didn't want to be labeled a crackhead. For some odd reason, heavy drinkers are acceptable and drug users are considered to have crossed the line. As a former user of both, I can say there is no difference in what you are using. The only difference is why.

I started to segment the groups of people I hung out with. I couldn't mix certain types of people with each other because of the unwritten politics and distorted ethics of different groups of people. I hung out with everyone. There were nights when I would simply drink and ride back roads and there were nights that I would smoke weed and chill. Maggie went where I was usually, and one particular night she decided to make out with someone at a party we were at. I was too trashed to care at the time, and when I finally confronted her about it, she convinced me that it was innocent and she was drunk. I accepted it and moved on.

A few months later, we all began to hang out at a mobile home that was out in the middle of nowhere with these two individuals who used it to have sex in because they were both in active relationships. Maggie, Cedric, and I started to hang out with these two and would play drinking games until we passed out or ran out of alcohol. What I would later learn is that Maggie and Cedric one night engaged each other sexually after I had passed out. This went on for several weeks until I was told by several people, including my sister. I denied it for the longest time, thinking that a best friend wouldn't do that and my girlfriend wouldn't betray me. I was wrong. I confronted Maggie after hearing about this one too many times. Her response was, "I am sorry." She then went on to tell me how this had occurred and why, putting blame on me for neglecting her. The perfect words to tell someone who already has low self-esteem and depression issues. I instantly grew so angry with Cedric that I honestly had my first real thoughts of murder. The betrayal that I felt from Maggie did not compare to the betrayal I felt had been inflicted on me by Cedric. This event burned me deeply, affecting my ability to build friendships and allowing myself to become vulnerable. After this event, everything seemingly started to push me out of my hometown. My parents had grown tired of me using their home as a hotel. I had taken Maggie back, resulting in my having this feeling that everyone was talking about me. The embarrassment of the situation was overwhelming. I had to get out.

All the teens who graduated from our high school who didn't have college or career plans would frequently say they were going to the local community college. To study what? Well, of course, to study the basics! Which I assumed meant to register for community college and blow off classes while playing Ping-Pong in the recreation center. The truth is, I went to college because I wanted to find purpose. I could see that the cement was setting quickly around my feet, weighing me down to drown in my own mediocrity and failures. What I know now that I did not know then was that it was me putting those figurative cement blocks around my feet with my decisions and actions. Outside of my parents and sister, my life was full of strangers. When I say strangers, I am referring to outsiders, and in all honesty, I started to question everybody in my life. Not vocally, out loud, but in my mind.

My sister was living in Waco at the time with her boyfriend because he was going to Texas State Technical College (TSTC). She wanted to move back home, but their apartment was still under a lease agreement. I took that opportunity to move to Waco by taking over her lease. Of course, Maggie wanted to move with me.

In late 1999, I was ready to start my new life, and we moved in together. I enrolled at Texas State Technical College and started classes almost immediately. For the first time, I felt like I had some type of direction. My first semester I made the dean's list. It was my first real accomplishment on my own and I reported home quickly to seek the approval of my parents. Sadly, this would be the last time I would make the dean's list, because my focus on school was distracted by the new friends Maggie had met at her job and the friends I made at school. What I discovered about the Baptist, Bible Belt, and Christian town of Waco was that drugs were everywhere and everybody seemed to have them. What was even more surprising for this country boy was the amount of drugs that came in and out of Baylor University, a Baptist school, and how widely drug use was accepted at Texas State Technical College among the student body.

Within six months of living in Waco, Maggie had found a group of friends at her job as a health care billing agent. I had made acquaintances around the school and began a growing friendship with Patrick, who was a bartender at a local famous hangout where many Baylor students worked as well. My first day in class I sat next to Patrick, and his first words where, "Did you dye your hair?" I had attempted to pull off a hairstyle that a white rapper by the name of Eminem had made popular. Needless to say, I did not pull it off very well. On top of that, my rapping skills consisted of attempting to rhyme every last word. Kind of like, "I have a cat, it has a hat, I hit it with a bat," Dr. Seuss style, or over-the-top vulgar rhyming everything with truck; that was my rapping style. I started to hang out with Patrick, studying, drinking beer, or just sitting on the couch; he would be my voice of reason.

Then there were Maggie's friends we started to go to bars and clubs with. Brad was a six-feet-eight-inch-tall redhead with multiple ear piercings, a tongue bar, and a lip ring. His girlfriend, Jackie, stood five feet two inches tall or so, was slightly older, and had a daughter. Brad lived with her off and on, and we always partied at Jackie's apartment. The clubs got expensive, so to avoid overpaying for liquor, we hung out at Jackie's all the time. Our nights consisted of one of the couples bringing a bottle of liquor and a couple of cases of beer. Most of the time, it was just four of, us, but sometimes we would have some tagalongs. We would drink and smoke weed. At this point in my life, I had started to smoke weed and drink daily. I had a job at a banking data center in downtown Waco, down the street from where Maggie, Brad, and Jackie all worked. I always considered myself a partier and not a dopehead. The night I crossed that line was when all four of us gathered enough money to buy a brick of weed.

We had all agreed that we could save money by buying in bulk rather than just small portions, and we had agreed to sell some of the brick and split the profits. First rule in drug dealing: You cannot be addicted to your own product. Brad and I took our $500 and proceeded to Dairy Queen. This is where the drug dealer worked. We placed an order, drove up to the window, took the burgers out of the bag, and put the money into the empty Dairy Queen bag. The dealer was also the night manager. I guess you could say he multitasked. Later that night, the night manager from the Dairy Queen, a.k.a. Razor the drug dealer, arrived at Jackie's apartment with a backpack full of drugs. It was the first time that I had actually seen someone carry a gun. As he opened his backpack, I caught a glimpse of a pistol. I assume it was a 9 mm, which is, of course, standard issue for drug dealers,. At least, that is what the movies had taught me. He took our brick out, laid it on the table and then proceeded to up-sell us. Brad bought an array of pills and an "eight ball," or roughly four grams of cocaine. That night would end up being my moment of shame. As I sat in the middle of the couch during the early morning hours, I had a moment of clarity that I believe God allowed me to have. It was as if time had stopped. I looked around, looked at my reflection in the TV, looked at the people around me, and it hit me: I was what I had always said I would not become. What does a person do when he comes to that realization?

After I got myself together and made a drive home that I really don't remember, I headed to my 8:30 a.m. class. There, I was met by Patrick who noticed that I had had a long night and was still feeling a few lingering effects of my intake of narcotics from several hours before. This would become a regular occurrence for the next several months. I liked Patrick and knew in my gut that he was a good guy, so I tried to make everyone happy. I once mixed Brad and Jackie with Patrick and his group of friends and realized quickly that I was trying to mix oil and water. I started to hang out with Patrick and party with his group a couple nights a week and hang out with Maggie, Brad, and Jackie the other nights. Sometimes I would hang out till midnight with Patrick and then shoot over to Brad and Jackie's for the remainder of the morning.

It was definitely a crazy cycle. I was going to school during the day, working at the banking data center till nine, and cleaning a real estate building for a janitorial firm. After all that, I was partying till the early morning hours. I would hit my limit at times and just crash for hours, usually missing school, but never missing work, because I needed the money. Maggie's life was just as chaotic, but when her nineteen-year-old cousin was killed in a boating accident, she totally lost it. Maggie found relief from her mourning by indulging in cocaine and trying to contact the spirits through the Ouija board. We had gotten into these rituals and dabbled in summoning spirits before we moved to Waco, but with Brad and Jackie and their passion for darkness, it would become an unhealthy addiction. Don't get me wrong, I was participating and wasn't innocent, but I also had Father Folk's stories in the back of my head that spoke of the dangers of invoking spirits and opening the door to the devil. I knew this had reached a level that I was not prepared for when I walked into my apartment and saw Maggie working the Ouija board by herself. There are many verses in the Bible about conjuring or summoning spirits, and most, if not all, instruct us not to. I can tell you firsthand that this is when the evil in my life took on a mind of its own. I firmly believe that the gates of hell were cracked open, and I would have nightmares that were so intense, vulgar, and sexually disturbing that I would wake up praying that they would just go away. In an attempt to silence my mind, I increased my intake of drugs and alcohol.

Jackie broke up with Brad one night. I later found out that it was because Maggie and Brad had started to sleep with each other. Again, I was in a situation that involved Maggie destroying the little trust I had in her. This exploded one late night as we drove home, screaming and getting physical with each other while driving down the road. She had begged me to take a ride with her so that she could explain herself. She was very high and was tweaking (or acting acratic) from the cocaine ingested earlier in the night. As we fought and screamed, the car jerked and swerved; this is one of those moments that God had to have intervened, as a cop pulled us over. I was convinced that we were both going to jail because of her erratic behavior and talking a hundred miles per hour and me smelling of weed and alcohol. I'm not very sure what was all said, but the cop handed me the keys and told me to drive home, saying that he would follow to make sure we got there safely. I am still speechless about this moment.

Once home, our fight intensified and resulted in our getting physical with each other. I can say this with confidence: This was not my, or Maggie's, proudest moment. The relationship ended that night, and if we were honest with each other, the relationship had ended long before this point. It was a relief when I was able to finally have the courage to say the words and agree with her about ending the relationship. After we both agreed, and after a long drawn-out argument, we woke the next morning not really knowing what our next steps would be. Obviously, one of us had to leave. We had just gotten into a rental lease in a trailer park just north of Waco that was literally down the street from my school. Also, the trailer house was every bit of what you would imagine a three-hundred-dollar-per-month rental of a two-bedroom trailer would be in an area that was considered the slum of Waco. The one thing this trailer house had going for it was that I had room on the property to plant a garden. It was my little escape from the reality of my life.

When Maggie moved out and I was in the trailer alone, I was truly scared. I quit sleeping in the bedroom and slept in the living room. I would spend as much time as I could away from the trailer. It became a reminder of all that I had failed at. This is not what anyone pictures when they move out, but I was living up to everyone else's expectations and merely breathing air. I had lost a big segment of my life when Maggie left, because the people I had hung out with the most were Maggie, Brad, and Jackie. I was heartbroken, not because Maggie left or because she violated me once again, but because I realized that I had no real friendship in life. I was growing sour and bitter toward relationships, but I adopted a mentality that I would start to protect myself by using women instead of pursuing relationships with them. Basically, I was harboring un-forgiveness for those who had hurt me.

At this point in my life, friendships with other males consisted of brokenness and shallowness, friendships with no real substance. My relationships with females were measured against my mother's relationship with my father, always staying true and loving unconditionally, even through my father's toughest moments. I had been with Maggie for almost six years. Most of that time was full of distrust, hurt, and pain. Maggie putting me in situations that would cause me to question myself. There was a lot of anger toward God in this moment in my life, and I was already so far from God and His truth, but I found a way to go further. The trailer house became a symbol of who I was—worn, broken, and ugly from the outside and full of nasty, dirty, disgusting thoughts, actions, and anger on the inside. I had become a creature, a man taken under the full power of sin. I was so far from understanding divine revelation that I had no reason or direction. The apostle Peter speaks of this in great detail as he describes false teachers who are far from the truth (2 Peter 2:11-14, HCSB). Have you ever seen a dog that has been beaten? It reacts in one of two ways. Either it cowers to the aggressor and runs, or it uses growling, barking, and an aggressive stance to drive away the aggressor. The problem is, a dog that has been hurt cannot discern whether the aggressor is truly there to hurt it or to help. I had become a brute creature that was solely relying on the instinct of my appetite, following my carnal mind, and refusing to apply understanding and reason that was naturally placed in my spirit by God. My life became a confusing array of mischief that was deceiving me into what I believed was freedom and happiness.

With Maggie out of the picture along with Brad and Jackie, my drug connection was gone. Patrick, being the stand-up responsible guy he was, made sure that I was not home alone very often. He was the only person in my life at the time I respected and admired because of his contagious, joyful personality. He brought me into his world but it felt too closed in, choking me and making me feel somewhat like a sellout for hanging out with Baylor people. There was a real disconnection between Baylor students and the rest of Waco. They were the preppie, rich kids who would occasionally slum in some of the outlying areas if they were in need of drugs or didn't want to be seen on campus acting out and doing things that might impact their prominent status as Baylor students. Now don't get me wrong; Baylor is a Baptist school, and there are some good Baptist Christians there, but from my side of the fence, Baylor students were the biggest hypocrites in Waco: not to be trusted but used for money and access. Also, if you put a Baylor kid in a pinch, they would always choose the institution out of loyalty. Again, these were the students playing Baylor elite, but their core was darker and more devious than mine and were some of the craziest guys around Waco because they were backed by money and influence. I had adopted Waco as my home, the part that rummaged around in the twilight in their own misery, looking for new recruits each night. Patrick seemed to always be right there trying to cheer me up, bringing me into his world, meeting new friends. We would drink and smoke really crappy weed that made your throat sore because of all the seeds, twigs, and dirt in it. They were into bongs and going to local Baylor hangouts. I always felt as if I was being stared at and lots of times would get the question, "What year are you?" or "What is your major?" Instinctively, I would go ahead and downgrade myself, responding with, "I just go to TSTC." This was usually followed by a smirk or a comment that I laughed along with, usually at my own expense. What I really wanted to do was unleash an attack of obscenities followed by a beer bottle across the head of the cocky, self-indulgent, two-faced Baylor student, but I would just shrug it off, laugh, and act out the violent response in my head. In addition, I was smart enough to know I was outnumbered and that this was not my crowd.

That semester at school I met Travis in my DC Circuits class. I met Travis right as I was ending my relationship with Maggie but never had hung out with him because Maggie didn't like him. He was a country boy from South Texas who seemed to always have the right things to say, seemed to pick up women everywhere, and always had a stash of drugs. He didn't have a care in the world. What was most frustrating was that school came naturally to him. While I struggled to keep up a nightlife and pass classes, he seemed to pass with ease. Travis came into my life at the right moment, from my standpoint at the time. Patrick didn't particularly care for him but tolerated him, and rarely did I hang out with them both at the same time. Travis introduced me to strip clubs. I had been a couple times with Maggie, Brad, and Jackie, but Travis made it even more enticing. Travis was a stranger in a van, showing me bags of every dirty little desire that my flesh wanted, that I felt I wanted and needed. I looked to him as a friend. Everyone else looked at him as a stranger luring me into a dark, twisted celebration of my sin.

When I agreed to go to the strip club with Travis the first night we officially hung out, he brought this older guy who had a weird German name, I think Baca. When we walked into the BYOB (bring your own beer) club, I didn't know what to expect. I had that same sinking, scared feeling I had the first night I drank beer. I didn't know Travis that well and sure didn't know this Baca guy, but I played it cool. We stopped and bought two twelve packs of beer and a couple of bottles of liquor that Baca paid for. Travis had leaned over and whispered to me that Baca didn't have any friends and he usually paid for everything. Deep down, I felt bad for him, but I was so caught up in the moment that I ignored this feeling. I went right along with everything, taking advantage of this mid-thirties, lonely man who was overweight, prematurely balding and obviously paid for friends. When we arrived at Sonny's BYOB, right outside the Waco city limits, we walked into the corridor to get our IDs checked and stamped. As we proceed into the club it was dark, with lights flashing and smoke. The bar floor smelled like it had had a long night of spilled drinks on it. We picked out a table, iced our beer down, and started to drink. Travis immediately got the attention of a girl by offering free booze and a promise to pay for a lap dance when a good song came on. I watched in amazement because I had never seen anyone work girls the way he did. I wish I could say I sat there innocently, but when you are in the lion's den you act like a lion or get eaten alive. We stayed until the club closed at around 2 a.m. and hung out in the parking lot afterward, seeing if any of the girls wanted to go to Travis's apartment for an after-party. After we with several strippers, none of them took us up on our offer. I was relieved, deep down, because I was not sure what Travis had in mind, and I certainly did not know what my role would be. I want to say that this was my last night at a strip club, but over the next year or so I became a regular patron of them.

Travis had earned my trust. He addressed my immediate emotional needs of feeling wanted, desired and important. Patrick was there as well, but I just couldn't handle my old feelings of sitting in that Catholic class with all my hypocritical classmates who were partying the same as I was and acting like godly children around others, acting one way at their austere Baptist institution and another at parties and bars. Patrick truly cared about me as a man, and he knew that I was struggling and going down a bad road but he smoked weed and drank too, so I just never got his reasoning for not liking

Travis. The difference was that Travis was using me. Patrick saw it and I did not. Yes, Patrick did some of the things I did, but he was a good man who had fallen away from God out of anger over his sister's premature death. Travis was a self-proclaimed atheist. Patrick had been hurt, and instead of turning into an angry beaten dog, he retained his natural personality and was very open with his struggles. He challenged me, and growing up in a household where I wasn't challenged and was taught to pursue comfort, I chose Travis over Patrick many times. Travis would challenge me in different ways and I wanted to rebel.

In Revelations chapter 2, an ancient church or temple was believed to have been raised up out of the ruins of Troy, which was a place where the Gospel of Christ was preached at one time, but now was devoted to emperor worship. The Church of Pergamum was overrun with men whose minds were corrupted and who purposely corrupted faith and the church. In Revelations 2:15 (HCSB), the doctrine of Nicolaitans is referred to and God hates it because it taught that unlawful actions were lawful. The Nicolaitans was a heretical group that when compared to Balaam from the book of Numbers (Num. 17–19 HCSB) had very similar teachings. Sacrificing to idols and simple fornication was no sin to them—this resulted in impure practices. When I went to Travis or when he called, I was invited into his version of the Church of Pergamum. Travis was a stranger, a person that I didn't know at all until I allowed him to lure me in with his own version of the doctrine of Nicolaitans. He offered me the solutions to the issues that I was facing—loneliness, anger, frustration, depression—with the promise of a good time like sex, partying and friends. He was teaching me that there was nothing wrong with having a good time and being happy. These friends I had found with Travis held mirror images of what was going on in the congregation of the Church of Pergamum, with the doctrine of Nicolaitans being taught. The only difference was that I had allowed Travis to minister this doctrine to me, turning me into an idol worshipper of pleasure and self-hate.

My whole basis of belief of who God, Jesus and the Holy Spirit are was formed by everyone around me that I had given authority to speak in my life. My view of the Trinity was being formed by Satan. I am not calling Travis Satan's minion, nor Maggie, Brad or Jackie. But the reality is that, every day, we make hundreds of choices to either glorify God or Satan. Not believing in anything is still glorifying something—Satan. My choices, feelings and beliefs were a reflection of my relationship with God. I was hanging out with people who made the choice to either not believe in God or simply live in some delusional state that this was a lifestyle that could actually fulfill our purpose. Brian Warner wrote these lyrics in 1999:

> *A pill to make you numb,*
> *A pill to make you dumb,*
> *A pill to make you anybody else.*
> *But all the drugs in this world*
> *Won't save her from herself.*
>
> *You were from a perfect world,*
> *A world that threw me away today.*
> *Today, today to run away.*

When Brian Warner wrote this song, I was totally drawn to his music because it made sense to me. What many may not know is that Brian Warner is more commonly known as Marilyn Manson. Take away the shock rock drama and makeup, and Brian is just another kid who grew up with a distorted view of God in his Catholic household, with plenty of strangers along the way who lured him into a world of false teachings. I would sing this song with such emotion and passion, but it was not until Travis would teach me another portion of his doctrine that it would be revealed to me what "a pill to make you anybody else" actually was.

7

A religious fashion show plays out each Sunday, sometimes known as the most hypocritical hour of the week. This weekly fashion show of those who walk around polished, well dressed, and measuring others by a set of standards that are out of their own judgment they call God's laws (Matthew 23:3, MSG). They walk on their red carpets with their beautiful garments and jewels in the attempt that no one will see the maggot-filled souls full of greed and gluttony (Matthew 23:26, MSG). This fashion show of religion and of proclaimed scholars is church. This image issue of church and religion is nothing new, as you can read in Matthew 23. There was an extensive issue with hypocrites leading temples and judging people by God's law that they would immediately be dismissed by their very actions and words. Religious leaders, priests, and preachers never had a chance with me because there was no credibility. Sure, in some cases, there were years of study of the Bible, well-organized lectures, and no doubt they were passionate about what they had learned in the Bible. In my experience, there was no credibility, and honestly, I don't ever remember any real Christian approaching me without some hidden agenda. Some of this mistrust and judgment did come from my parents' view of not needing church or a community of believers to have a relationship with God, and this is true to a certain extent. The most obvious and glaring problem with the viewpoint of not needing church or community is that, inherently, a person finds a church and a community without even realizing it. Think about it. When you sit at a bar, movie, strip club, or around a table full of drugs, you are sitting with others, while the bartender, actor, stripper, or drug is ministering to you. A doctrine is being taught. Many doctrines are taught each day in various ways, with various levels of challenges and commitment. The hidden truth is that many, if not the majority, accept and follow those who offer the least amount of resistance and challenge and offer the most comfort. Travis was a renegade, deserting the institution of religion and claiming to be an atheist, but a more honest assessment of our status would be truth-seekers. Maynard James Keenan was quoted as saying

> I witnessed first-hand the hypocrisy of this particular form of Christianity....My views against Christianity or religion in general are directed towards the middle men, those who are in power and use religion as a market force by which to manipulate human beings for their own personal gain.

Maynard was raised in a Southern Baptist church and is the founder of the rock bands Tool and Perfect Circle. His music is heavily saturated with symbolism. He mocks the institution of Christianity but, strangely, never denies that Jesus was special. Obviously, I see now that his viewpoint was that Jesus was way more than just special, but Maynard's assessment of the institution of Christianity and the church was not far from my own. Travis and I connected with music and this disgust with Christianity and any religion. We would throw in Tool's album *Lateralus* and jam the whole album as we took our trips away from reality. Ignoring the fact that we had become professionals at polishing the outside of our cup while our insides were rotting away (Matthew 23:26, HCSB), essentially becoming the same hypocritical people that we stereotyped about Christians.

Everyone has experienced that exhaustion that is past tired, where your legs are achy, mind foggy, and attention span at a bare minimum, just like an emergency generator running on a boat stranded out in the middle of sea. Running the bare essential functions of the boat to keep it afloat until assistance arrives or the captain can limp the wounded vessel back to port. I was beginning to feel like that boat, stranded in the middle of the sea of confusion and exhausted from the journey of life. Travis was the only one who seemed to truly understand me. Right at the beginning of my friendship with Travis, we were trying to learn where each other stood. We decided to have a barbecue at his place on the Texas State Technical College campus. This was the first time we had hung out at his place. It was more of an interview process, deciding whether we could trust each other. There were some small houses that students could rent that had been built back when the campus was used for a military base. These were hard to get because they were usually set aside for single mothers or small families attending the college. The same rules apply to these houses as the dorm rooms, but they were rarely enforced unless there was an over-the-top, outright lack of respect for the campus authorities. Most of the time, as long as it was out of sight, it was out of mind for the campus authorities. It was more work for them to arrest a student because they would have to involve the Waco Police Department. Just like most campus police, they are not seen in the same light as "real" city police officers. This particular evening, Travis was cooking steaks on the grill—his specialty.

Travis was somewhat of a grill master and really enjoyed grilling outside. He invited several guys over to throw back some beers this particular evening. This was your average red-blooded male gathering for the purpose of approval or affirmation from our peer group. A group of males seeking approval and affirmation is a process as old as man himself. What makes us different from one another is who we allow to give us approval and affirmation, what downward spiral we are going into or coming out of. Travis and I shared a desire for authenticity in people because of the amount of hypocritical people we had encountered throughout our lives, especially those who claimed faith in Jesus Christ and God. There is something organic or natural about a person who embraces his or her struggles and sin. In hindsight, a person living in sin and worshipping his or her sinful nature is acting as a hypocrite as well. Ecclesiastes says that man has sought out great inventions that have become as great as gods (Ecclesiastes 7:28-29, King James Bible). God has not called us to be worshippers of things that are fading away. He has called us to live in truth and to be upright. I placed so much blame on hypocrites in the Christian faith for my failures and struggles that I had become a master at hypocrisy. I was holding down a banking job at night as a data processor and a janitorial job and was passing my classes, all without question. I was working hard at shining the "outside of the cup," but the rottenness and filth was running over. This particular night, while standing around the pit waiting for Travis to flip the steaks (and learning a valuable lesson: that if you flip the steak more than once you're playing with your food), I hinted that I might not be going out that night. This was met with a loud and abrupt response challenging me. The consecutive nights of getting hammered and hanging out till the early morning were taking its toll on my body. One of my jobs at the banking data center was a long drawn-out ten-key process. I had actually fallen asleep in the middle of the job I was working on a couple of times. In my defense, data entry isn't the most invigorating jobs, looking at thousands of checks and entering numbers into a database. When I fell asleep for what seemed like hours but was really only a few seconds, I realized that I needed to recoup to prevent losing my job. As I explained my reason to Travis, he invited me in his house, pulled out a little baggy with multiple colors of pills in it, and told me to take some.

In high school, I had started to take NoDoz, a caffeine pill, to fight the long nights and mornings while going to school and working a job, but that had long lost its effects to keep me moving along throughout the night. I had also taken codeine pills for a knee injury in high school, but I never mix anything with alcohol out of fear of death, or at least that's what I had believed till this moment. There was something about how Travis asked me. So with confidence and conviction that resulted in my throwing out all reason and common sense to trust his professional medical prescription, I said, "Okay, friend who has no medical background nor any pharmaceutical training, yes, I will take this brightly colored pill from a Ziploc baggie. This seems okay." I still remember his words as he noticed some concern. "Just take half," he offered as a compromise. After taking half of a Xanax, I did not really feel an effect, so I followed Travis's lead and dropped one in my beer and swallowed it, chasing it with more beer and a pull on my cigarette. Oddly enough, I have a reminder of this night that stays with me in the form of a chipped tooth. It is not visible, but it is there. Even as I write, I rub my tongue on the back of the chipped tooth and remember Travis's dog jumping at me while I was putting a beer bottle to my mouth, chipping the back of my tooth.

Nine Inch Nails' front man, Trent Reznor, wrote an album that would open the door to the mainstream public that would build an acceptance of this mostly unknown underground band. His breakout album came in 1994 and is still referred to as a work of art in the music world. *The Downward Spiral* was the name of the album; Trent Reznor was able to articulate a man's downward spiral into the depths of the dark, isolated parts of his soul in fourteen uniquely designed songs that combined all sorts of genres. Robert Hilburn wrote in a *Los Angeles Times* review that "'Spiral' isn't a celebration or acceptance of nihilism or decadence. It is, instead, an anguished cry for something to believe in during a time when such traditional support systems as religion and family have failed for so many." The first song that Reznor wrote for this album was "Mr. Self-Destruct," which starts off with a screaming voice that ends each verse of the song with the last line whispered, "And I control you." The character in the song realizes that an alter ego is responsible for all the negative aspects in his life. A downward spiral usually refers to a situation that is getting worse very quickly. Since my breakup with Maggie and the emergence of Travis in my life, not only was my drinking, partying, and marijuana usage getting to its highest levels, but fear, negativity, anger, and selfishness that I had never experienced was growing in me. What was more frightening was that as my life got more and more risky, my soul became darker. I was not suicidal, but I really did not care if the morning came, either.

Many people don't know that drugs such as alcohol and downers reduce activity in the brain and central nervous system. This eases tension and lowers inhibitions, increasing sociability and decreasing self-consciousness, basically enhancing the drunken state. The problem with mixing downers with alcohol and marijuana is that it creates a high risk of overdose and dependence. The night I popped pills was the first time I truly felt out of control but totally relieved to take a break from being myself. To escape the place inside my mind where I would hide all my dirty, disturbing, corrupt secrets and thoughts. I was somebody else. Marilyn Manson's lyrics would ring true, "A pill to make you numb, a pill to make you dumb, a pill to make you anybody else." The mixture of alcohol, weed, pills, and sex was a high that was so addictive. And throughout history, it has put many people in the grave prematurely. I now understand how a person starts to mix and increase drugs and behaviors, because you are always chasing a high that beats the last. The endgame of a journey based solely on the search to alter your reality, in most cases will force you to face your reality. This in turn creates aggressiveness or brokenness in facing the reality. This combination was like a boost to my confidence that resulted in my seeking out situations to showcase my newfound reckless demeanor of increasingly risky decision-making. I got involved with the strip club scene to the point that I knew the girls by name. I was a regular, and in my mind, these girls wanted more than my money, and they did. They wanted access to alcohol and drugs, and I could provide that with great success because of Travis's skill to make so much accessible that was otherwise difficult for an everyday person to obtain. Strip clubs are filled with pain, and everyone is trying to alleviate and escape their issues of doubt, failures, and purpose on both sides of the stage. I never thought much about it. It was a gradual progression, and everything felt natural about this culture. I didn't feel like a hypocrite, but I wasn't sure what I totally believed in, either. If there was a God, then I was failing all His tests, and he must be massively disappointed. This thought drove me in ways I didn't really understand or even realize till later in life. I would think about the parties that Maggie and I had together but in reality were rituals and attempts for medium readings through the Ouija board or tarot cards. Even with the negativity and darkness of those moments, there seemed to be a spiritual connection. What was this spiritual connection, a feeling simply manifested in the moment? The Christians I knew and, in some cases, the ones who claimed to be born-again believers participated in gambling, pornography, petty thief, consuming alcohol, messing around with psychics, using profanity, using drugs, or lying to different degrees. I felt more righteous than Christians did because at least I wasn't faking. I was who I was. The Christians prayed to God as in most other religions, but there was this icon at the center of Christianity, Jesus. I never prayed to Jesus, just to God, and ran through the rosary prayers a few hundred times while in the Catholic Church as a kid. Was this spiritual connection Jesus? There are people who justify their actions and personal addictions by mixing it in with Christianity and saying things like, "Jesus hung out with sinners." Yes, that is true, but for a young man searching for purpose and Jesus's followers on both sides of the spectrum, there were too many inconsistencies and seemingly powerless, empty words backed up with impactful actions that would lean more toward a relationship with the opposing forces of Jesus.

A strip club is much like a person sitting in prison. He is there because of his own sinful desires that caused him to make a series of decisions that eventually led to his being immersed and reminded each day of the result of those decisions. In my case, I was sitting not in a cell, but in a dark, smoke-filled room with a girl dancing on a stage as if on an altar where I worshiped my god with money, food, and drink. A church is defined as any division of a body of people professing the same creed and acknowledging the same ecclesiastical authority, or in other words, a lawful assembly of a community of believers with the same denominational characteristics. This was my church, my place of worship—the place where I would become more evil.

Paul warns Timothy of the fatal end that the seducers of evil offer: "Unscrupulous con men will continue to exploit the faith. They are as deceived as the people they lead astray. As long as they are out there, things can only get worse" (2 Timothy 3:13, MSG). My comfort and progression in my sexual temptations led me to celebrate my lust. Satan had subtly been invited into my life through the power of my own corruptions that grew worse and worse. Like people who take their faith in Christ seriously and aggressively and who seek out rituals, places of worship, and who offer up personal prayers, I had established my trailer house as my personal temple. The trailer was about thirty years old, the age and neglect were obvious from the hole in the back bedroom covered with insulation and carpet. This was the same trailer where Maggie and I had had disturbing arguments, parties, and dysfunctional sexual experiences. The trailer had a backroom with a computer on a cheap, water-warped desk with a Walmart discount quality look to it. The carpet in this room was a light brown with several black stains on it. A small closet smelled like an old storage shed; the entire small room smelled of a mixture of way-too-old carpet and mildew, strangely, very similar to the wrecked RV that Wayne and I had played in as children. The computer was a Gateway, a popular PC in the nineties. The name was fitting because this became my gateway to the world of porn addiction. Before Maggie left, I had a porn habit similar to that of an occasional binge drinker. After Maggie left and Travis became a permanent fixture in my life, my porn habits began to become darker and more secluded. Even when I was by myself in the trailer house, I would close the door to the room because I felt too exposed. Something about closing the door and locking it made me feel like I had another layer of protection from the truth. This room became my private prayer room for offering up myself to the growing addiction of pornography. No one but me and the spiritual counterparts of heaven and hell would know the truth. Not even Travis knew the amount of time I was spending surfing, chatting, and participating in webcam sessions. I was ashamed even in front of those who were living less than moral lifestyles.

Patrick was still around during this time of my life; he had started to date one of the servers from the bar and grill he was working at, a famous local college hangout that was known for the extremely large beer glasses and authentic Texas country music played essentially all day, with an occasional visit by one of the artists. Once, I met Pat Green, a local Texas music star, but I did not realize it because it was not really my scene. All I knew was that he bought beer for the whole bar that night. The server Patrick started dating was a Baylor student from Houston who was an outspoken, vibrant suburban girl with lots of friends and a very open-minded view about sexuality. She and Patrick were a bit of an odd couple, but the relationship worked because of the party element that she and her Baylor friends desired. Patrick began to hang out with more of the Baylor crowd, and I tried my best to hang out with them as much as possible because I felt like it was the lesser of two evils. I used the relationships that Patrick had with the Baylor crowd and at the bar he worked at to work over for free beer and food. I went to a few parties, but what I found was that many Baylor parties consisted of a bunch of rich, entitled young adults looking for an outlet to protest their predetermined lives by the parents being held hostage by money and greed. I had a hate toward the Baylor establishment and really any highly regarded educational establishment because it represented control and hypocrisy. I secretly wanted to destroy and expose the very ones at these campus because of the face value, high-moral, and ethical lives they lived in the open as they slummed with guys like me and Patrick who were merely survivors looking for some sort of affirmation. I was also jealous of Baylor students and alumni because of the high level of respect they received and also that someone had invested so much in their education while I merely existed without anyone really investing in my well-being. Well, besides Travis. I felt like Travis was looking out for me. It is hard to understand after what you, the reader, know about Travis up to this point, but I never had to try to fit in. I was encouraged, affirmed, and respected—everything a man looks for in a fulfilling relationship. I was always torn between Patrick and Travis because I respected them and both of them treated me as a brother. Take out all the drinking, drugs, girls, and there were moments—granted, small moments—when I felt a genuine friendship. When I started to get to know Patrick's girlfriend and her friends, I tried to fit in with the Baylor crowd, and I did. If you have not realized yet, I have a talent for finding a way to fit in with any type of person. The upside to Patrick's newfound relationship was that I would have access to another type of women, not the usually bottom feeders of society. That might sound terrible, but it is truth. The women I was with most days were victims of some distorted, dysfunctional relationship. They were not lesser than anyone else, but they just didn't have the resources or desire to get out of the situations they were in Women with resources and people who care can create a way to prevent themselves from being bottom feeders. Come to think of it, I was a bottom feeder. I guess the old saying is that "misery loves company." These newfound Baylor girls that Patrick had brought me into connection with were women with resources. They liked to party with alcohol and, in some cases, drugs. The difference, and my biggest barrier from fully committing to these relationships, was that they did it out of boredom and rebellion. I saw them as posers because I did not have any light at the end of the tunnel (or at least this is what I perceived at the time). This was my life, and there was no graduation or career awaiting me. I never made the comment "when I graduate" or "this is just temporary" because this was my reality. But this was seemingly a game to these girls to slum with a couple of naïve boys.

Patrick was a good friend and still to this day is a good man. He is genuinely a gentlemen and one of the few people in my life at the time who was willing to step into my trash. After Maggie and I split, he had seen the demise of my character. The evil in me was at war with the good, or to paraphrase Paul in Romans 7, there is a predictability about sin. The moment I decided to do good, sin was there to trip me up (Romans 7:21–23, HCSB). I truly did want to be good. I wanted to delight in God, but it was blatantly apparent that a large part of me didn't enter into that same enthusiasm. I wanted to rebel, and there were moments when that rebellion would lash out with the enhancement of drug and alcohol-induced moments. This rebellion was always self-inflicted, for the most part. The drinking, drugs, and pornography were actions I was using against myself. The anger and frustration that I bottled up inside me were typically saved for my own self-punishment.

One particular night, my emotions and need for affirmation overflowed onto some somewhat-innocent bystanders. Travis, myself, and a few other guys were drinking and smoking weed, and, at this point, I was fully into popping pills. I actually chose to pop pills over doing cocaine, as cocaine made me hyperactive and paranoid. All the depressants took me to a place of escape, a carefree state with no cares and certainly no worries. One of Travis's neighbors across the courtyard/pool area had a party that wasn't much of anything. I still don't remember how we ended up going to this guy's apartment, but before I knew it, we were going through this guy's fridge and stuff while he lay passed out. We ransacked the place, taking CDs, movies, and games and even emptying out his medicine cabinet. Someone started throwing his stuff from the balcony into the pool. I hesitated but joined in quickly. I remember finding a Jesus movie that was frequently handed out throughout Waco by a group of Christians. I looked at it for a moment and chucked it. This was a symbolic moment in my life of literally throwing out Jesus, not too different from Peter denying his affiliation with Jesus in Luke 22 (HCSB) when faced by the public. There was even a Bible floating in the pool. This in itself was a low point, but to make matters worse, the guy's girlfriend showed up about halfway through this whole event. She was not mad. She laughed, mocking him by saying that he always passed out—he was no fun. As we started to head back to Travis's apartment, we invited her to join us. A conversation started about the girlfriend who had showed up, whether any of us had a chance to have sex with her. With everything that had already happened to this poor guy, it was about to get worse. With the confidence and boldness of a man who had been affirmed by my participation in these devilish destructive acts, I took them up on the bet. I proceeded over to the apartment, said what I needed to, and then we took her boyfriend's truck and stayed out for a few more hours, stopping at a convenience store for condoms, smoking some weed, and eventually having sex. Nothing romantic or euphoric, just shameful, guilt-filled, animal-like sex; no emotions connected at all.

As I woke up the next morning on Travis's floor, the pit of my stomach ached, mostly from the hard night, but also for the events that had unfolded. In Romans, Paul closes up chapter 7

(HCSB) by explaining that he has tried everything to follow the law of God, but he is at the end of his rope. The chapter ends somewhat desperately. My life was becoming desperate.

Desperation results in decisions that a person would not make under normal circumstances, but what is a normal circumstance? My "normal" had gradually morphed in a nihilist viewpoint.

"Nihilism is a philosophy based on the idea that reality alone is important. It rejects belief, faith, wishful thinking, ideology, morality and socialization as in any way a form of reality and/or 'inherent'; these are human projections" ("Frequently Asked Questions About Nihilism," Center for Nihilism and Nihilist Studies, nihil.org, April 13, 2013). Paul concludes in the last verse of Romans 7 (HCSB) that Jesus Christ came to set things right in this life of contradictions where people want to serve God but are pulled by the influence of sin to do something totally different. Having a nihilist mindset and just focusing on reality alone is dangerous and leads to sin, because without a God, without a savior, we are all doomed to meaningless existence. When life seems meaningless, you start treating others the way you feel on the inside.

Travis and I, along with a couple of other guys, went on a rampage of Waco for several months in late-night intoxicated events of vandalism—shooting signs while driving down I-35 or trashing streets by launching full trash cans onto cars parked on the side of the street. Our vandalism was not limited to cars and signs. We would take our "talents" to people as well, walking into bars full of Baylor students for the sole purpose of hitting on guys' girlfriends in the hopes of finding some opposition. Sometimes I participated and sometimes I didn't. It just depended on how much I hated myself that night. The way I was treating women would haunt my sleep because of my mom's history with abuse. She ground it in my head about respecting women. I held that true in my heart, but I was with a group of guys whose sole purpose each night was conquering women as part of the journey. That night, we went back to some stripper's house for an after party, which took place after the club closed at two in the morning. The young stripper had to pick up her baby first before we went back to her apartment. Something died in me that night. As she laid the baby down in the room, we proceeded to party the night away. When I left her apartment at about six in the morning, going back to the trailer to get a couple hours of sleep before class, I thought about the reality of the moment. Treat other women as if you would want your sister treated is what my mom would say to me, but justification of my actions would kick in. The reality of justification in most cases is that it is a submission of guilt and admission of the wrong.

I have always considered myself a Christian more or less because of a cultural background and not necessarily because I believed. Unbeknownst to my parents, I had grown quite attracted to the darker side of life; it was starting to become apparent to those I had grown up with. A couple of times, my parents came down during this time of my life, but I can imagine it was quite uncomfortable and disappointing for them to see their son's transformation. They were not naïve at all. They knew what was going on. They just did not know the details. Friends from my childhood would come visit me, but it only happened a couple of times because I would put them in very uncomfortable situations, not respecting the fact that my lifestyle was not normal for them. People who knew me before Waco approached me as you would approach a stray dog, not knowing what to expect because of the beaten, battered look on its face. Since the breakup with Maggie, I had started to leave a wake of destruction sexually and emotionally, both for those who were a part of my devious acts and myself. I had become totally convinced that those who didn't understand me or were judgmental about my lifestyle, either by words or nonverbal communication, and I was better off without them. In verse 15 of Matthew 23 (HCSB), Jesus points out to the scribes and Pharisees that they have gone out and made more hypocrites, and while they pride themselves heirs of heaven, they are in judgment of Christ. Jesus uses strong words, saying that they have made legalistic followers, calling them children of hell. Anything against Christ is for the opposite, which is the devil, Satan, and/or hell. My newfound friendship in Travis was educational in how to go through life not caring. Not letting people, circumstances, or myself hold me down. Essentially, how to clean the outside of the cup no matter what was in it, or how to have a smile on my face no matter the turmoil inside. Therefore, I distanced myself from the people who didn't understand me. The proclaimed Christians that I knew up to this point of my life were blind guides putting importance on the Bible, but nothing about their actions or speech resembled their convictions. I was drawn to real, transparent people. Even if those people where living out their sinful lifestyles, at least they were transparent. I did, however, have a secret that I did not tell anyone.

My current wife would be the first person I would reveal this secret to: If I was conscious and physically able, I would pray. Not your Sunday service cookie-cutter prayers, but rants full of obscenities, anger, and emotion. These prayers would usually take place alone, either in bathrooms at people's houses as I stared in the mirror, or at my trailer where I would physically hit myself, sometimes burning myself with cigarettes just to make sure I wasn't dreaming or that I hadn't lost feeling. These prayers usually involved something to the effect of, "If you want me to stop, you are going to have to make me," or "Take my life tonight if this is all there is." Not your most uplifting motivational prayers, but definitely a reflection of where I was. God was a distant memory.

As you have most likely realized, I relate a lot to music; Jonathan Davis's song, "Blind" was written to describe his own emotional battles. He sings about a place in his words, "Another place I find to escape the pain inside." That place is inside the brain, where another kind of pain exists. This pain causes a lost reality, low self-esteem, like trying to look through thick clouds of fog. The harder you strain to see, the harder it seems to be, which is similar to going blind. There was so much blindness in my life, not anything to do with actual sight but with the "blind guides" (Matt. 23:16, HCSB) I had allowed to shape my view of Jesus Christ and His followers, Christians. You have heard hundreds of times that prayers are always answered, but we never realize it because we get caught up in our one-sided, self-motivated, childish outlook of what the answer should be. God's plan is always in motion, and all play a part, regardless of your willingness to acknowledge. I expected my desperate prayers to be answered by a genie or wizard, but God had something else in mind. Learning to trust in Him and be introduced to Jesus wasn't going to come through by giving me what I wanted, like giving a toy to a child after a tantrum. The child doesn't know the importance of the gift and the sacrifice that was required for the gift. God was going to start giving me an opportunity. I would never have thought it would come by a last-minute decision to go partying in Houston.

8

The most overwhelming and fearful thought I would have at times was a spiritual tug that continued to strengthen its grip: "What if God is real?" This spiritual tug at my soul would torment me at night. It was something like the result of cheap Chinese buffet sushi. Let me explain: Sushi is one of those glamorous, hyped foods that has international clout, and it is inevitable that you will run across someone who will ask, "Have you ever had sushi?" If you respond no, then that person will go on and on about how incredible sushi is. If you respond yes, and you are comparing it to cheap Chinese buffet sushi, then that person will go on and on about how you should go to a *real* sushi bar. It is the same with Christian faith, and it seems to be the only faith that is presented to people as sushi. Sushi is an art. I am sure that it infuriates the highly trained sushi chefs who make it their lives' work to create an artistic, flavor-packed, fresh, made-to-order food experience to be compared to cheap Chinese buffet sushi. Chinese buffet sushi has been thrown together with, let's say, less-than-par seafood with a film that has formed on it, which I can only compare to a catfish fillet that has sat in the refrigerator one day too long. Add that to a poorly-rolled, falling-apart sushi roll and place it behind a sneeze guard under the ultraviolet light, and you have an average American experience with sushi/Christianity. This was my experience with Christianity. I would meet people who would go on and on about their church or their experience with church and how I just hadn't been to the right church. Or people who would not touch church because of the hurt and pain it had caused. Ever had bad sushi? It is extremely painful, and you will most likely be scared and be very hesitant about trying it again. Same result with a church or preacher. A cheap Chinese-buffet approach to presenting God and the importance of Jesus Christ will leave a person sick of fish. The problem for me is that I was stuck with these questions: What if God is real?. What if Jesus is real? What if Jesus's teachings and the Bible are true? This is what drove my prayers of desperation and fear that fed my night with horrifying dreams of death and hell. One prayer that was common and, as I have discovered, is true of many people was, "If you are real, then prove it to me." Words offered up to God do not go unheard even by the unrighteous if there is a mustard seed of faith. Jesus tells his followers that because they are not taking God seriously, their faith is compared to that of a kernel or poppy seed (Matt. 17:20, MSG). He did not say they had no faith. Their faith was just immature, lacking growth, and they wanted more.

My faith in God — and certainly, my faith in Jesus —amounted to that of a mustard seed, but that is all God is looking for, a flicker to ignite fire. I had a very unfavorable image of Christianity and Christians. They were judgmental, hypocritical, insensitive, and confusing. There are so many religions and so many versions of doctrines. How does a person know what is right? For a young man in his early twenties, the choice was easy. Do not choose. Growing up in an age where men are allowed to wander aimlessly around with no vision or direction, with an entitlement mentality that is encouraged by our society, will increase a person's level of dependence. There is a subtle whisper in the modern culture to simply submit to what makes us happy. A very dangerous approach to life is seeking out that which can offer instant happiness or relief from pain. Consider the simple fact that we are all born with a sinful nature, which means we are drawn to that happiness that offers a temporary relief, which means we go back for more. Do not believe it. Do a quick experiment the next time you sit to watch a sporting event, sitcom, or even the news. You will see numerous advertisements and commentary within the program that are meant to somehow degrade your current version of life. I heard a comic once say that he got a new TV and was super excited about it. Until he went over to a friend's home to watch the football game and saw that the TV was bigger and better than his. When he went home, all he could think about was how much his TV sucked. Presenting an upgrade that will help you have more friends, more fun, more sex is highly tempting and addictive. It is sickening how blatant these attempts have become, even attacking the youth with a message of lust and greed within mainstream cartoons and commercial breaks. As I was sitting with my son watching *Dora the Explorer*, the commercial break was a swimsuit advertisement with grown women stripping clothes off to go swimming. Really? The earlier an addiction can start, the better chance they will be a repeat customer for years to come. Fifty years ago, it was cigarette ads depicting the happiness that is created by smoking certain brands of cigarettes by beautiful women, getting the attention of all, or a strong, handsome cowboy, by revealing strength and confidence from smoking. Cigarette companies have been upfront about their marketing efforts to target youth. In 1998 there was a master settlement agreement signed to stop these efforts. What was pinpointed in the agreement was stopped, but next time you are in a convenience store, take notice at how many signs and ads are at the eye level of a child. Obviously, the happiness is short-lived because we know now that cigarettes cause all sorts of health issues and, in most cases, a slow death brought on by lung cancer or some other type of disease. The kicker is that even with all that is known about cigarettes and the taxes that the cigarette industry has had to incur, and even with the prognoses printed on the label, millions of people still flock to this product. Why? Temporary relief from stress, anxiety, depression—the list goes on. Is this an idol? Are resources (money, time) being offered up? Has this taken the place of God, allowing this product to alleviate the pain of life, even if only temporarily? Even when this is read, people using cigarettes to somehow manage emotions will become defensive and begin to defend the cigarette, in most cases defending a cigarette more than God. Why did I go down this rabbit trail? Because there must be an understanding of the origins of the issues we have with God.

My secret prayers out of desperation and fear were the result of the idolatry in my life. Idolatry isn't *an* issue, but *the* issue with all of us. If we dig deep into our feelings, emotions, and actions, we will uncover false gods and areas of our lives that have demanded worship and have distanced us from God. Idolatry is the foundational sin for so many of us. What we believe about God has huge implications. How we address the idolatry in our lives has equal-weighing consequences. One of the homes my wife and I owned had some foundational issues. There were cracks in the outside brick and interior walls. When we remodeled the home, everything was patched and painted, but we ignored the foundation issues because the cost of the foundational repairs would have eaten up our entire remodeling budget. The house looked great after the remodel was complete, well, until summer came. The cracks reappeared and in some cases were worse. No matter how much paint and filler we used, the cracks would reappear. At some point, we were going to have to address the foundation issues with the home, or it would eventually give way to the weight of the structure on top of it. Sometimes that involves some painful and costly maintenance. God was going to begin to work on some foundation issues. Just as in our house we owned with the foundation problems, there were parts of the house that were in great shape, but the whole house was suffering because of the few areas that were weak and failing under the pressure of the whole house. My foundation issues of who I was, the relationships I harbored, and the overall presentation of Jesus Christ was badly put together. Every time I would try to have some substance to a relationship, it would crack and crumble because of my lack of foundational truth of who God is. My foundation was built on lies and misconceptions of who and what I was. My reality—and I fear that many share this reality—is that there is a God, but because of the misrepresentation that many of us have been presented by trusted individuals in our lives, we are confused. In confusion, most build assumptions and fears out of the unknown that unfortunately are fed by our relationships. The end result is pockets of people searching for purpose and meaning, all the while trying to remain safe and secure and to retain their individualism. This was the truth with me. God, to me, was something you go to in desperation. My father went to God in a desperate plea to heal him of his addictions, and my mother cried prayers of passion and deep yearning for healing in her marriage. Both my parents relied on God in desperate times. The other relationships and friendships I had revealed fear, anger, and misunderstanding with God, which led me to put my faith in things of the world first rather than God, running to the modern-day idols of the world and only praying to God in desperation. The problem with this approach is that there is a great truth that we all have to realize sometime during our short existence. There is a God, and but one God. This God is to be worshiped. Only He, with no other Gods before him. In stress, we don't run to ourselves and temporarily fix the stress with cigarettes, drugs, or porn. When we are sexually aroused, we turn to God for self-control and to put sexual relationships and activities in the proper place, under the sanctity of marriage (Hebrews 13:4, HCSB). But I was taught this in my world, my circle of influence. I was taught that masturbation and porn all a part of being a man. That when stress of life hits, you grab a bottle. When you don't agree with something, you get angry and throw fits of rage. That, yes, there is a God, but there is no need for a church relationship, and there is a time and place for God. God is a jealous God, and not in the negative context our world has associated with the word *jealous*. In Exodus 20:5 (HCSB), it is describing his passion for His holy name, the enthusiasm he has for the exclusive devotional relationship between him and his people. This demand for an exclusive devotion to Him is employed with that fact is endangered by the deities, or in other words, those things, people or relationships that attempt to align equal or above the one true God. Those prayers of desperation, those prayers full of corrupt motives and distorted beliefs were being heard by God but not the way I envisioned. The first step to understand God is to tear down all that you think you believe all the way to the foundation. If needed, destroy the foundation altogether to reveal raw land. God works through his people, and he was charging me to abolish and extirpate all those things that I had utilized to serve my idol-gods with.

My life built one big altar full of sexual impurity, murderous thought, angry rages, and disappointments that I allowed to depress me into a state of false pretenses. On the outside or with my speech, I would tell everyone that I was okay or that nothing was wrong and even prep myself with a smile and a fictitious joy. This works till you run across someone who calls your bluff, who calls you out on your lies. That person came to me by way of a part-time job. Toward the end of my tenure at Texas State Technical College, I was entering my third year of employment at the banking data center, but not only was I entering banking data into a database, I was also learning how to update full banking platforms. I was learning all about how ACH payments, account structures, and ATMs actually work. The guts of the banking system. It wasn't the most exciting job, but it was the one stable function of my life at the time, and it felt productive versus the destructiveness of my personal life outside of work. I had grown a friendship with the day manager, Janice. Janice was an African-American, early fifties mother of four, Christian women. Janice was the first person that really dug into my life in a way that didn't rub me the wrong way, and honestly, I really didn't even think of her as a Christian because she didn't fit the stereotypical Christian approach that I had grown familiar with. Janice was the same each day without apology. It was effortless for her to show genuine concern and interest into other people's lives. Nothing was normal. Or what I had grown to accept as normal about her even from our first encounter. When I had applied for the position and interviewed with Janice for the open data entry position, she called me the same day to offer me the position; however, I couldn't report to work when she requested because my sister was giving birth to her first son. Without skipping a beat, she inquired about my sister, the birth, and even congratulated me about it, dropping a praying remark at the end of the short conversation. I accepted the compliment and prayer, but as I got off the phone, I thought that it was a little weird for her to congratulate me because my sister was the one doing all the pushing and screaming. I was just driving to Bryan to meet my new nephew. Now that I have a child of my own, I realized her response was driven from a deep excitement brought on by the birth of a child. Janice and I would work together for long periods of time most of the time doing small talk, but she so cleverly would enter into conversations with me about life. Now that I am walking with the Lord, I still remember her approach wasn't that unique. It was actually a genuine concern and love for people. It would never fail that I would somehow start talking about my disappointments, frustrations, and anger with life. She always had an open ear and would offer up the most straightforward advice—pray about it. Sometimes she would simply ask the most open-ended question, "Why, Gerald?" She was a mother of four, and she knew that I was in over my head in personal junk. If I made a comment or revealed something to her, she would simply ask, "Why do you think that?" or "Why do you feel that way?" or "Why do you do that?" These are questions that deserved an answer. Sadly, most of the time, I couldn't honestly answer them, or, sometimes, I really just didn't know. She was the first person to say "I love you" that wasn't a family member and had to. She wanted to tell me that. She invited me into her world. Never by force and never by judgment. There is something about a stranger reaching out and helping. Family is important, but the truth is that family is sometimes used as a crutch and enables our behaviors and beliefs. God knew that I wanted more, and my silent prayers that went untold to anyone was that God would show me people who were really living the life He desired and demanded and, boy, did he come through with Janice. She wasn't perfect by any means, but there was a genuine love and respect that flowed out of her that I still desire from her at times. To this day, I can call her, and we pick up where we left off. No matter how long or short the conversation is, she always ends it with, "I love you, Gerald." She wasn't too fond of Maggie either, and when we broke up, I think she was more excited than I was.

Patrick and his Baylor girlfriend, Jennifer, invited me to a long weekend in Houston. We were joined by one of Jennifer's friends and one other guy named Todd. Todd was invited to stay at Jennifer's parents' house for the weekend. Jennifer's sister was graduating high school, so there was going to be a big graduation party at their parents' house. We would also find time to break away and got to a club in Houston, maybe even party with some Houston girls. I hesitated mostly out of fear but was quickly talked into it by Patrick with the promise of partying and girls. Why not? What did I have to lose? A part of me thinks that Patrick was overwhelmed with the thought of meeting Jennifer's parents, and in the event of an awkward moment, we could bounce off each other to move the conversation along. We left on a Friday midmorning in

Jennifer's Chevy S-10 Blazer and headed to what I considered the rich part of Houston in a suburb called Sugarland, which was southwest of Houston just off Highway 59. The only other time I had heard of Sugarland was when I had overheard my dad and mom talk about a friend from their past who was in prison in that area. As we made our way down to Sugarland, I thought of my previous limited experiences driving through Houston. My parents made at least annual trips to Galveston Island. We would take Highway 290, hit the 610 loop, and exit Interstate 45 south. Still to this day, my parents continue to have a vacation in Galveston, and we still accompany them when we can. Remembering the times that I had the opportunity to drive through Houston and how Cedric and I had snuck out to Galveston Island for a weekend of, well, let's say more of the TV-MA-rated (FCC rating meaning Mature Audience Only) activities. My experiences in Houston and the surrounding areas were a hodgepodge of experiences. I went on this trip expecting nothing but a rerun of events, slam some alcohol, go clubbing, and make some bad decisions to regret later. I was already told that we would not be bringing any drugs since we were staying at Jennifer's parents' house for the weekend. Her parents were liberal and allowed the drinking and smoking of cigarettes, but I guess their liberalism had boundaries drawn at illegal drugs. As we pulled into Jennifer's parents' neighborhood, Patrick and I commented about the obvious financial social status that was nothing we were accustomed to. Our thought process was ignorant and short-sighted, because we tied everything to materialism and the assumption was that we were in an extremely wealthy community. You have to understand that most my life was spent in a small community and so was Patrick's. We both had a preconceived notion and expectation for big city people. As we drove up to Jennifer's driveway and was welcomed by her family, I was quickly thrown for a loop as this laid-back Louisiana family welcomed us with an abundance of southern hospitality. Take away the huge two-story house, in ground swimming pool, and upscale neighborhood, and Jennifer's family could have easily been mistaken for a small-town country family. We all got settled in and were hanging around the living room as Jennifer and her family begin to attempt to get to know these three mystery guests. I realized that I had forgotten my belt and we headed up to the local mall, and as any clubber knows, you can't go out to a club without all the accessories. Well, of course, I am only assuming that there are some people out there that know what I am talking about. Maybe the BC crowd or "before Christ." When we returned back to the house, there was another car at the house. Jennifer's sister's friend had stopped by. As we walked into the house, my eyes immediately connected to her. She was a blonde bombshell. The first thing that I connected with her was her amazing smile, it was infectious. The next most-glaring attribute of this beautiful woman came as she got up from the ottoman she was sitting on and her flip-flop got caught under the ottoman and she fell to her knees as she went to shake my hand. She got up quickly to her feet as if no one just saw her trip and fell to her knees, eye level with my crotch. As the room erupted with laughter, she played it off and joined in with the laughter. She went right into her introduction, "I'm Tabitha." This was incredibly impressive because in the midst of an embarrassing moment, she exuded confidence that demanded respect from the room. She had my full attention.

As the evening went on, we all just hung around, talking. Tabitha ended up staying over the entire evening and had decided to go out with us all. We all came to the consensus that we would hit up a club. These Houston girls kept raving about one in particular. It was called Rehab. Yes, that really was the name. I guess it was more of a premonition insinuating that, after a few hundred times at the club, you would be seeking rehab! As we all prepared for the evening, Todd, Patrick, and I all changed in the same room. We were getting our game plan together and deciding who was going to pursue who. I hadn't even dated or spent any significant time with Tabitha, but I already felt a connection with her. I told Todd that Tabitha was off limits, and he responded that he wasn't interested. This all sounds a bit like a Neanderthal, but this is how guys act around women. We lose all sense of reason. We all went downstairs to meet up in the entryway of Janet's parents' house for a photo before we hit the nightclub scene. It felt like some weird grownup prom moment where your parents line you up with your date for a picture. Strangely enough, I was standing behind Tabitha, which symbolizes and resembles our near future relationship. As Tabitha entered the picture, I remembered thinking how stunning she looked. Quite honestly, I had never seen a woman and instantly felt so connected. There was a natural joy that poured from her very presence. It was comforting. When the photo was taken, we proceed to the vehicles to load up and head out to the club, Rehab. When we got there, I jumped out the vehicle and pulled out a cigarette. Noticing that Tabitha had done the same thing, I pulled the only smooth move appropriate for a couple of smokers and, might I add, incredibly classic. I pulled out my lighter and, as smooth as possible, offered her a light, in which she accepted. She might as well have said she loved me right there! Well, she did. Or at least I thought so with her eyes and little giggle. After a few glances of innocent flirting, we headed into the dance club. As we entered the club, I noticed that Tabitha had a bounce to her step. She loved to dance, still does. Every once in a while, I will catch her singing and dancing to a song, but these days, it is worship or country songs, not the gangster rap that we used to bounce to. It is all part of her natural joyful personality. It is beautiful. Even in those first moments of meeting her, she instilled a confidence in me that I hadn't seen in a long time. Even when she ordered her drink, a screwdriver, she said it with great confidence and joy. She was underage, so I offered to purchase the drink for her. When I asked to buy her a drink, the last thing that I would have thought that an eighteen-year-old would have ordered was a screwdriver. These drinks are usually reserved for the older, more astute crowd. As I walked back to the bar to order the screwdriver, I remember thinking that it was a little odd and even felt weird ordering it. Later on in our relationship, I would learn that she wasn't a big drinker, and the only drink she could think of was a screwdriver. Funny thing is that she doesn't like orange juice, so at this point, we were both doing some out-of-the-ordinary actions. It was a fun night of dancing and feeling each other out. Of course, we both hung out in the hip-hop dance room because both of us had a shared liking for rap music. I did sneak off to the techno room. I would always jump at the chance to jump around in a pitch-black room, waving glow sticks and playing around. It was the only room that I was a good dancer in. But is techno dancing really dancing or just organized jumping? Either way, I was good at it! The night finished out, and we left the club at about closing. Of course, I did my usual self-inflicted damage by getting highly drunk, but honestly, it was a light night in comparison to a typical night.

We retreated back to Jennifer's parents' house and Patrick, Todd, and I went directly to the backyard to hang around the pool. Tabitha went upstairs to lie down and turn in for the night, but Jennifer and her sister came outside for a moment. The exact details of the night evade me a bit, but at one point, I went upstairs to tell her good-night. She sat tightly and nervously on this single wide bed. I learned later that she did not want to give the wrong impression; therefore, she made sure that she did not give out any signals that we would be, how do I say this, having sexual intercourse/sex. I said my good-nights and retreated back downstairs and eventually to bed.

As we all started to wake up and meet at the breakfast table, I was talking about Tabitha but not calling her by her name. I was calling her Trinity. I have no idea where I got that from, but I did have a small crush on the character Trinity in the *Matrix* trilogy movies. Jennifer quickly corrected me, but then I learned Tabitha had been calling me Julius. So our first official night, we referred to each other with the wrong names. I am assuming that there was so much attraction between us that we never noticed that we were calling each other the wrong names. Or the alcohol and loud music could have muddied our communication abilities. We all shared a laugh at the breakfast table and proceed with the day. Tabitha had gone home to get ready for Jennifer's sister's graduation, and we all hung out around the house, recouping from the previous night. When the graduation rolled around, Tabitha showed up to ride with us all. We all drove over to the then Compaq Center where the Houston Rockets played for many years. Today, the Compaq Center is megachurch pastor Joel Osteen's home base. We sat through the long extensive high school graduation. I was overwhelmed with all of this because my graduation was conducted in our high school gym in about an hour. I graduated with about ninety people. This graduation had upwards of a couple thousand students. Patrick and I, being the small-town, guys, sat in amazement of this massive ceremony for high school graduates. After the graduation was over, Tabitha yet again revealed her graceful entrance into a room by tripping on the steps as she went up to Jennifer's sister to congratulate her. Yet again, she gracefully recovered and joyfully recollected herself. Tabitha was and still is a little clumsy, but she has the unique talent of recovering so quickly while making some sort of remark that totally takes the attention off her. This girl was the total opposite of me. She was naturally joyful, positive, and beautiful inside and out. I was drawn to her. There was an uncontrollable force that was drawing us together like the old science experiment with the positive and negative ends of a magnet. Put a positive and negative together and there is a connection created. Put two positives or two negatives, then the connection never forms even if you force it together. That was the feeling I had with Tabitha, the natural force of polar opposites drawn together because of their natural God-designed purpose. This attraction would even become more apparent later that night when we all agreed to see a movie as a group. We decided to see the hit movie *Pearl Harbor* starring Josh Hartnett and Ben Affleck. This movie was based on the events surrounding the attacks on

Pearl Harbor in the 1940s. We went to a ten-o-clock movie, and the movie was approximately two and a half hours long. About thirty minutes into the movie, I glanced over to my side and noticed that Tabitha has started to doze off. She was trying too hard to stay awake, but as the next few minutes passed by, her head began to fall slowly toward my shoulder. She was cold asleep on my shoulder. I often wondered if this was some move she pulled to get closer to me, but she swears she was fast asleep, and over the years, I have learned that if we are going to a movie, to make sure we are out of the theater by eight. As she slept on my shoulder, I looked awkwardly at Tabitha, but deep down, I enjoyed it. I didn't even mind her drooling as she fell deeper and deeper to sleep. It was actually quite amazing to see someone sleep through such an action-packed movie, but she did, and she did it well. I never said a thing as she drooled all over my shoulder. Even as we got up and she was so embarrassed, I ended up laughing it off and making light of the situation. She had already started to impact my life because, usually, I would have been extremely upset, and I also would have woken the girl up if they had fallen asleep, but not her. Her positivity and joy had started to impact me, and we weren't even officially dating. Later that night, I proceeded to get Tabitha's phone number. I very smoothly handed her my phone and asked her to put her number in it. That is when I realized that she went by the name Tabby. I gave her my phone number as well. She left to go back home, and I left the following day. Tabby had, had some issues with relationships in the past, which resulted in her developing a low expectation of men; therefore, she didn't put much expectation on me contacting her. She was totally off base because I called her as soon as I got settled in to my trailer in Waco just to let her know that I had arrived home safely. We weren't even dating! Ever since that day, I would always call her to tell her that I have arrived home safely.

A couple of weeks after our first meeting, Todd and I had made plans to go down to Missouri City, just southeast of Houston, to visit yet again. We couldn't stay at Jennifer's parents' house. The reason why evades me, but Tabby was all too willing to offer up her parents' home as a possible refuge. We had driven in for the night and gotten to Tabby's parents' house. It was a beautiful two-story white home with a nice yard and pool. In my eyes, it was a rich person's house. When Todd and I walked in the house, there were two sleeping bags set out. That in itself was good, but this wasn't just an everyday sleeping bag. Tabby's parents, Kathryn and Bruce, had laid out little girl sleeping bags, one with some sort of princess theme, and the other a My Little Pony theme. That is enough to freak out a couple of six footers, I being six foot one and Todd six foot four. There were little stuffed animals laid on the pillows. Let me remind you that this was going to be the first time I had met Tabby's parents. I stood at the door awkwardly looking at the floor, and Todd just kneeled down, swiped the stuffed animals to the side, and curled his large frame into that tiny sleeping bag. He jumped in that situation all too quickly and comfortably, but Todd was a little strange. Yet again, another moment that was way out of the ordinary or at least what I was accustomed to in a relationship. Remember, I was reeling from a six-year destructive, toxic fiasco of a relationship with Maggie that was full of anger, depression, and sexual impurity covered with identity issues. A relationship with joy, fun, and love was a foreign concept to me, but I enjoyed it. It made me feel special that someone took time out to make me laugh. As Tabby laughed in her embarrassment of her parents' antics, I was filled with a welcome relief of happiness and joy, and it felt genuine, not made up. Tabby knew that I was a heavy drinker and drug user, but she didn't really know the extent of what was really going on. Her parents weren't fully aware either, but they both had backgrounds that gave them some wisdom about what this guy who is courting their daughter was into. Tabby's dad is an Episcopal priest, so I had drawn an assumption about who I was going to meet. This assumption was generated from the only other priest I had ever known back when I was consulting with Father Folk. This guy was not that at all. Full of dry humor and one-liners, he would slowly demolish my stereotype that I had built about him. When I learned about Tabby's dad, Bruce was her stepdad, this blew me away even more because it was my knowledge and experience, although limited, of course, that people who did not get divorce were Christians and certainly a man wouldn't marry a divorced woman who was a leader of the church. Tabby's family broke all the stereotypes I had built over the years about Christian families and leaders of churches. In all honesty, I felt like I was seeing something I had never seen before. A single man meets a woman with two daughters, both of them with messy pasts covered with their own sins, addictions, and struggles, and yet they went on to marry each other. Weird or, at least, that is what I thought at the time. Up to this point, I thought Christians were a hypocritical nightmare, trying to present something that were only words but no actions. Tabby's family was open, honest, and up front. Was I uncomfortable? Yes!

But I was drawn to it. Especially when Tabby's step-dad, Bruce, was getting out of my truck one afternoon after running a quick errand and a liquor bottle rolled from the backseat. He never said a word. Just pushed the bottle back and closed the door. Those are the things I am talking about—weird. Why didn't he run and tell Kathryn, Tabby's mother, and forbid me from seeing Tabby ever again? Why not scold me right then and there? Getting to know Bruce and Kathryn blew my mind. They were open, upfront, and sometimes a little in your face, but I never flinched. The honesty was a relief. The progressive and in-depth questions about who I was intrigued me. Why does someone I barely know want to know so much about me? I know I was dating their daughter, but most parents would give you the same old dull, honestly ignorant speech that you can find on sitcoms or movies about dating. This was different. They took an active interest in me. The only other people that put this much interest in me up to this point were my parents and Janice. Why? I would drive back from Houston to Waco and think the whole way about what in the world I had gotten myself into. Dating a Houston girl with her Episcopal priest father and charismatic mother who talked about Jesus like he was in the room! This was a very freaky moment for me, a Catholic holding onto a lot of dark secrets of drugs, pornography, addiction, drinking, and hanging out with band of misfits in strip clubs late at night and early in the mornings, in off-the-beaten-path bars and drug-infested rooms.

Mind being blown, yes, I would say so. The reason why was because I had prayed for real people that were Christians. Not fake or part of the massive hypocrisy that takes place one hour a week each Sunday as people sit in pews for selfish agenda and not real relationship. I knew those people. If Jesus Christ was so special and if he really did die on the cross and people really did believe the promises of God, what would that person look like? This was my prayer for many lonely nights spent lying on the floor or curled up in the corner of a room, crying out after a porn-surfing session that lasted hours, or a night of partying. I wanted to meet people that really believed in Jesus Christ. I begged for that. I knew enough about God and Jesus to know that there was something powerful in the message of the Bible. When my mom bought that praying Jesus picture on sale at Walmart and hung it up in our home, she did not realize the impact that the picture had on me. Yes, the picture was obviously driven to the American culture version of Jesus, but still, there was a symbolic power in the portrait. When my dad made the decision to drop his physical addictions, he thanked God for that. But why? Where was the power in my life? My mom and dad had prayed for hours behind closed doors when life's situations would hit. What was that all about? The message of Jesus is not obscure to me or anyone. Someone might look at me and draw the conclusion that I was holding back in some way or not filled with the Holy Spirit. As so many Christians or so-called Christians have blasted people only to further push them away and pass unjust judgment with those accusations. The honest truth is that I was looking and going the wrong way in finding truth. My eyes were fixated on the fashionable god of darkness that could give me what I want and desire without believing any truth of Jesus. Microwave happiness, quickly delivered hot and ready, but after an hour or so, you regret the whole experience, wishing you would have just cooked a homemade meal. The Gospel of Christ forces a person to bring light in those places of darkness. Paul has a hardened truth about the Gospel in 2 Corinthians 4:3-4 (MSG). There are lost souls that the true message of the Gospel is hidden or ineffectual, but that is the whole purpose of the Gospel of Jesus Christ to save the lost. In 2 Corinthians 4:4 (MSG), Paul points out that the evidence of the lack of knowledge of the Gospel is the ruin in our lives. "The god of this world has blinded their minds" (2 Cor. 4:4, MSG). When a person is under the influence of the power of evil, which is the god of this world a.k.a. the devil, our understanding is darkened, therefore, creating a blindness. This is exactly where I was at this point of my life, blind to truth. Where some of you find yourself. Under a façade of surface level Christian religion with no real relationship but just legalistic actions or no knowledge of the truth at all. This only leads to the circle of struggle, pain and joyless living that is not different than those who have never heard the Gospels. I was looking for authentic, real, truth-seeking followers of Jesus Christ, not the watered down, politically correct, safe Gospel message that so many accept. I wanted to know and experience the Gospel message that changed the world, which set the church into motion as pillars of refuge, restoration, and mission, the same message that people have died for thousands of years. You know like the Bible speaks of. It all looks different because we are in a world that sets out to blind us to every decision. Like my favorite comedian, Jim Gaffigan, says when describing our blindness about the result of our food choices, "No cake for breakfast, but here is a piece of fried circle bread with a hole in the middle with sugar icing on top, and Oh yeah, let's keep believing that the double expresso Frappuccino from Starbucks is *not* a milkshake." This is funny, and I laugh hysterically each time I hear Jim's comedy and his right-on-the-money food jokes. Apply to the Gospel of Jesus Christ, and we have allowed the world to hijack the validly and power of the Gospel only to be wrapped into something that is less appealing. Instead of the healthy meal that strengthens, empowers, and heals, and, in most cases, the better tasting meal that takes time and careful measurements. We go against all that is good for our bodies and accept a burger from the golden arches that is slopped together with low-grade ingredients, which makes us slow, sluggish, and unhealthy. We are blinded by the deception of the world. We have allowed the world to dictate what church is and the power of the Gospel. When I say the world, I mean Satan, the dark one, the devil, whatever you call it.

After years of prayer and crying out in my lonely places, God had started to present people in my life, but as we all do, we question whether our answered prayers are really from God or is it just coincidence. God was about to get a whole lot more intentional to prove this was no coincidence.

9

Walking down the hallway of St. Mary's Catholic Church felt more like strolling down a museum hallway. The floors were polished marble with a shine that reflected the hundreds of lights shining down from the huge cathedral ceiling. The main room of the building was huge and could hold approximately one thousand people. The doors were massive to each room in the church, at least eight- to ten-foot doors that were made of solid wood. Statues of saints seemed like life-sized replicas of the actual people that they resembled. All of these were finished off by a huge altar with a ten- to twelve-foot Jesus statue, and there was no doubting what this statue was depicting. This Jesus statue was posing as if on the crucifix with holes in the hands and feet Blood was painted on these areas along with the crown of thorns and sword to the side. It was very accurate of what had happened to Jesus. (well accepted for Jesus's white skin tone and his blue eyes). In all honesty, the Jesus statue was a bit overwhelming and a little creepy. It had those type of eyes painted on it that followed you wherever you were in the main part of the cathedral. I remember sometimes walking from one end of the room all the way to the other side, staring at the statue and watching its eyes follow me. Sometimes I would head down one of the hallways and quickly turn back to peek around the wall just to see that Jesus statue staring back at me. Weird. Before I go any further, let me first tell you that I have great respect for the Catholic faith, and what I am sharing is my own personal journey and feelings of being a Catholic. The statue was weird, but the confessional that evening was weirder.

Our church had the traditional confessional where the priest sat behind a curtain or screen to somewhat disguise the individual spilling his guts, or there was an equally intriguing opportunity to sit in a room with two chairs directly across from the priest while you share your recently committed sins. Confessional for me was so stressful and frightening. First off, it was down this hallway that seemed a little shady and shameful; second, the priest spoke in such a way that kind of made it weird. "Come in, have a seat. How are you today?" Well, I certainly didn't volunteer to walk in this incredibly awkward situation and force interaction. *You tell me how I am doing!* Obviously, I didn't say that, but I certainly thought it. You see, to be a Catholic, you have to go through all these steps, communion, confessional, confirmation, and confusion. Well, I added the last one because it was confusing what and who the heck we were doing this for. God or the priest? In those days, I was doing everything for everybody else. When I went to my first confessional and the other handful of times, I learned how to tell just enough truth without telling on myself or exposing anything. I guess that is still technically lying. *Yes, Father, I disrespected my parents this week and said a cuss word.* Apparently, that is like four Hail Mary's and three Our Father prayers in the sanctuary; still trying to figure out the math for repentance, and, yes, this was in front of the massive white, bleeding, blue-eyed Jesus statue staring down at me in disgust. Confessional would be my training ground on living a dual life, telling people what they wanted to hear and doing what I wanted. When I was asked to be an acolyte or altar boy as we called it, I said yes. On Sunday mornings, I would get up earlier, and we as a family would head up to church. It was not unusual for us to be early to church because my dad was so anal about getting the right seat before anyone else got there. When we went to movies, we were so early that when we would purchase tickets, the person selling the tickets would ask if we knew that the movie didn't start for another hour. My dad would confidently respond, "I know," like the ticket person was crazy. So, yes, we were at church early. I would go to the dressing room and put on a robe, buttoning it all the way up, and wear this white blouse-type of clothing that went to about mid-chest. Basically, it looked like something my grandmother would have worn as an outfit. I would stand up there, lighting candles, ringing bells at certain key moments, handling the sacraments, which was either the water, grape juice, or the thin circle wafers. I honestly couldn't tell you one sermon or witty comment that I heard during this time at the church. I could tell you who was there and what people were doing. Honestly, what I was doing was counting the women in the church that I would have sex with if the world was ending; which guy would I like to beat up and what weapon would I use; who would I save in the event of a major fire; what if this huge Jesus statue fell, would it kill a lot of people? Yeah, you can see a lot of things were going through my disturbed mind on top of the fear of screwing up with the handful of duties we had on the altar. I would sometimes look at the crowd of faces and wonder if everyone is doing the same thing I was because I can't remember one person who looked like they wanted to be there. Everyone looked like they were in defensive driving, like they had something better to do.

From my point of view from the stage or altar, I had a view of the church. I saw a group of people who nodded their head, kneeled, and made the sign of the cross on command by the priest's instructions. To a teenager and some adults, this is nothing more than the church version of Simon Says. Walk in, dip your fingers in a bowl of water, and make a cross gesture on your forehead. Walk to your pew and kneel before stepping into the row. Once seated, pull down the knee rest from underneath the pew in front, kneel with your elbows resting on the back of the pew in front, and repeat. Stand, sit, kneel, and repeat where it says "all" in the bulletin when prompted by the priest. One day, I just decided in my head I was not going to follow a bunch of rules and demands that made no sense. It certainly was not a motivating factor to come back to church. Again, I want to say that I understand and respect the great significance that all of these gestures and mannerisms reflect, but that is not my point. The point is that it can be intimidating, from the perspective of someone not truly understanding the whole relationship we are called to in Jesus. However, what is truly a relationship? The definition of a relationship is the way in which two or more concepts, objects, or people are connected or the state of being connected. This can be emotional, association, involvement, or a connection between persons by blood or marriage. Gallup's (Gallup.com) most recent poll on the state of Christianity in the United States revealed that nearly 80% of the US population considers themselves a Christian. That is roughly 250 million people in this country who believe that there is a God and believe in Jesus Christ. Mormons are added in this number, and it should be noted that they believe in Jesus Christ but in a very different light. Regardless, we have a large amount of people in the country that will tell you that they believe in God and Jesus Christ. Odds are when you walk in a mall or down the street that 80 percent of the people you encounter will tell you they believe in God. Craig Groeschel wrote a book called *Christian Atheist*. This book really attacked the very fiber of knowing God and really knowing God intimately. Just as Craig points out in his book, "A quick glance at Scripture and our culture makes it plainly obvious that nowhere near 94 percent [of Christians] actually know God." Craig used the stats from Gallup as well but was using numbers for Americans who believe in God or a universal spirit. He is right! The apostle Paul gives us great insight on what the ideal Christian church looks like and how Christians should behave. In Ephesians 5 (HCSB), Paul gives us direction for our relationships within marriage. He describes and compares this relationship to that of the love of Christ for the church, which if compared to Jesus Christ, this love is sincere, pure, and consistently affectionate and notwithstanding imperfections and failures that the church is guilty of. This love for the church is presented as an example for husbands on how to treat their wives in verses 25-32 of Ephesians 5 (MSG). Paul goes on to say that if husbands love their wives in the manner laid out in these verses, it will be returned by the wife in abundance. In verse 26, Paul explains that Christ's love for the church serves as the ultimate example because Jesus gave his life for the church so that he might sanctify and cleanse it with the washing of water by the word. This is a relationship, willing to die for the sake of the relationship, the love. Understand the landscape of the book of Ephesians; Paul is under house arrest as a prisoner in Rome for his relationship with God, Jesus Christ. How many of you have this type of relationships in your life? How many of you are willing to face imprisonment or die for God, your faith in Jesus Christ? I can say that I am to that point now, but there is still a fear. There was a time and place that I would not have offered my life up for anyone or anything. When you hear words of dedication and power, but they come from a mouthpiece that is weak and unfaithful or disloyal, the words are worth the paper they are written on. Paul speaks from a place of arrest and prosecution for his relationship. Paul was notorious for heading right back into the face of prosecution once he regained energy from being imprisoned, beaten, and tossed. That is a relationship.

With my relationship fresh and new with Tabby, there was an excitement for the unknown. I was obviously impressed with her and certainly admired her personality that was authentic and genuine. She had an innocence about her that intimidated me. Even with that intimidation, I felt she was inviting. She had a calming presence that created something in me that I had not felt in a long time, joy. As our relationship grew from a distance, with me living in Waco and her living in southwest Houston in Sugarland, we learned a lot about each other through communication over the phone. Ever since the first day we met, I can only think of one day we have not communicated with each other over the fifteen-plus years we have been together. That one time was when Tabby had to have her tonsils taken out in which I still drove all the way to Sugarland to just sit with her throughout the weekend. I really enjoyed her. It was a relationship that wasn't built on sexual immorality but on communication and an effort that took both of us to maintain. Before you start thinking that this was a romance made in heaven, remember that I still had a life that was outside of this newfound relationship with Tabby. I had a lifestyle that Tabby had some idea and suspicions about but really didn't know to what extent. I started to silo my life even more than ever before. Here is an overview of my schedule when I added Tabby into the mix: Monday, I had class, worked usually till ten to ten thirty, headed over to a strip club called Two Minnie's to meet up with Travis for drink specials till about two to two thirty in the morning. I would call Tabby when I got off work either while Travis and I got primed up in his truck or while I was on my way to Two Minnie's. Tuesday was usually easy night. Get off work, maybe head up to the bar and grill that Patrick worked at. These nights were usually designed for whatever. We would go to different bars or just stay in Travis's apartment. Sometimes I would go to Scuff and Murphy's, a Baylor hangout with Patrick and his coworkers. Wednesday nights was Sonny's BYOB, a strip club outside of the city limits of Waco where you bring your own beer, hence the BYOB. This was usually the hardest night of the week because at Sonny's, Travis and I start to get to know some of the strippers. It was nothing to stay out till four or five in the morning after attending an after party. Thursday nights, I would hang out after work at George's Bar and Grill, where Patrick bartended. This is where I would drink till he got off, and we would go to a dance club that night. There were several clubs that we all rotated. Sometimes I would join Travis and his crew at a hole in the wall called Chapter's 11 where the liquor was cheap. When Friday rolled around, I would usually get off about 9:00 p.m. to 10:00 pm and either head to Sugarland, head to my parents' were Tabby would meet me or go back to Janet's, Patrick's girlfriend's apartment, where Tabby would either already be at or would be driving to from Sugarland. The weekend would consist of hanging out with Tabby. Of course, others were around, but when she was around, I really didn't care who else was around us. We just had hands and talked with each other, looking into each other's eyes. There was a physical attraction, of course, but we seemed to both have this unspoken commitment of getting to know each other from the inside out. This is how it went for several months, joyful reunions on Friday and tearful good-byes on Sunday evenings. When Tabby left, that is when I would start the downward spiral. I didn't even realize that I had begun to live a somewhat double life. Tabby only knew one set of people that I was hanging out with, which were her friends who lived in Waco, and Patrick, who was my friend. What she didn't know was the other side of my life, which consisted of Travis, among numerous other guys, and the places where I went with Travis.

One particular time that I cannot remember clearly but has been told to me in great detail by Tabby is the night I called her cell phone and left a message for Nikki. If you didn't catch that, I called the girl I was dating and left a message for another girl. Yeah. Not good. Nikki worked at a strip club and had parties at her place many times. Travis and I were headed over to Nikki's place, so I had called her from my phone to let her know we were on our way. To this day, I have a hard time remembering this, but I did get a chance to hear the message when Tabby played it back to me, wanting and expecting an explanation. I lied about the whole situation and said something to the effect that I was calling on behalf of Travis. I lied because that is what I had been taught through my experience of how to protect feelings. The truth was that Nikki was just another point person to a whole other set of people whom I partied and did drugs with. She was a stripper and one of the more well-known ones for a certain demographic of patrons. I was leading a double life and not the glorified secret agent, Mission Impossible–type double life. A person can't lead a double life. This was my first of many wake-up calls that I would not answer. I would blow up and believe that I could continue to carry on a productive relationship with Tabby and keep an alternative lifestyle the other half of the time. I would try at times to bring the two lives together by slowly bringing Tabby into my other world, but they were so radically different that it was impossible. One life was pulling me in a direction in which I felt I should be going, but then I had this other life pulling me in a direction I didn't want to go, but it was comfortable and easy. It was also stressful. The demand of managing lifestyles and trying to keep everything nice and tidy was virtually impossible as my emotions and feelings became stronger for Tabby. I wanted her around. When Tabby was around, it was like a fire being contained by a fireplace, burning and providing heat and the smoke being properly dealt with through the chimney. When Tabby wasn't around, I was a forest fire, burning everything in sight, consuming life to leave a trail of gray ash. Ever seen a raging forest fire? There is a reckless motion that strikes fear and death with its wild motions and unpredictable direction. This is what I felt. Tabby was my fireplace. When she wasn't around, I was devouring whatever would burn. Tabby was seeing the best of me but was not aware of the personality traits that would shine through when I was alone or with those who inspired the darker personality traits. She definitely had no clue on my sexual issues in the form of a growing pornography addiction and how that was slowly decaying me from the inside out. This lie that I told her would be the beginning of the end. God would allow this lie to put me in a downward spiral that he alone would be the one to rescue me from.

The experiences I had with God up to this point were nonexistent or, I should say, unrecognizable from my point of view. My experience or relationship with God was built more on memories and reputation. I remember the work and restoration that was credited to God through my own parents' issues and woes. God to me was something of a fairy tale. I had heard some of the more culturally popular and accepted Bible stories, but it was more secondhand knowledge. I would equate it to me knowing one of the all-time greats of basketball, Michael Jordan. Sure, I know him, but my perspective of knowing him is purely built on his past accomplishments and stats in the National Basketball Association. I really didn't know the actual person and character of Michael Jordan. When I was a kid, I only caught the tail end of his career. I looked at this guy and thought to myself he had it easy. He was a millionaire, talented, and had a lifestyle to accompany his fame and idol-like status. I am sure that his family, friends, and teammates had a totally different perspective of him. Michael Jordan was known for his incredible work ethic, endurance, and commitment, but talk to his wife or teammates and you might find out that their perspective of him is of a man who was reckless with his marriage and money with a life of gambling and women off the court. My point is that our relationship with people is defined by our intimacy level. I had been a part of the Catholic Church and read only what I was directed to in the Bible. Everything was secondhand and was directed under some sort of pressure from what others expected. My memories served my stagnant faith. I do believe I always had some sort of faith, but like a hammer sitting on the shelf, it was useless unless put into action. Hammers don't build; people using the hammers build.

Even in my darkest moments, I would think of the times that something happened in my family that was special and was attributed to God, but where was that feeling and why was it not something I hung onto or clung to in times of my own struggles? No intimacy. Relationships are a two-way street. Think about how many people you love and can say are influential in your life whom you don't talk to, call, or spend time with. I have friends I have become distant with, and we call every once in a while, but it is a little awkward and hard to get the conversation going. Also, I don't have the same comfort level with a person I don't spend time with or do life with. However, with friends I see and talk to frequently, the relationship gets closer and closer naturally because there is a level of intimacy growing. How many people do you talk to whom you graduated with from high school? I would venture to say fewer than three. If it was more, then ask yourself another question: Do you share your struggles, pain, and happiness with those friends? What about God? Most likely, if your relationship with God is weird, awkward, and forced, then you are lacking intimacy. And when those moments come up when you shake your fist and say, "Why me?" remember that it is like going to someone on the street for help. We are strangers, not because of God but because of our lack of effort in the relationship. This is where Tabby stepped in and revealed some challenging relationship issues that I had. Unbeknownst to her, she was going to step right in the middle of a mess of a man.

I have heard for years people say, "I believe in God." Really? Try to imagine the writer of James saying these words, "Do I hear you professing to believe in the one and only God, but then observe you complacently sitting back as if you had done something wonderful? That's just great. Demons do that, but what good does it do them?" (James 2:19, MSG). Obviously, there is more to being a Christian than just saying, "I believe in God." Even with all my experience with Catholicism and Christianity in more of a cultural sense by going to church on the major holidays and helping people in need, I felt there was more than just simply believing in God. We prayed at every meal as a family, but that was the extent. There was nothing that really made me or my family stand out that said we are Christians, or that Jesus is our savior. All I knew about Him was mostly through my parents' experiences and a few little things here and there. There was no relationship with God. In Deuteronomy 4:28 (MSG), it says that our sin will be made our punishment, and we will serve the gods that we have served, whether by our will or through our own stupidity and drunkenness. Moses goes on to say that we are the only ones who can assist ourselves because we have cast out all that is good with God; however, in Deuteronomy 4:29–31 (MSG) he encourages us to have hope in God to grant us mercy through His judgment and bring us to repentance. I was more accustomed to seeing people state that they believe in God but then be enslaved in a world of their own sin, whether it be drugs, alcohol, or a reckless lifestyle that puts multiple people at risk in their family. They may be saying they believe in the one true God, but they were definitely serving their own gods, and there was no repentance, only justification on the sinners' part to protect their brokenness and pain. It is not enough to simply "believe in God." 1 John 2 plainly lays out how to know for sure if we are following God in the right way by keeping His commandments (1 John 2:2–3, MSG). John goes on to say that when someone claims to know Him but doesn't keep his commandments, that is an obvious liar, and his life doesn't match his words (2 John 2:4-6, MSG). This is where I was when Tabby walked—or, should I say, tripped—into my life. If people claim to be in a relationship with God, shouldn't their lives somehow resemble the kind of life Jesus lived? Not exactly, but something like that. These started to become my prayers as I fell deeper and deeper into lifestyles of destruction. Deep down, I knew I was ignorant and stupid about the ways of God. I knew that some of the justifications for my actions and lies were wrong. They would end badly, or, as Moses points out, these actions I was participating in would eventually become my punishment. I would be left running to the very gods I had served, letting them fill me with more lies and deception of truth. All the while, thinking about what could have been with the one true God. What an intimate relationship really looked like in the real world.

Some might relate to my desire to find believers who were actually believers, whose actions and lifestyle at least resembled a desire and an attempt at having a relationship with God. I wouldn't think that would be too difficult, with the stats earlier in this chapter about the amount of self-proclaiming Christians, but it is. John reveals a straightforward truth in 1 John 2 (HCSB). Remember, he actually walked with Jesus. These words are coming from a guy who laid his life on the line and had established many Christian churches throughout Asia. To say the least, he had some credibility. When Tabby and I started to really get to know each other, it became a bit difficult, not for her but for me. Our relationship wasn't built on some initial sexual experience, and we seemed to never run out of things to tell each other. The relationships I had before with girls were usually built on some twisted event or sexual experience. Sadly, that is how most misplaced identity issues for people play out—identity in our sexuality. After my six years with Maggie, I had gone through a destructive time where I tried to find happiness in sexual experiences. When Tabby walked into my life, I never thought of her as another victim or another attempt to find myself. She was more of a solution. In Micah 6:8 (HCSB), the prophet speaks of what is required by our Lord, "Act justly, to love kindness, and to walk humbly with your God." I looked at Tabby as a person I didn't want to taint or hurt. After meeting her parents, I would find out later that her parents started to pray for me as if it had become apparent that I was not a Christian. I was one of those saying, "I believe in God," with no action to resemble that belief. When I had dinner at her family's house and we would pray, we would hold hands. I would stand there awkwardly looking around while they prayed prayers that seemed like they were talking to someone. They were. They were talking to God. A relationship has lots of communication, not scripted prayers for certain places and for certain buildings. By no means was Tabby perfect, but she did have this faith that couldn't be shaken. She talked about God like a family member. I would oftentimes comment in a negative or condescending way, which was rude. She would get angry, but it wouldn't shake her faith because she knew God. My rants or obscenities about Christians or God were just a reflection of my own ignorance and stupidity. The more I learned and got to know Tabby, a part of me wanted to drive her away and a part of me wanted her right by my side. As corny as it may sound, Tabby almost forced me to be a better man. I desired that. I wanted to be a better man for her, but I also wanted to push her away before my mess overflowed on her. I knew that if our relationship was going to move forward, she was going to have to face some hard truths about me. Like someone once told me, if you walk around in mud, you will eventually get it on you.

Her first truth to discover was that I lived in a trailer park. Seeing where she lived and her home and her being from the city, I had not allowed her to see where I stayed. One weekend, I decided to have her meet me at my trailer in northwest Waco, an area notorious for white-trash meth labs and gang activity. We met up at the trailer, and I gave her the grand tour, complete with the bedroom with a hole in the floor and bathroom that was not air-conditioned. Thinking she would have a grim outlook and create some way out of this incredibly awful place, she rolled with the punches and never missed a beat. Once she came into town early, and I had left a key for her. When I drove up, I found her sitting on the front porch with the TV pointed to the outside as her chair on the porch was pointed to the inside. She was watching TV from the porch. Apparently, something creeped her out about the place, but I was impressed with her finding a way to deal with this incredibly uncomfortable situation. Needless to say, neither the trailer nor the neighborhood scared this woman off. Tabby never really knew a lot about Travis, and that was on purpose. I was always nervous that Travis would release some information about past events that included me that would tarnish me, not allowing me to bring her into my mess slowly. It was like boiling a frog. Place the frog in a pot of water at room temperature, slowly turn the heat up, and before the frog realizes it, it is being boiled to death. I was trying to slowly expose Tabby to my reality, sometimes by accident or sometimes purposely. She knew I clubbed and went to bars but was never really under the impression that I went to strip clubs until I was in a position where I could tell her. She never really asked where I was, just whom I was with. If I was with Travis, it was a very somber "Please be careful," If I was with Patrick, it was "Okay." I ended up moving out of the trailer shortly after Tabby's first visit because I started to see the safety issues that this neighborhood posed. I moved into some apartments right next to one of my hangouts, Tom and Jerry's. It was a hip-hop club that was small and loud. This was the first place I had ever been that had a shooting. Lots of drug dealers came to this place, and lots of fights happened. When the arguments ran over into the parking lot, it would go to a whole other level. Needless to say, I would quickly run back to my apartment because I would usually walk to this club.

Tabby had changed up her schedule and come up to Waco on a Saturday morning versus the Friday I was accustomed to because something had come up and she couldn't drive up that Friday night. That night, I called up Travis because I was so looking forward to Tabby being there that I didn't want to be alone. Patrick wasn't always available because he hung out with Janet's friends, and I just didn't get the same satisfaction with them. When I called up Travis, I knew that he would have a plan, and I would soon be blown out of my mind. That night was a blur. We had gone to the strip club for a while then came back to the apartments where I was told we invited several people to come back with us. The next thing I heard was a knock on the door, which sounded like a gong in my eardrum. I woke in my clothes from the night before and in a panic because I just realized that Tabby was going to be arriving, but it was too late because she was at the door. I frantically stood up and ran into the living room to see Travis passed out on the couch. Pills, seeds, stems, and white residue were left on the small kitchen table that my parents used to use as a breakfast table in their home. I swept all the stuff I could onto a paper plate, throwing it into the trash, while waking up Travis. I answered the door cautiously. Awkwardly standing there was Tabby looking at Travis and me as if to say what the hell was going on. She may have said that, but I don't remember. I do remember Travis quickly cutting out of the situation. I told Tabby that we had been sleeping, but I would later learn she heard these two drunken, hung-over guys frantically hiding and destroying evidence. I can only imagine what the smell was like. We had smoked in the apartment and not just cigarettes, so there must have been the stench of beer mixed with an aroma of substances. Later in the morning, Tabby would locate two large blue pills that were under the table, which evaded our eyesight during the cleanup. I conveniently blamed it on Travis. Later, when she was in the other room, I retrieved the pills that I had thrown in the trash for later use. I thought for sure this would be a breaking point, but she said nothing. I could definitely tell she wasn't happy and that she was disappointed, but I didn't find myself picking a fight to try to justify my actions. I felt embarrassed and sad that I had allowed myself to be the person who took her smile away. We eventually got back to a good place and had a great weekend. This would be a truth that I have come to grips with, something so beautiful and joyful as Tabby would be destroyed by the opposing force. I compared this to something I heard from Corey Taylor.

Did you ever get that headache that is just not going to go away, and you end up sticking your thumb and your middle fingers so far into your eyes just to stop the pain? It usually has to do with making a choice. You get to that point in everyday life where you have to make a decision that you may not want to, but you're kind of pushed into making that decision.

Corey Taylor said this describing a song that he wrote for the band Slipknot called "Duality." The song is fast, hard, and contains the ups and downs of decision-making that we all experience by visualizing the process with words, music, and crazy antics. "Duality" is the state or quality of being two or in two parts. Corey Taylor wrote this song to vocalize the mental insanity that sometimes happens when you have to make a decision. Either a wrong or right decision. I felt this torment in my mind and in my soul, knowing that Tabby was the right decision but tormented by decisions to feed my underbelly of depression and sexual immorality. Either way, Tabby was making the same decision to be in a relationship that she knew had some potential pitfalls to say the least.

The teachings of Jesus and the Gospels reveal an intentional ministry. Jesus's purpose was not to be a genie or some form of Santa Claus going around and granting wishes. When I talk with people about Jesus, I never once tell them that their life will be easier, but I do tell them that they will find passion, purpose, and joy in life. Some people argue with and harbor anger toward God, thinking that he could instantly make a situation better or solve a problem with a simple thought. But "Wealth obtained by fraud will dwindle, but whoever earns it through labor will multiply it" (Proverbs 13:11, HCSB). The hard truth is that we all have—and I mean all—have a level of selfishness, entitlement, and greed that we fight against each waking minute of each day, but just as the Scripture implies, something worked for with sweat, tears, blood, struggle, and pain tends to lead to growth. Once a person walks through the fire and trial of life, he or she learn and grow because the next trial is just around the corner. We live in a fallen world (Genesis 3, HCSB) where there is a god of this world that is manipulating and deceiving us at every speed bump along life's road (2 Corinthians 11:13-15, HCSB). Therefore, when Jesus is on the scene, healing and raising people from the dead, he is always aware of His surroundings, atmosphere, and people group. When the man with leprosy approaches Jesus in Luke 5:12, Jesus could have simply waved His hand, healed him with a thought, and looked at him. However, what did he do? He touched him, in verse 13 (HCSB). In those days (and still today) people kept their distance from terminal or contagious illnesses, and in the timeframe of this story, people with leprosy were put out of town and away from the community. Think of the sickest person you have met or seen and think about touching them skin to skin. Most of us would not do it. We would quietly mumble something about prayer and move on, because their lives are too messy to get involved with. Jesus was aware of the context of what he was doing when he touched the man afflicted with leprosy, as if to say he was going to step right in this mess with him and help him through it. Tabby was the first person I had met who was willing to step right into my mess and make it hers. It was not about judgment or her trying to change me. It was about a relationship developing between us. Relationships are hard. They require intentional actions. They require communication. They require a willingness to be there no matter what. A good relationship has arguments, praises, encouragement, unconditional love, and disappointment. I did not have this type of relationship with God. I had prayed about it. I had recited a song that the band Korn did called "Somebody Someone" on their album called *Issues*, and believe me, I felt like I had issues! The song ended with a rant, a cry out that I truly understood. I was not just singing this song. I was feeling it. This song would cause me to be an angry and tearful mess, drinking and smoking on the couch by myself, singing right along with Jonathan Davis.

> *I need somebody, someone.*
> *Can't somebody help me?*
> *All I need it to be,*
> *Loved just for me.*
> *I look, I sign,*
> *I need someone*
> *Inside to help me out*
> *With what I'm trying,*
> *I'm crying, I'm* frying
> *In a pile of sh**, I'm dying, I'm dying, I'm dying.*

Tabby had come into my life, willing to help me and love me, but the adventure was just beginning. Tabby was the catalyst to this adventure. God was going to start throwing gasoline on this small flame of faith!

10

We make thousands of decisions every day that have ramifications. Some of these ramifications are seen, and some are unseen. Some are instantly realized, and some are not realized immediately. These decisions lead and direct us to say either yes or no to Jesus, yes or no to Satan—those are the only two responses. Each day is peppered with small decisions that have an eternal outcome. Think about that for a moment. As soon as you wake up, your decision journey begins. Some decisions stem from previous decisions you made that either hindered you or helped you. For example, if you decided to cuss out your spouse because of a disagreement, you might decide to go to a bar to cool off just think of how to make up with the spouse later on. There is certainly another side to that brief example, but I was often the one grabbing the cigarettes and stumbling around the trailer while getting ready for class or work, sometimes even spicing up my coffee or Coke with what we called "the hair of the dog that bit you." The best symbolism for this colloquial expression is displayed in a scene in the cult classic film *The Shining*. The main character, Jack, seats himself at the bar in the Gold Room for the second time and asks Lloyd the bartender for a drink. Lloyd asks, "What'll it be, sir?" Jack responds, "Hair of the dog that bit me." Lloyd says, "Bourbon on the rocks?" Jack responds, "That'll do it." If you have ever seen *The Shining*, you know that Jack's "hair of the dog that bit him" was started by going against the family's and his initial gut feeling on taking a job as an off-season caretaker at an isolated hotel called the Overlook Hotel. Jack was a recovering alcoholic and a failing writer who was stressed by the evil and tempting environment. Jack's decision to stay there has placed him and his family in a very volatile situation. The Overlook Hotel is completely empty besides Jack, his wife, and son. Therefore, Lloyd is, well, you get the picture. Decisions make or break us. Jack in *The Shining* ended up making a decision, which he and his wife had some reservations about, that ended up destroying their family. I saw the movie several months ago and realized something that I had never realized before. There was not a decision to pray, go to God with the decision, or even really consider the consequences. There was an absence of God in this huge decision in the midst of Jack's ongoing struggles. What was present was evil. Yes, this was a movie based on a novel by one of the great writers of our time, Stephen King, but this was how I processed my decisions. There was no real thought about the reeling consequences or ripple effect that my decisions would cause either for myself or others around me. God was never in the decision-making process. As I have mentioned before, my relationship with God was more of a child's approach to the belief in Santa Claus, nonexistent until I needed something. So when Tabby and I started to get serious in our relationship, and I started to think that this was going somewhere other than a boyfriend-girlfriend relationship, I had a decision to make.

As each weekend came and went, the roller coaster of emotions got more vigorous and intense. As the weekend approached, I would start to get giddy like a child waiting for a trip to Disney. My conversations with Tabby would go from a somber mood to that of excitement as the week gradually got to Friday. The other side was that as Saturday night ended and

Sunday morning started, it was a funeral-like experience between us because we knew that we were going to be separated for another week. This up-and-down battle would tear us up emotionally. Tabby handled the week differently than I did. She would go to work at an inner-city day care and, most of the time, hang out at her home. She has always called herself a homebody. She was perfectly comfortable curling up at home with a book or a movie or visiting with friends. For myself, I would fill the week up with as much as I could simply to not be alone. This led to some questionable and risky decision-making that further put me in the hole of loneliness, fear, and depression. Most of the activities and risky decisions were not revealed to Tabby unless I was with Patrick. Patrick had more respect and never let me go too far into my own addictions, or at least the ones he knew about. Patrick was an overall good guy. He may have drunk and smoked a little weed here and there, but overall, he was genuine. He had a big heart and truly liked hanging around me. He cared. However, there was a need for my corruptive side (Romans 7:20, HCSB) to be satisfied. Travis, on the other hand, was a vault full of secrets and lies. To this day, there are things that he has done or told me that I have not repeated. This worked both ways. Nothing was ever agreed on or said between us. It was an unwritten agreement between us. We encouraged and inspired each other in our corruptive nature. Together, we were a match made in hell. With all the week's events that were unseen and unheard by Tabby on the weekend, she never really got into what I was doing during the week. Tabby never asked. I honestly think, at that time, she may have been scared or nervous to ask, out of fear of what I would have told her. Either way, I would have lied or told a partial truth to attempt to protect her. Remember, truth was not my strong suit, especially when it came to personal struggles that were buried deep in the abyss of my emotional battles when I was alone. I was so frightened to lose her. It was always a relief when I went to Houston to hang out with her because when I was in Waco, I was always looking around restaurants, movie theaters, and anywhere we went to avoid people I knew from the other life I lived when Tabby was not around.

One night, as Patrick and I rode around Waco downtown, barhopping, it was well into the twilight hours when we popped into the player a CD of the band Staind, Aaron Lewis's band from the late 1990s to early 2000s. *Break the Cycle* was the title of one of their top-selling albums (Electra/Flip Records, 2001). The song "It's Been Awhile" was the top single on that album. Patrick had a small after-market stereo system in his truck, but at the early morning hours, the song seemed to carry as if we were the only two guys in the whole town, as the music bounced off buildings and echoed down empty streets. This was the first night when I had the thought that Tabby was more than just special. As we sung, the lyrics hit me as I hung my head out the passenger side of the window in a drunken stupor, screaming the lyrics alongside Aaron Lewis's raspy, intense voice:

> *And it's been awhile*
> *Since I could say*
> *That I wasn't addicted.*
> *It's been awhile*
> *Since I could say*
> *I loved myself as well.*

And it's been awhile
Since I've gone and f***** things up,
Just like I always do.
And it's been awhile
But all that sh**
Seems to disappear
When I'm with you.

While I was singing these lyrics, it hit me. I realized I am a better person when Tabby is around. I really like being around her. Just thinking about Tabby made me feel good, as if I didn't want to let her down. I started to get so pumped and excited; I think Patrick saw the intensity with which I was singing and put this song on repeat. A couple of dudes riding around, singing as loud as they could to "It's Been Awhile." There weren't too many guys I would have done that with. Sometime during the night, we decided to take this huge Baylor banner saying "Welcome Home Students." It was on the third floor of this hotel where the doors were exposed to the outside. Kind of like a La Quinta Inn or Best Western. This hotel sat right next to a Jack in the Box, and we decided to get some food before heading back to the apartment. While in line, Patrick said something about how cool that banner would be to hang up in his room. With a shot of adrenaline, I darted up the stairwell to the third floor, cut the sign down, rolled it up, and took it back to Patrick's truck just in time to get my food and head on our way. This is one of those nights that will remain with me forever. That night, I realized that there was something more than special about Tabby. The night I got an oversized Baylor banner that was symbolic for the oversized appreciation and love that was growing in me for Tabby.

Tabby and I grew emotionally close. The relationship we had chosen to enter with each other forced us to have a well-versed line of communication. At times, I would call her just to hear her voice. It would remind me that someone believed in me. Someone had an interest in me that was not forced by ties to family, hometown acquaintance, history, or participation in my addictions. Sometimes, before I would drive off to go either meet someone or go to a place with the sole intent to get drunk, high, or sexually stimulated, I would think of the consequences. This was not some long drawn-out process; maybe just a second or two of processing the what-ifs. This touches on something that would turn me away from a person, whether a Christian or a concerned individual. When someone would try to relate or express concern by throwing stats and the consequences of actions and decisions that I was making, it would just come off as judgmental and hypocritical. Here is a little secret that some of you individuals who are less exposed to addictions—whether drugs, alcohol, sex, gambling, or whatever—need to know about those wrapped up in these worlds: Everyone knows the consequences. Everyone knows the end game is destruction, death, and dismay. People in gangs know this all too well. It is ingrained in youth at an early age that the goal is to "get rich or die tryin' " (a shout out to 50 Cent). We look from the outside looking into a world of which we have no understanding or bearing, yet cast judgment and offer our socially accepted way to fix the problem. When, in reality, people in that world don't need another person telling them what is wrong with their life. We all are at this level in some way. It is natural for people to feel as if they are one social status above another, and that empowers them to judge another's situation in an attempt to help. The truth is, it is not a single person's teaching and judgment that save people, it is the willingness to simply walk with a person to communicate knowledge by actions, not laws or dogmas. In John 18:19 (MSG), the high priest questioned Jesus while processing him to prepare his trial in front of Pilate. He asked Jesus about his followers and teachings. Jesus explained that he had spoken openly and honestly with no secrets. One of the officials struck Jesus because they were offended. They had laws and dogmas that they followed and inflicted on others instead of loving and walking with people to reveal a love of God. They burdened the people with laws and dogmas that drove people away or drove them to serve out of fear. I wanted to know the God revealed in loving and walking with people. Sadly, the example of Jesus in most modern, mainstream cultures is one of little power or with no real application—in most churches or in my experience. The Christians I had met or encountered were not willing to walk or spend any amount of time with a person who was truly searching or struggling in life. Tabby was a unique person, and when I met her parents, I could see why. Tabby was not perfect, but she had this knowing, child-like approach, what Jesus tells us to have in Matthew 18:2-4 (HCSB). In my eyes, I needed Tabby close to me. People who struggle with knowing God or faith try to have someone close to them who has these things. It makes a struggling person feel as if they have hope. The problem was that I wanted Tabby close to me but did not want her to know all of me, just the part that she liked. I worked hard at showing her the part of me that was respectable and honorable, not the disgusting, perverted, destructive, deceiving man living with secrets that would keep me awake at night.

When I went out, I knew what I was going to do and the consequences. People often assume that people do not know or do not think about the consequences of their decisions. I am here to tell you they do. I did. When a person bases their sense of worth on the success of their own personal plans, life is a never-ending roller coaster of emotions. My life was terribly off track from what I had planned, which resulted in three major emotional attacks I had to fight through: anger, anxiety, and depression. When I think about my plan for life, I honestly cannot think of any plans I made then. I wonder how many people have no plans at all. Are they just plans that are predetermined by our circumstances and social influences? I certainly was not sure of my goals nor was I sure of a purpose or the direction to go. From about middle-school age to before meeting Tabby, my life resembled the path of a plastic bag blowing in the wind. Going whatever direction has the strongest force, hanging on to whatever catches it. Eddie Vedder, the lead singer of Pearl Jam, wrote a song that he will still to this day say, "Here is Pearl Jam's longest title song, 'Elderly Woman Behind the Counter in a Small Town.'" The song was released in 1993, four years before I would graduate. The song is about a lady who has been trying to get out of the small town she grew up in. Sadly, she has become the elderly woman behind the counter telling her testimony of being stuck on "the shelf," as the song says. The song explains that she has changed by not changing at all, allowing the small town to predict her fate, wanting to scream "hello" to warn people of this vicious circle. This song was all too telling of the reality of others' expectations becoming your own. People in my small town assumed and even counted on my fulfilling my father's role as the local partier, troublemaker, and wild man. Honestly, I hated that. In a small town, I struggled for my identity. Before I knew it, I was fulfilling those small-town expectations for my life. It takes a person to step in, willing to get dirty, and work hard to make something incredible, to speak a truth and inspire a journey for identity. My journey had led me to Waco to meet a girl three hours south in Houston through mutual friends who worked in a bar where I frequently drank. This girl, Tabby, stepped into my life and was walking with me already in our young relationship, unaware of the dirt and nastiness of who I was without her around. We knew one thing. We loved each other. A natural bond was formed so quickly and firmly between us that we knew this was more than just another relationship.

When Tabby's father accepted a position in Bay City, Texas, as the rector of the local Episcopal church, Tabby and I discussed how the driving would be murderous. It would extend the already three-hour drive to five hours, quite daunting to drive every other weekend. We discussed the option of living together; it was bold and a little crazy for me because her dad was an Episcopal priest. Thinking that this idea would never see the light of the day, Tabby was already preparing to present the idea when her parents made a bold statement of the possibility before we did, seeing that Tabby was miserable and a complete wreck throughout the week without me. Yeah, she was already head over heels for me! Three to four weeks into our relationship, Bruce and Kathryn, Tabby's parents, wanted to talk to us. Tabby had already warned me of this meeting. I did not think anything of it, but she was incredibly nervous about it, which made me nervous. One weekend when I came to Houston to see Tabby, Tabby's parents had planned on meeting with us. About what, I really did not have a clue. I was counting on some long drawn-out list of fatherly warnings and motherly disagreement with our relationship and our decision-making. Boy, was I wrong. Bruce and Kathryn summoned us from the upstairs living room to their personal bedroom, which was a little intimidating in itself. Bruce locked the door behind us as we all entered the bedroom. That was a whole other level of weirdness. Later, I would learn that the locked door was to keep Tabby's curious younger sister, Kellie Ann, from barging in. The last two women I had been involved in a relationship with before Tabby both had absent fathers, and I had come in and out of their homes with little to no interaction with their families. Bruce was a whole other kind of father. It was weird to me only because I wasn't used to a father being so engaging with me, but no matter how engaged a father he was, nothing had prepared me for what he was about to say to us, more or less directing it to my side of the room. Bruce and Kathryn, in their calm but direct voices, sat us down and explained to us a few expectations and what I can only describe as premonitions. I don't remember all the words and subject matter that was spoken, but I do remember the words "sex" and "marriage" coming out of Bruce's mouth, his Episcopal priest's mouth nonetheless. He told me that he knew we were going to get married, and that he knew we weren't having sex yet, but if we did, we had better be careful. No matter how hardcore or gangster a man feels like he is, if the father of the woman you love looks you in the eyes and says these things, you had better believe there are a lot of "yes, sirs." I was intimated a bit by Bruce, but not because he was some guy that threatened my life or said crazy things to scare me. It was more of an intimidation driven from respect. I caught myself many times watching how Bruce interacted with Tabby and Tabby's sister, Kellie. How he treated his wife, Kathryn. As I mentioned before, he never judged me, only loved me unconditionally, even with his discernment of the junk I was involved in. He had plenty of moments to judge me and push me further away from Christ, but he took opportunities to share simply truths about the Gospel, not by word but by his actions. I remember the first time I saw Bruce open the car door for Kathryn as we jumped in to go eat out. It wasn't a special occasion, so I was shocked to see him do it. I jumped right in the car as well as Tabby did, but as Kathryn went to the passenger side of the door, and Bruce followed to open her door. I thought to myself, *Yeah, right; this is all for show.* However, he did it again when we got to the restaurant, went into the restaurant, left the restaurant, and got back home. This man opened the door for his wife everywhere, which influenced me and my warped mind of lust and selfishness. Later that day, I asked Tabby, "Does your dad open the door for your mom all the time?" She answered, "As long as I can remember."

I had dated Maggie for over six years, and not once was marriage a real option. It was a nice conversation to have to pass time, to factiously move about the relationship under the façade of love. I bought Maggie a promise ring and bought one other girl before her one as well, so the meaning behind the promise ring had lost its promise. Sadly, I had recklessly thrown around the word "love" in such a way that when I said, "I love football," it held the same power as "I love you." Up until meeting Bruce, my father had been the only other man in my life who loved me unconditionally. The only man who made decisions based on the betterment of my life and the family and not out of some selfish ambition. Here I stood face-to-face with another man who was making decisions that were above his own selfish desires. My father had made some huge decisions that radically changed the landscape and sent a ripple effect throughout generations to come in our household, which was obviously a selfless act for the betterment of his family and generational line. As impactful as my father's actions were, Bruce's actions of simply walking around to the other side of the car to open the door for his wife was just as impactful. In the early goings of my relationship with Tabby, I would find myself getting anxious and embarrassed of this man going out of his way to open the door for a perfectly abled wife.

Sadly, men as a whole have allowed a culture of seductiveness, darkness, and passiveness to define us as men. In the past, when I saw a young man or group of teenage boys, most of the time, if not all the time, I would have been part of the masses calling them irresponsible, immature, careless, and negligent in their roles as men, husbands, leaders, and fathers. How's that saying go about children? "Children are reflections of their parents." If this is true—and I can assure you that in most cases it is—then isn't the same judgment or assumption we place on some other person's shortcomings in life turn right back on us, as if looking into a mirror? In the Apostle Paul's letter to the Corinthians, specifically, in 1 Corinthians 13:12

(HCSB), he stresses to the people that they have partial knowledge built only by what they have been exposed to; therefore, he emphasizes the dependence on God's grace. This is during his sharing of his personal knowledge and experience with God's grace, explained in the previous verses how walking with God has matured him. See, what Paul is saying and telling these Corinthians is that they are passing judgment on something they don't understand, using the knowledge they have up to this point. The Corinthians are reminded not to be boastful and prideful. Paul is focusing on the intimacy and immediacy of God's knowing. Here, Bruce had a deeper understanding of God, Jesus Christ, and the Bible. Here I was with limited knowledge, passing judgment, feeling embarrassed and almost angry that Bruce was doing all these little things for his family: opening the door for his wife, holding his tongue during disagreements, calmly approaching situations, not judging or condemning me with words but bringing conviction to me by his actions. My feelings were just a reflection of what was inside me, embarrassment, anger, frustration, and judgment. My limited knowledge and immature relationship with Jesus were being challenged by Bruce's self-controlled, intentional, unwavering, unconditional loving relationship with his family and his God.

What Tabby, Bruce, and Kathryn never realized was that their relationship with God challenged me and forced me to think. When a person slips into a world of drugs, addictions, and evil plagued and peppered with generational sin and evil, a relationship with God is not the focal point. The Gospel is destroyed by assumptions, frustrations, hurt, and disappointments of past experiences either firsthand or through secondhand experience by family, friends, or culture. The one thing that hurts my heart, that keeps me praying, and sometimes that keeps me awake at night is the number of people who have been fed a truth and identity in God, Jesus Christ, by the environment, friends, media, and, in almost all cases, family. People are born into a fallen world with sin, pain, and hurt, and life never pans out the way anyone plans because it is not our plan. The devil, evil one, Satan is always there to point us to instant relief, a place to run and to simply escape our issues with life. How does this play out practically in life? It depends on what side of the cross you stand, your knowledge, and your proximity to believers. For myself, it was an addictive personality to accommodate my realization, my limited prospective that no one really believed in God. For some, it is jumping churches or leaving altogether because people in that church offended them by attempting to be truthful. Truth hurts and often offends. These churchgoers who leave churches because they are offended or are told a truth do one of two things: either to find another church until they build some relationships and get offended again *or* convince themselves that they don't need other people. Both are dangerous approaches. One leaves a person in a constant state of limbo, never allowing himself or herself to become too attached; the other will eventually lead to an absence of a relationship with God and the creation of all sorts of idols. Don't believe me? Think about yourself and your struggles with church or lack of a struggles. If you have a grounding in church, your parents most likely taught you some hard truths at a young age, forcing you to make your own decision about God. If you go to churches and have difficulty building relationships or feel like people are judging you, you were taught that churches are judgmental and hypocritical. I totally left the church. Slipped in and out of belief of a god at all but accepted the existence of some type of spiritual world and evil. Why? Well, my family went in and out of churches, not really staying in one place too long, eventually accepting the response and mantra that our family didn't need church or a community because we could just talk to God and deal with life ourselves. Yes, we can talk to God, but referring back to the apostle Paul in 1 Corinthians 13, this left me with limited knowledge and experience with God. I had a great life and childhood, but something in me always yearned for more. Those walks as a child through the woods revealed a passion and desire for more. But more what?

My struggle for purpose, direction, and respect was not being met; therefore, my approach to filling a lack in these areas was unhealthy. I knew how to work, provide, respect my elders, and make hard decisions and that it was right to protect women from the world's evil. My parents had put a foundation of hard work up under my feet that had protected me and enabled me to find work and be successful; however, any deep-implanted passion and purpose behind it all was missing for me. As I have mentioned previously, my parents had their encounters with God; mine was only secondhand knowledge. I was spiritually dead, and my parents' stories of redemption were great—for them. I felt like I was becoming one of those guys who just retell the same old stories and listen to the same old music while losing their individualism, basically, a poorly made sequel to their parents' or guardians' lives. Not my purpose, not my passion, but out of a desire to see satisfaction and enjoyment on my parents' faces for something I had done drove me to start repeating the same song, second verse. Before meeting Tabby, I had slipped into seeking out all sorts of artificial substitutes in the form of addictions such as drugs, alcohol, pornography, sex, and self-hatred. My decisions were driven out of a desire to escape my life—the life that seemed small and insignificant, the life that I felt was headed in no direction or great purpose. Most, if not all, of my decisions were for my own selfish desires. But were they really for my desires? Take a step back and look at these decisions. What do they have in common? Below the surface, decisions to turn to a substance or lustful behavior come from a place deep within and are driven by fear, anger, disappointment, hurt, and pain. I did not just wake up one day and want to be the most destructive person I could be to myself while having no drive or sense of purpose. It is a process that happened over years of believing a lie. James 2:24 (HCSB) states that a person is not justified by what he does, has an opinion on, by his or her profession, or obeying all the rules, but by having a faith in Jesus Christ. The lie I believed was that I did not belong to this seemingly exclusive group or club called Christianity.

Where were the Abrahams of faith, people so sold out for their faith that they would offer up their child as a sacrifice, as described in Genesis 22, only to have God provide a lamb to stand in the child's place. Even though Abraham did not actually sacrifice his son, his mind was made up. God wants unapologetic faith that would destroy our flesh and our desires, to step out without knowing what to expect or having some predictable result. The spiritual leaders and church leaders I had met were great men, and I am sure they would be highly offended if even asked if they live by faith. However, what destroyed my faith was the attempt to copy their works in an attempt to believe what they believe—so frustrating that it will cause a man to simply give up. When the apostle Paul writes the Corinthian church in 1 Corinthians, he is straightforward and truthful, blaming their weakness and nonproficiency by calling them mere infants in Christ. I love what he says in 1 Corinthians 3:2 (HCSB), "I gave you milk to drink, not solid food, because you were not yet ready for it. In fact, you are still not ready." It was like a shot right between the eyes, basically telling them that they have received some of the first principles of Christianity but had not grown to understand them. The Corinthian people were notorious for being proud of their wisdom and knowledge; this is all too common today. People have a surface-level knowledge and understanding that somehow grows into a self-conceited approach that far outweighs actual wisdom of faith, holiness, mercy, grace, and sacrifice. These are usually your church-hoppers and those who think they do not need a church. They are conceited and proud but have a faith that is a calculated risk for a deep-down, selfish desire. I would get so overwhelmed by the dos and don'ts of religion that I never understand that this started with a relationship with Jesus Christ. Think about it this way: When I was a child, I mowed grass and folded clothes when my parents asked, sometimes doing these chores without being asked. If somebody in another state or country sent me a letter stating that I needed to mow the grass and fold clothes, I would not do it. Why? Because when it comes down to it, do chores to please my parents because I respect them and love them. I have a relationship with them. The letter from some stranger holds nothing but rules to follow, no relationship.

What the apostle Paul made very clear about it is that we need a relationship with the one true God. That if we attempt to put our faith in man, it will turn contentious and quarrelsome about religion because people will be guided by their own passions and pride (1 Corinthians 3:4–5, MSG). Paul is driving home the fact that he is simply the leader, the one to plant the seed, but God makes it grow. Between the planting and growth, there must be water, sunlight, and nutrients. If we simply allow a man to plant a seed of knowledge in us and never act it out or allow it to be watered by more knowledge and experiences, then it is simply a seed in the dirt. It has no direction because it is confined to the shell of the seed, but with limitless potential and a purpose ingrained within the seed. What I needed was some water on my life. But what does that look like in reality?

I wavered between belief and disbelief to fear and acceptance of a purposeless life with no point or direction, but I was merely a seed planted in the ground. I was in a spiritual drought, and I believe that this is where a large majority of people fall. Atheists, compromisers, those picking and choosing what to obey and believe, those who have been in churches for years without joy, the church-hoppers going through life unchallenged within their faith, and, of course, the lost. Oddly enough, I fell in each one of these categories to some degree at some time in my life. A seed with no water is simply a seed. Sure, it might have the purpose to grow tomatoes, cucumbers, onions, or eggplant, but without the water of life, the seed will never realize its purpose and certainly never have the opportunity to reach its potential. Where does the water in our lives come from? The Samaritan woman in John 4:9–13 (HCSB) received "water" on her "seed," and her eyes were opened to a purpose and direction in her life. What was the source? Jesus Christ. Jesus tells her as she was drawing water from the well that he can give her water that will never cause her to be thirsty again. Revealing to her that the life she has lived was nothing in comparison to what he has in store for her. She was led to the well because of thirst, then met Jesus there. I am sure this woman's life was not perfect and that she encountered hardships, but receiving this water from Jesus Christ allowed her to grow. It was up to her what she did. Obviously, we do not know, but she would have to make the decisions to act out her newfound purpose. She does take off running after her conversation with Jesus, telling everyone about her encounter. My point is that she was led to the well out of a need. I was led to Tabby because I needed unconditional, unwavering love. I was damaged and incredibly darkened and hardened by my lack of purpose and direction. I did not need someone to tell me everything I was doing wrong or hadn't done right. I needed someone to simply provide a glimpse of hope. Tabby had a relationship with God that amazed me, and when Tabby moved in with me, I thought for sure I would expose the fraud of this relationship with God.

Once a plant has been watered, it reproduces. You can cut a plant off right at the ground, and if that plant continues to receive water, it will grow up once again because the roots are deeply rooted in a soil and can retain life even in dry times and pull more resources if needed to grow. That is Tabby. Deep-rooted in a faith that she leans on like a rock. When we moved into our apartment together, it was like a line from a song by the band called Powerman 5000: "This is what it's like when words collide" (Dreamworks, 1999). Of course, you had the little things couples deal with: dishes, garbage, and clothes washing. My biggest pet peeve was closets and bathrooms. I preferred a more organized approach versus Tabby's free-spirited approach. As the newness of Tabby's moving in with me wore off, my destructive cycle presented itself again. It was one thing to visit every other weekend and talk on the phone during the week, but now that she was in my daily life. I would attempt to include her, to make her more of a part of my world. At first, she participated, sometimes by going to clubs or bars. She never seemed comfortable in those environments, but I did not frequent the most attractive places. I once talked her into coming to a strip club with me and a group of people. This was my attempt to reveal to her that these places were not that bad. Yes, this really happened. Nevertheless, as I watched people purchase a lap dance for her and seeing her face of disgust and concern, I knew that this was wrong. Honestly, at that moment in time, I never saw anything wrong with strip clubs or pornography. Boys being boys, right? Is this not what we teach our male youth today and the same mantra that men follow throughout life? It is sickening now to think of the utter disrespect and horror I inflicted on Tabby, but it was not on purpose. This was a part of my life. Like it or not, a side of my personality was very deprived and dark, but there was also a loving, caring, and compassionate side. Our worlds as a couple may have been colliding. A collision inside my mind and heart was happening as well. The weird thing was that I liked it. I liked when Tabby challenged my decision-making by her actions. Now, do not get me wrong; we have had our share of outright arguments, but what was most effective was when she would sacrifice and stay home while I went out drinking or barhopping. These words actually came out of my mouth: "Hey, I am going to Two Minnie's tonight; be home after midnight." Two Minnie's was a strip club. I said this to the woman I loved. Wow. Even writing that makes my stomach knot up. She would respond with a disappointing tone, begging me to be careful, along with a couple of sighs.

Even though I was an idiot and a total jerk at times, we had good moments. I would say that when it was good, it was very good. I absolutely loved being around her. I loved her family. Her joy in my life was like that moment when a dark storm cloud is broken up by the sunlight peeking through. She was light breaking through my life; I believe God ordained it. We moved in with each other in early 2002. Several months later, I made one of the biggest decisions of my life—to commit myself to one woman. I tossed and turned about this decision, not really whether I wanted to marry her—that was always a given. What I tossed about was the pain and hurt that I had the potential to inflict—the hurt that I could cause with my use of words, manipulation, and fear. Tabby had seen glimpses of this, but, like I said, when it was good, it was amazing. I decided to ask Tabby to marry me. I planned a weekend getaway at Hyatt Reunion Towers in Dallas. As we drove up to Dallas from Waco, I thought the whole way, not what if she says no, but when she says yes, how is this going to play out? I was praying to God at that moment in my weak, dormant faith—which was definitely the size of a mustard seed—that I would not ruin her life as I felt I had mine. I begged that if there really was a God, he would not hold my sins against her.

On that drive to Dallas, something happened. My seed was watered just a little but enough to start to question life. For one of the first times, I was going with my gut feeling to attempt to build a life with an incredible woman who had a natural overflowing of unconditional love. For the first time, I had met someone who inspired me to be better, not by words or criticism but with action and faith in action.

11

"If you really want to understand a man, don't just listen to what he says, but watch what he does," (Brennan Manning). Manning nailed it when he wrote this in his book, *The Ragamuffin Gospel* (Multnomah, 2005). This is why entering into a community of Christian believers is so difficult. It has already reported in great detail by the Barna Group that the number one reason people either don't go to church or leave the church or have a negative view of Christianity is because of their perception that the church is full of hypocrites. Is that true for you? It was certainly true for me, but if I am honest with myself, the reality is that this is a cop-out and an easy way of discrediting the whole Christian faith. It is similar to that one person in your family or circle of friends who is always jumping jobs or relationships. Usually, their response involves something someone else did or did not do, or that there is some sort of universal conspiracy against them. Their response is the same each time, something like my manager does not like me, or I didn't get along with the manager. We all think the same thing after hearing this for the umpteenth time. It's probably not the manager. It's you! Divorce rates are significantly higher among second marriages. Why? I cannot speak from a women's perspective, but I will tell you from a man's point of view. We have a natural ability to place a large portion of marital issues on our spouse, not looking into the mirror of how we as men have led the marriage down a destructive path by a lack of leadership and failure of responsibility to guard the wives' heart.

"'The man who hates and divorces his wife,' says the Lord, the God of Israel, 'does violence to the one he should protect,' says the Lord Almighty" (Malachi 2:16, NIV). This powerful verse is all about hypocrites and the power of a hypocritical testimony. In the last book of the Old Testament, the prophet Malachi wrote about the corruption of the temple sacrifices. Malachi's concerns mirror those of Nehemiah's as he wrote to the people of Judah while the Persian Empire ruled over the promised land. Overall, the people of Judah had turned away from the true worship of the Lord, resulting being under judgment and in need of salvation. Sound familiar? In our current culture, we are a massively confused bunch of people under government leaders who, in their attempt to govern, have created corrupt boundaries between the church and the state. All types of believers and nonbelievers on both sides of the argument scream, beg, and curse our government leaders about various issues; however, the leadership is a mirror image of what the people have become. Corrupt, perverted, and obscene, attempting to create equality and fairness while removing God's name and the law that was put into place to protect and guide. How did we get here as a people? One broken marriage at a time. The divorce rate is seemingly rising each year, according to statistics, and marriage has become a debate about legal rights rather than a gift from God for a people to enjoy. The current culture is ruled by groups whose sole purpose is to take the Bible, God's word, and twist it to fit sinful lifestyles. Malachi was writing those words in Malachi 2:13-16 (HCSB) to serve as a warning to the people, the men, particularly, about being on guard with their marriages. God's word is truth. When men fail their wives, repercussions ripple further than the eye can see. A wickedness accompanies complaints about the law of marriage as confinement. We are to be confined to one person, a man-woman relationship, as demonstrated in the first marriage ordained in the Garden of Eden between Adam and Eve.

Most concerning to me about marriage was not the fact that I would be stuck with one woman or that my life was over as I knew it or all the other clichés that men have come up. My biggest concern was taking another human on this journey of marriage. Remember, I watched my parents struggle through their issues and sins, and I only saw the last half of that journey. As I have gotten older, I have been led into a little more of their beginnings. Granted, they are still married to this day, which was thirty years plus, but to know how they got to that point is overwhelming. I just was not sure if I wanted to put a woman through that, and after my relationship with Maggie, I knew what I was capable of. I had seen an affection between two people grow into an angry, lustful, distrustful, and painful existence. I did not want to go through that again. Shortly before entering into a relationship with Tabby, I had grown strangely appreciative of the superficial, empty relationships that did not require any energy or intimacy. It was purely sex, nothing more than what I would compare to a bull pursuing a cow in a pasture with a burning passion of lust in his eyes. That is what I would compare my relationship experience before Tabby with—no intention, no direction, just a burning desire to satisfy my selfish and lustful desire. I certainly knew what a toxic relationship looked, smelled, and acted like. I did not want that again. My experience with relationships and marriage was somewhat disturbing but all too normal within the group of people I was associating with, which had no real obedience to or realization of God. Look at the book of Malachi and how he explains and points out the way the priest profaned the holy things of God. Malachi observes that their sin has aggravated them, and they are severely threatened for it. These were priests, supposedly holy people. Not only that, these people were living in the Promised Land, a country that was supposedly honoring God. But as you read Malachi's book, they seem more like the average person you meet today—lots of words to tickle the eardrum but with questionable, diluted, powerless actions that prove otherwise.

It seemed like everyone I ran into or had a conversation with on long drunken nights believed in God, but their lives told a whole other story. The funny thing is that I could be with some of the heaviest drug users, everyone blown out of their mind, but spiritual discussions would be going on. It never failed; God, the devil, or why none of the above existed was a topic of discussion. When people are faced with their own mortality, they question. I have always said that when atheists face death or a moment when their mortality is put to the test, they will call out to God. When the power of self is challenged, the prospect of how totally out of control we really are becomes all too apparent. When I was faced with mortality, when my maternal grandfather passed away of a massive heart attack, something changed. There was a realization of death and a fear of the unknown. As a child, I suppressed this with activities, but as the fear grew and no one led me to Jesus Christ, the Holy Spirit, I was left with only words. I remember being told in one of my highly emotional states, when the fear overwhelmed me, that was life. People die and life moves on. I could never shake the image of the graves of people, over the portraits from Nazi concentration camps, of dead bodies literally stacked up like piles of dirt. Death, our own mortality, will take us to some strange place without grounding in God's purposes for this life we have been blessed with. For some, depression or fear keeps people captive in a life that ultimately becomes a prison sentence with fear dictating where, what, and whom to interact with. You could go to Scripture like Philippians 4:6-7 (NIV): "Do not be anxious about anything, but in everything, by prayer and petition, with thanksgiving, present your requests to God. And the peace of God, which transcends all understanding, will guard your hearts and your minds in Christ Jesus." More times than not, the person telling this Scripture has little to no action behind his or her presentation of this verse. It is a nice feel-good verse, but if you have no understanding of prayer, peace of God, and Jesus Christ, this sounds like an insane plea. Many people are walking around right now with a pieced-together, dilapidated, and distorted view of who Jesus Christ, the Holy Spirit, and God are. People are allowing other hypocritical testimonies to determine their foundation of faith. It is suicidal to put our faith, our declaration of whom we serve, and the purpose of our lives in such a flawed system. When I say flawed system, I am speaking about the underlying idolatry and belief that we put into other people to transform our lives. The term *transformation* scares off people. It certainly kept me away until I was introduced to justification. Justification means that we have been saved from the penalty of sin, which is even weirder, because if we have been saved from sin, then why not indulge? The bottom line is that it is a choice; transformation in our life is not automatic. We must choose at each moment whether we are going to resist the temptation to sin and live according to God's plan for our lives. You hear people say, "He [or she] is real," as a positive trait. I certainly use this to describe people as well, but this is the problem with presenting the Gospel—no realness, no transparency. It is hard to understand these insane notations and teachings throughout the Bible with people saying one thing and doing another.

The apostle Paul wrote a letter to Titus and very bluntly told him there a lot of rebels full of loose, confusing, and deceiving talk were among them. Those who were brought up religiously and ought to know better are the worst. Paul goes on to tell him they've got to be shut up because they're disrupting entire families with their teaching and all for the sake of financial gain (Titus 1:10–16, MSG). Walking throughout my early life with no concept of the living God, Jesus Christ, and the power of the Holy Spirit hindered me in a big way. Not having an identity and understanding of who I was and the purpose of my existence resulted in a lot of displaced feelings. When Paul was telling Titus this very- up-front, honest, and hard-to-swallow truth about the people he was involved with, you have to think that Titus had a moment of denial, but do we not all want to believe the best of people? My lack of understanding of Jesus Christ and his overall purpose was not all to blame on others. Everyone has good intentions. It is just that those intentions are developed out of the person's personal convictions. Therefore, a person struggling with identity and purpose may approach advice or guidance to another with a large amount of fear and the illusion of comfort while stating a belief in God. Jesus tells the disciples in Matthew 16:24–26 (MSG) if they have any intention of going with him, they have to allow him to lead. When there is suffering, they are to embrace it and not run. In addition, self-sacrifice is the way—Jesus's way—to finding themselves; their true self is to sacrifice all. I picture Jesus telling his disciples in a matter-of-fact way, what use is it to get everything you want and lose yourself? After all that, Jesus lets them know that all they have to do is follow him and he will show them. That does not sound like a lot of comfort, stability, and safety, and there definitely wasn't anyone in my circle of influence putting their comfort and safety at risk for Jesus. The question must be asked: I believe in God, isn't that enough? Many people don't believe in God, but I do—or do I? In the book of James, the author says that even demons believe in God and tremble. Tremble? Really? They tremble because demons know that they are relationally separated from God (James 2:19, MSG). Eternally separated from God—what does that feel like? If the demons believe in God and are in torment about the separation, then why did my separation from God seem more like a relief? Don't you think there is more to the Christian thing than just merely believing in God or stating that belief with empty, useless words?

The combination of a mustard seed of faith and a reckless direction in life was coming down to one decisive moment. As I was driving to Dallas with this special yet peculiar young lady who had come into my life with her faith in Jesus Christ and this invisible God, I had every intention on not letting her go. I used to say that she made me want to be a better man, and that is true to a certain extent. However, something unseen was occurring within me. I wanted to be around Tabby because of her faith, and I liked her family, respected them because of their unapologetic approach to serving God. Not caring what people thought but more concerned about serving God. I respect that about my own parents for taking a stand for the betterment of our family in the midst of severing contact with family members and secluding themselves to protect us from the sin of our family. I always respected them for that and understood why but never could wrap my mind around why we never let anyone else in. Our family is tight-knit, and being a tight-knit family is somewhat like being on an island. We developed a deep love and care for each other, but a tight-knit, small family can have a downside. Just like a group stranded on an island, there is a fear of the unknown and a protective obligation that is not entirely bad, but when that protective action is constructed out of fear or being in isolated relationships for so long, it can prevent growth, opportunity, and produce large amounts of fear and frustration. An overprotected, fearful approach tends to lead in small families to an overall pessimistic mindset. This is all out of love and protecting those closest to one because so much has been lost through pain and, most importantly, so much has been overcome with each other. I have always been the one to step out and naturally believe that things will work out, fighting through the fear and discomfort. I do not know why I gravitated that way. Even with my overwhelming fear of death, I did not allow that to prevent me from pushing forward, and I am not talking about necessarily positive things but anything that would make me feel alive. Evil is so much easier to get ahold of. The world is full of evil and people who depend on the world for comfort, purpose, and safety. On the other side, there is a whole other life that is meant especially for us by God's original design.

Jesus reiterates Scripture from Genesis 2:24 (HCSB) in Matthew 19:5 (HCSB): "For this reason a man will leave his father and mother and be united to his wife and the two will become one flesh." He says this after being heavily questioned and tested by the Pharisees about marriage and divorce. This comes after yet another miracle of healing of a large group of people that the Pharisees totally look over to pin Jesus down with his own words and convict him of breaking the law. Without getting too deep into divorce and marriage, I will say it is very clear that we as men and women are to come out from under our parents and build our own life. This is very important overall. Additionally, I believe this is a very important element of my own recovery walk with Jesus and in my experience with other men and women my wife and I have counseled with. Your purpose and identity is found in God by the acceptance of Jesus Christ and the direction of the Holy Spirit. It is not to fulfill and attempt to earn your parents' approval. Let me be clear about this because we are to honor our parents, and by no means am I saying that children should desert their parents. I am saying that my parents', your parents,' most important relationship should be that between each other, through their own relationship with God. Sadly, unbeknownst to the parents, their own struggle with brokenness, fear, and striving for acceptance overflows into their children. In addition, a child's viewpoint and foundation of the Gospel of Jesus Christ, feelings, and emotions attached to God are usually, in most cases, a reflection of those of the parents. This obviously looks different for all types of families, whether divorced, stepparents, or no parents, but the bottom line is that the parents are the biggest contributors to the child's struggles in how they handle rejection, success, disappointments, anger. Pick any circumstance of life or emotion, and odds are that it is similar to a parental influence. I bring this up because I had so much fear and guilt and a deep yearning for acceptance from my parents. It was at an unhealthy level, to the point where I was seeking that fundamental law of marriage with my parents, seeking a relationship with them that was never meant for that level of intimacy. I know intimacy can come off a little weird when talking about parental relationships, but we search out and put things on our parents that are just not their roles. Eventually, a man must leave his parents to cleave to his wife, but why? To see the divine power instituted by God that will result in a union stronger than the highest obligations of nature. Two people becoming one flesh (Matthew 19:6, HCSB). This union is closer than that of parents and children. This was a hard truth, and I struggled with this throughout the early goings of my relationship with Tabby. The hard truth is that any guilt that I felt toward my parents was my own and nothing to do with my parents. It was my guilt and the unhealthy relationship I was seeking from them. Isn't it amazing how God's commands from Genesis, reiterated several times in the New Testament, ring true and bring a wonderful, painful conviction?

A few weeks before Tabby and I were headed to Dallas for a weekend to remember, I had asked my mom about marrying Tabby. I told my mom, "I think I want to marry her. I really love her." My mom responded by telling me to respect my feelings, and if that was really what I want to do, she would support it. She also said it did not surprise her because I treated Tabby so much differently than other girls I dated.

Tabby was already well-liked by my family. She was unlike any other girls I had dated and brought to the house. It was a breath of fresh air to my parents when I started dating Tabby. Deep down, they knew she was good for me, and Tabby was way out of my league. Tabby was stylish, hip, beautiful, and had a sweet transparence that people accepted. She still is that blonde bombshell today! I was somewhat in my own world with my personal wardrobe of style and definitely thought I was hip, but as I would learn later, wearing club shirts everywhere was not exactly a style, as it was a little weird. If you do not know what a club shirt is, well, let me enlighten you. It is usually made out of some material other than your typical material that had a shine to it. My shirts had some designs on them; pair that with gothic-type big jeans, Dr. Martens boots, and a couple of choke necklaces, and then you have my style in a nutshell. I cannot forget the mustache that I insisted on growing in an attempt to look "playa." Sadly, I am challenged in the facial hair department; therefore, the mustache looked more like catfish whiskers. Now you can see why my parents were a little surprised I was able to woo Tabby! As you can gather from my story so far, my selection of women was more or less, well, you get the point. Mom helped me pick out the ring. As I bought the ring, I was overcome with fear, happiness, and anxiety, and my mom was smiling from ear to ear as we shopped around the ring store. It is not normal for a man to have his mother with him shopping for a ring, but honestly, it was a special moment between us. Before going to Dallas, I tucked the ring away in my bag, checking the bag a hundred times before we left and every time we stopped for gas. I was paranoid about losing it or getting it stolen.

We arrived at the Hyatt hotel in downtown Dallas at the Reunion Tower. I had it all planned out—an amazing room and dinner in the restaurant, which is 560 feet up in the observation tower that overlooks the city. As we checked in, my nerves were all over the place. I would say I was the most nervous I had ever been. As we checked in, got our bags, and walked to the elevator, my heart beat tremendously with excitement and fear. When we got to the room, we set our bags down and got comfortable, looking out the window on the city, and admiring the view and accommodations. We rested for a little while before our reservations at the restaurant, watching a little TV and talking. Eventually I went into the restroom and started to get ready. I sat in the bathroom, going over all the reasons why I should not propose a marriage to Tabby. I thought back to all the things I had done and participated in that were evil and distrustful, some of which Tabby was aware of and some not. Thinking of how I had treated and been treated in the last relationship with Maggie—the yelling, darkness, fighting, drugs, and dishonesty between us. I thought of my dad and the pain he put my mother through in dealing with his own addictions and emotional issues. I really sat there almost frozen, just staring in the mirror, looking at my reflection. This is something I often did as a teenager and still today. It is a way of examining myself and focusing, ensuring that I am not dreaming. When I looked in the mirror, I saw a filthy, destructive, depressed, angry young man, but one thing superseded all of this. It was the girl in the next room waiting on me to make a decision. I knew that when I walked out of that bathroom, my life would never be the same. I was about to take this girl and drag her alongside this mess of a life I had built. I thought about my parents who had fought through so much and stuck it out to only experience a deep, intimate love with each other for thirty-plus years. With all the reasons not to ask Tabby to marry me, only one superseded them. Outside of this bathroom there was a girl who loved me unconditionally, and as much as I had attempted to shock her or scare her off with all my antics with drugs, alcohol, strip clubs, pornography, and an obsession with gothic entertainment, she never flinched. She did not actively participate in those things. She was unconditional in her love. I concluded that she had made her choice, and it must be real. For a guy struggling with his relationship with Jesus and a fading belief in God, Tabby was that person who revealed to me that there might be some truth to it all. I fell in love with Tabby and her faith.

I walked out the bathroom and took Tabby's hand, led her to the chair in the corner of the room, got on one knee, and asked her to marry me. My voice was shaky, and I struggled to get the words out, not out of fear but from being overwhelmed with the moment. With tears in her eyes, she said yes. We hugged with watery eyes and embraced each other for several minutes. At that time in my life, only one other woman brought my emotion out, my mother. Now, a woman had entered my life not connected with my family or hometown or in any means connected with my circle of influence. Almost forcing me into a place of desiring to serve her, to be a better man, and to throw all my own selfishness out the door just to be by her side. She entered my life, and in a short time, our souls connected. We were on a mountaintop that entire weekend, loving each other intently, taking walks and having moments to just talk about the journey that had just been accelerated. As we returned to our daily grind of work, paying bills, and dealing with everyday issues, it was very apparent to me that the only thing that had truly changed for me was that an amazing woman had just agreed to go on this intense war of finding myself with me. She had just enlisted whether she knew it or not. Love is an emotion. It starts with an emotional feeling or drawing to another person. Love is most of the time downgraded and misused to describe a love for music or a certain food. A perfect example of this is when we say, "I love this movie," or "I love that color." The problem with connecting the emotion of love that people have or say they have is that it is just that—an emotion. Every emotion requires an action to demonstrate it. Paul describes love in 1 Corinthians 13:4–7 (HCSB) as patient, kind, does not envy nor boast, and is certainly not proud. Love does not dishonor others, is not selfish, not easily angered, and never keeps a record of wrongs. Love does not delight in evil but loves truth while always protecting, trusting, hoping, and persevering. When I asked Tabby to marry me that night, I was all of those things in that burst of emotion. When I returned to my everyday life the following Monday, I became the opposite of the apostle Paul's description of love. Not because I wanted to, but because I did not have a relationship with Jesus Christ, or a knowledge of the Holy Spirit. There was no truth in me about the love of Christ and a loving God. I had felt moments of spiritual emotions with God, but I had discredited many of those as just coincidence or luck.

So many people have 1 Corinthians 13:4–7 posted in their homes. Pastors recite this during weddings, and singers make feel-good songs about these verses, but these verses are only one-half of the story. The apostle Paul moves on to explain further about love in verses 8-13, essentially saying that our best knowledge and greatest ability in our current condition will result in this emotion of love being narrow and temporary. My love for Tabby never left, nor did the emotion of that moment and the moments that led up to our engagement. What happened was exactly what Paul wrote in verse 8 of chapter 13. That the words that come out of our mouth, the praying and understanding, has its limits—that our knowledge is limited and what we know and say about God is always incomplete. My understanding was so lacking and my faith was so distorted that I was essentially still drinking spiritual milk as I did as an infant. However, now, as an adult, I had left those foods that had fed me physically as an infant because I needed more, but without other food, I would be malnourished. In my relationship with God and things of the Holy Spirit, I was severely malnourished and starving because I was still drinking spiritual milk. Deep down, I knew there was more out there. There had to be, or what was this life for? Why are there these emotional responses throughout our bodies for other human beings? Why, when the name of Jesus Christ or God is spoken, does it instantly promote a response to rejoice or an onslaught of anger and obscenities? Paul closes out 1 Corinthians 13 (HCSB) with the demand to trust steadily in God, hope unswervingly, and love extravagantly, explaining that love was the best of these. He was right. Love is the best. The love I felt for Tabby was like no other feeling. Still to this day, after all that we have been through and that I have put her through, I am thankful for love, our love, and the gift of love God allowed us to experience with each other.

As I have mentioned, Tabby and I chose to live with each other before we were married. It was never really an issue with me then because that was the example of how relationships progressed. It was a bigger issue for Tabby, but under my wavering, misguided leadership ability and her unapologetic love for me, she followed me right into my locomotive approach and confusing, disconnected existence driven by evil inspirations. Even as an engaged man, I would still frequent bars, hang out at clubs, and visit strip clubs, not to mention a heavy dose of pornography that I used to medicate on the areas I was struggling in as a man. These actions helped me feel alive. Not in a positive sense, but in a more of an erratic, erotic feeling that I wasn't really failing in life and that I had some sense of control. As amazing and beautiful Tabby was, she was sweet and had an innocence about her that I respected, guarded, and, sadly, took advantage of. Tabby was not unaware of the world's darker side. She had her run-ins and experiences in high school with partying, drugs, and promiscuous activity. It might not have been to the same degree, but she was battling with her own issues in her own search for purpose. She may have had a great set of parents, but there was a strained relationship with her biological father, not Bruce, that was less than desired and left some scarring. Even though Tabby was making choices that affiliated her with someone who was less than pure, spiritually lost, and searching for purpose, she hung on to a hope that only came from God. I never could understand why someone with such a faith and desire for God would have chosen a person like me to associate with, but that is the type of person she was and still is. She has a great gift of discernment with people and seeing past the immediate to look forward to the potential. At the beginning of our relationship, that was what drew me to her, but something was changing in me. Resentment had built up, not toward the person of Tabby, but toward what she believed. It states in 2 Corinthians 6:14 (HCSB) that it is wrong for good people to join with the wicked and profaned because of the two totally different ways they are going. It will result in grievous moments. What Paul was expressing is a trap that so many fall into, many relationships of all types, that the good will overcome the bad. The truth is that there is a greater danger that the bad will damage the good than that the good's hope will benefit the bad. Tabby's good was benefiting me, but my bad was damaging her tremendously; however, was I evil or simply misguided?

Tabby was a woman with a deep-seated faith. It was a relationship with its own difficulties, but it was between her and God. I had known God on a very surface-level manner, more like a historical account. Referring to Him more as I would someone like a sports figure or the president of the United States—to know some stories, stats, and even a little history. I ran into one of the all-time great basketball players once before, when Tabby and I were strolling around in a mall in Houston, Patrick Ewing. You may remember from an earlier chapter that I was a huge Knicks fan, and Patrick Ewing was the star of this team, not to mention that my first expensive pair of shoes where the Ewing. I knew everything about Patrick Ewing: where he went to college, his stats both in college and the NBA, who his kids were, his divorces, and not to mention his stats in certain situations in basketball games. I was a fan. When I saw him in the mall on this Saturday afternoon, it was then that I realized that I was nothing more than a fan. Ewing is a massive man, standing at seven foot two and weighing in at three hundred pounds, not to mention his current wife being a statue of a woman standing well above my six-foot-one frame. They were not hard to spot. When he was walking toward us, I froze because there was a little boyish shock to see the iconic figure I had always looked up to in basketball, and also I was thinking of what I would say. Not a word came out of my mouth as Patrick passed us by in the mall. I just stared like a twelve-year-old kid would at some boyhood hero. He did give me a nod to acknowledge this awkward moment of a grown man staring at another grown man. That has to be a little weird, but I like to think that the nod was Ewing acknowledging my mad basketball skills. This is how my relationship was with virtually everyone in my life. Very surface-level. Besides my parents and sister, I really cannot think of anyone I really took time to get to know and who took time to get to know me. God was foreign, Jesus Christ was a picture, and the Holy Spirit was just plain weird. What was real in my life was that I was just wandering around aimlessly, moving from one bad decision to the next, stacking them up like poker chips in the middle of a very high-stakes poker game. I was making high-stakes bets with my life and my eternity by choosing selfish pleasure out of my own shame and guilt. This lifestyle was ruining me. God was not part of my life and certainly was not a real relationship. Maybe in times of need or desperation, I reached out. I had the audacity to believe that if there were a God, he would somehow take up residence in a place where I was pushing anything that had to deal with him out and inviting in idols of my selfishness, shame, and pain. If I was honest with myself, I would have to admit that I loved to wander and go astray from God because that was easier than pursuing something real like an intimate relationship.

This was the first real relationship outside my parents, sister, childhood friends, and girlfriends and was different from what I would normally be a part of. Sure, I had relationships before Tabby, but I never really had a desire to be a better person or be drawn into an intimate situation that would create vulnerability. I was usually trying to protect or hide my true self behind some twisted display of emotions and actions in an attempt to deflect any type of deep, intimate relationship. In Jeremiah chapter 14 (MSG), especially verses 10–16, God has an intense dialogue with the prophet Jeremiah about people who had chosen to strive to seek out sinful desires that were ultimately separating them further and further from God. In this dispute, Jeremiah listed of excuses and desperate pleas to protect this group of people who had taken pleasure in everything that was against God. But now, in their desperate moment, they look to God. These verses communicate a life that so many have chosen, certainly myself. Taking pleasure in all that was against God and seeking relationships that served some selfish desire, whether sex to combat loneliness or simply someone who could make me feel good about my sinfulness. Like the saying "misery loves company," I found plenty of people to join or escort me into a lifestyle of rebellion against God. I formed distorted friendships and had destructive relationships with girls; however, this relationship with Tabby was different. Tabby was none of those things, and she certainly had something I wanted. I just could not pinpoint it, or maybe I knew what it was and I just didn't have the courage and wherewithal to pursue it or admit it. I knew her relationship was with God through Jesus Christ but did not really know what that meant. What and who was Jesus Christ? I mean, who was he really? Sure, there are plenty of stories and an entire book dedicated to his life, but my shortsighted view was that preachers, priests, missionaries, and nuns were the only ones chosen to do God's work. Then what for the rest of us? Catholicism has a way of disconnecting the pulpit from Jesus Christ that directly creates this unattainable god for people of the congregation. More of a separation between *them* and *us*. I knew one thing for sure: clearly, there was some sort of spiritual realm. In addition, t my experiences with the occult with Maggie and others had proven to me that some sort of spiritual experiences really existed.

One night as Tabby and I lay asleep in the bed, I was awoken by an incredible sensation in my body. It was a gut-wrenching feeling of fear running through my body like a shock of panic in my vines. I was awakened somewhere around midnight with the racing thoughts of dead relatives, of how short life was, and how everyone I know and see will die. I was racing with questions like, "If God made the Earth, then who made God?" Utterly full of fear of death, almost paralyzed. I did not go to Tabby with this fear. I picked up the phone and had this long conversation with my mom. Tabby later would reveal that she knew that I had called my mom and that she was somewhat concerned that I did not go to her, but you have to understand the landscape of my emotional state at the time. My parents were well aware of my unhealthy fear of the unknown, and at the very moment, I felt like my mom was the only one who would understand and be able to calm me down. As I was crying and shaking on the phone, talking to her about death and my fears, she had this very calm tone and talked me down from the ledge, so to speak. Tabby heard the whole conversation. In a one-bedroom apartment, there are not a lot of places to hide. This fear was so intense. I can only describe it as a presence whose sole purpose was to inflict fear. Granted, I had had encounters like this in the past as a child, but I had diminished the feelings with drugs, alcohol, and pornography. With Tabby living with me, I was forced into an abstinence to hide my hidden desires for those things. Before moving into the apartment and right before I met Tabby while I was living alone in the trailer house I rented, I had a similar but more intimate encounter with this presence. One night after a long night of partying, I came home alone and went to the freezer and put a pizza in the oven. I lay on the living room floor to wait for the timer to go off. I fell asleep on the floor or passed out—the jury is still out. As I was in the drunken sleep, I had the most vivid vision I had ever had in my life that instilled the most fear I had ever encountered. In the dream or vision, I was clawing my way out of this hole while I heard screams, voices, and evil mantras from underneath me. Hands were grabbing my feet, and I could feel the nails on my calves and upper thighs. In the version, I was being pulled, dragged to what I interpreted as hell. I felt the panic, anxiety, fear, and the overwhelming feeling that I should just give up. When I awoke, I was obviously sobered up. The timer had been going off on the oven for the pizza, and the back door of the trailer house was wide open. Yeah, you can guess how freaked out I was. Paul says in Ephesians 6:12 that our struggle is not against flesh and blood but against the rulers, against the authorities, against powers of this dark world, and against spiritual forces of evil in the heavenly realm. In a nutshell, this is a life-or-death fight to the finish against the devil and all his angels, and it is a battle for souls. These attacks were getting stronger and stronger as I and Tabby progressed in our relationship.

When Tabby found out the depth of this fear and panic, not to mention the whole "I think I encountered a demon or the devil in a vision," there was some concern on her part. Obviously! She reached out to her parents, and they entered into a prayer campaign on my behalf. They did not make me aware of this prayer campaign or the prayers being offered up on my behalf. I think they knew that would have pushed me further back because of my lack of understanding that resulted in criticisms. This goes back to how they know God. They knew God, and they knew lies. They knew spiritual warfare and how to combat it. My experiences with ghosts, spirits, or vivid dreams generated lots of fear and anguish, but when you grow up around a hybrid Christian faith with occult attributes and a focus on the spiritual realm as a welcoming place or a place to entertain, there is no faith in God or Jesus Christ. Just a misguided doctrine that is placed in misguided teachers. In addition, massively misplaced feelings are dealt with conditional situations and inspiration from the culture around us, which has occult attributes that are moving us into idol worship by the lures of comfort, safety, and immediate gratification. Call it what you will, and most people get highly offended when you start talking about these types of things because it demands conviction by the Holy Spirit to align our lives with the Word of God. This goes back to what Malachi wrote over a thousand years ago in chapter 2 about the people of Judah, the supposed priest of Judah. God hates—a strong word, but it reveals his passion—divorce. Divorce is a violent dismembering of the "one flesh" of marriage, as it states in The Message translation. We are to watch ourselves, not letting our guard down, but showing a lack of proper regard to these notions of "God loves sinners and sin alike." The ultimate truth is that there is a judgment seat and we all must make a choice whether we choose to believe it or not. My fears and anxiety were growing more and more intense. My sleepless nights had become more and more common, and with drugs, alcohol, and pornography, I was becoming more aggressive, dark, and isolated within myself.

Tabby and I grew closer and further apart at the same time. The areas of our relationship growing closer were the communication between us and the unconditional love we revealed to each other in spurts. These areas were developing when I was not allowing the influence of substances or others who would fill my head with lies and deceit. Our relationship was like ocean waves of emotions crashing beautifully over the white sands of our lives, cleaning the sands as a fresh slate. The wave crashes and hits the beach, and the wave retracts with all the debris and junk lying around on the beach. The problem was that, instead of locking hands with Tabby, walking along this beach and allowing the waves to crash and retract, cleaning the beach in front of us and underneath our feet, I would unclasp my hands from hers and walk into the depth alone. This allowed the undercurrent to pull me further and further into the sea of deceit and lies. When I was focused and intentionally seeking out relationship with Tabby, our relationship would experience great growth. In those times, I drifted and lost sight of what was truly important, my point of reference on the shore, while allowing myself to become lost in the sea of despair. In thinking about the difficulties, trust and distrust, encouragement and discouragement in my relationship with Tabby, it had nothing to do with Tabby. My experiences with Maggie and others filled my head with lies and inconsistencies. Feeling loved one minute and then suddenly to move to a place where I was totally questioning whether Tabby really loved me or was I just a stepping-stone or was this even real. When I think about how I would rationalize my thoughts in those days, I laugh because I can guarantee that she was not with me for any riches or great influence. This whole back and forth of the relationship was hurting her and destroying me from the inside out. The issues I was experiencing were a mirror image of my distorted relationship with God. I felt unworthy, angry, and untrusting toward a God I had heard good things about. I had even seen those good things played out in others' lives, but they were nonexistent in my own. My late-night ramblings of tears of fear of death and the desire for purpose were affecting me in ways that frustrated those around me. Usually as an excuse, to act out and find relief in others who could fill those needs in a way that was temporary but satisfying. It was my way of getting to God, taking something he created and destroying it. I have heard that suicide is the ultimate slap in the face of God. We are made in his image (Genesis 1:27, HCSB), right? Therefore, those who decide to end it on their own terms in most cases have decided to walk away from God and revel in their shame and despair.

Those prayers offered up on my behalf for my deep, hidden desire to feel wanted and accepted and to have a purpose were being stored up until the time was right. Tabby and I were preparing for our wedding in early 2003. Well, Tabby and her mother were doing most of the planning. In the earlier part of the year, I had started to feel the pressure of the impending marriage, and the weight of the decision was beginning to set in. This only caused more and more stress and fear. Not only that, but Travis and I had started to hang out again. We had never stopped, but I had distanced myself from him because I saw the discomfort in Tabby's eyes when I was with him. Sadly, Travis would call to hang out, and I would decline many times but call him up or accept when it was convenient or something I wanted to do. In some sense, I used him. When I wanted to make some bad choices, he was the one I called up. As I look back on that friendship today, it was a very selfish relationship from my standpoint. As the calendar rolled over to 2003, I reached out to Travis, mostly because I felt I was suffocating under the pressure of marriage. Most men, especially those without a real relationship with God, struggle with the process of marriage. Marriage is looked at as the next step in life, not a gift to us from God to enjoy. Men treat it as a prison sentence. I had started to burn the candle on both ends, working as a banking center manager during the day, working long hours and staying up late at night and sometimes in the early morning hours in bars, strip clubs, or at someone's apartment. My pill intake had hit the highest level in my drug experience, taking uppers and downers or, really, whatever I could get my hands on. We were hanging out at a local Waco bar that served crappy beer and had even crappier service, but it was cheap. You could get drunk for twenty dollars, plus, it was down the street from a local strip club. One night in early February 2003, Travis had this plan to go to Del Rio and across the border to Ciudad Acuña in Mexico. He sold it as a weekend of partying. The mantra for the trip was, "Let's Get *Messed Up!*" The word "messed" is a lighter adjective than what was actually used. All those stored-up prayers on my behalf, all those nights of fear, those nights of nightmares of hell and the devil, those intoxicate rants cursing God had led me to this point. A decision.

In Malachi (ESV), the prophet starts chapter 3 by saying,

> Behold, I send my messenger and He will prepare the way before me. And the Lord whom you seek will suddenly come to His temple and the messenger of the covenant in whom you delight, behold, He is coming, says the Lord of hosts.

After Malachi spends the entirety of Chapter 2 speaking about the Lord rebuking the priests and how Judah profaned the covenant, he foretells Jesus's coming in Chapter 3. All of those groans, complaints, curses, and disappointments of God I had recognized either with my words or my actions. In my immediate, controlled environment of Waco, my job, my relationships, and all the distractions of pornography, drugs, and just the culture, God had no place. Certainly, there was no place for Jesus. I was nothing more than a screaming person in Judah, profaning the covenant, but Jesus was coming, and he was going to reveal himself in a most radical and obvious way, in the most unlikely of places.

12

In 2002, Tabby saved up and bought me tickets to the Houston Texans' opening game in their inaugural season since the original Houston Oiler franchise left town when Bud Adams moved the team to Nashville, Tennessee, in the 1990s. Tabby knew I was a football fan and passionate about Houston sports. I was excited and extremely grateful for the gift. We had a whole weekend planned out. Tabby and I would spend the weekend together. It promised to be the perfect weekend until Travis and I were out one night at one of our local hangouts, and he told me about a music festival held all over the nation in selected cities, hosted by the rock icon Ozzy Osborne. Ozzy was in his late fifties to early sixties, headlining these festivals, and the wear and tear of the rock-god lifestyle had taken a toll on his abilities to entertain as impactfully as he did in the 1960s and 1970s. Even with his broken voice and shaky presence, a result of the amount of his drug intake, he headlined a highly popular music festival called Ozzfest, a collection of bands that ranged from seasoned veterans to up-and-coming artists. Ozzy himself even sung a few of his most well-known songs to close the festival. The festival had three stages, twenty-four hours of heavy metal and alternative rock, with a little rap mixed in, accompanied by a party scene made up of thousands of teenagers and young adults. There was also the crowd that looked like they had been to every Ozzy Osborne concert and did not realize they were adults attempting to live out some memories. In addition, a few were there for nostalgic moments. Travis described it as the ultimate party scene and the hardest music. He had been to this before, and as we sat talking about this in a bar with the excitement of his voice and actions, I immediately was hooked in. I had never been to a concert; well, I had gone to one with Maggie, which was Tom Petty and the Heartbreakers, the type of concert you sat around and listen to, smoking weed and singing along with people two or three times your age, if not older. Kind of a folk or bluegrass-type concert. Without regard to Tabby's feelings or the sacrifice she had made to save up the money for the Houston Texans tickets, I had the nerve to ask her if it was okay if I traded the tickets for Ozzfest tickets. Deep down, I knew this was a wrong move. I knew it was hurtful, and I knew it was more about the time we as a couple were going to spend together than football. Not to mention Tabby had taken time to think of something I enjoyed and to enjoy it with me. Still to this day, I regret the decision to trade those tickets, but the lure of darkness and a chance to medicate was overwhelmingly enticing. A part of me wanted Tabby to put her foot down, fight, and disagree with this decision, but she simply asked if that was really, what I wanted to do. The lure of drugs, alcohol, and a weekend of reckless behavior was more attractive than spending it with my fiancée. Even writing that puts a lump in my throat. It was nothing to do with her , but it was more of what I desired at the time and whom I was serving, if you will. Someone who internally tormented tends to keep people with some type of positive, loving element just close enough to make them feel human. A lot of truth is in lyrics sung by Trent Reznor in his song "Hurt." The whole song is about pain and how pain makes us feel alive. One particular lyric says, "I cut myself today, just to see if I still bled." I loved Tabby deeply, and she made me feel and realize the harsh truths in my life. Choosing to spend time with Travis was not some intense friendship; we were both hurting individuals running from God. Tabby was a reminder of all the areas I lacked and that I struggled with, which were essentially good; Travis offered up a venue and resource that ensured me that I still had an overbearing desire for the things that cause destruction and pain. I was in a circle of internal pain. I was in a place of depression where I continually beat myself up for all the things I wasn't and all the things I was.

When I went out to bars or clubs or out of town, Tabby would lay out a set of rules, which to many would seem insanely liberal and prompt the question why in the world Tabby would stay with me. I cannot speak to everything Tabby was feeling or experiencing, but I will say this: She had a relationship with God and knew Jesus. Her reasons came out of a deep-seated place of faith. Yes, her faith was not ideal, but it was real. She was going through her own struggles and issues with herself and her relationship with God and was obviously in a place of questioning why God had called her to this life with me. If you ask her, she saw past the surface, knowing there was much more to this craziness that was for the good. Still to this day, my wife can meet a degenerate soul, a woman or man in a sinful, destructive lifestyle, and have the discernment whether to pursue or walk away. It is powerful and a little weird, but I cannot think of a time it hasn't been spot on. Tabby's rules would get more and more specific as I pushed boundaries or when she realized the depth of my reliance on a lifestyle of darkness. When I approached her about this trip to Ozzfest with Travis, she did not judge or ask why; she knew why. She had gathered my cravings for those things but also knew the side of me that would come out when I was at a distance from those things, emotions of love, protection, and joy. She always would ask me to not do hard drugs. At this point, she knew that I smoked weed as easily as I would pull out a cigarette. The other rules were embarrassing, and I am ashamed that I had to be told these things. They were no slow dancing with other girls and not to drive drunk. The no slow-dancing rule was in place and possibly some can relate. In the club scene, especially the rap club scene, there is usually a mosh pit of people jumping up and down, grinding, or anything else in an attempt to recreate the rapper's intention of the lyrics. If I went to strip clubs, she would ask that I do not buy lap dances. I honored these rules in my own twisted, justified way; obviously, when you are in a lifestyle like this, the boundaries are always blurred, pushed further out. As I recount everything that has happened throughout our marriage, I have often just walked up to her as I write and ask, "Why did you stay with me and how?" Her response has been the same every time, and every time someone asks her, it remains the same: "I prayed for him, our relationship, and for protection when he was out. That he would see the things he was involved in and want to stop." I am paraphrasing, but you get the point.

In Romans 10:1 (HCSB), Paul starts the chapter by saying, "Brothers, my heart's desire and prayer to God concerning them is for their salvation." You have to realize that Paul was persecuted everywhere he went, and at the end of Romans 8 and beginning of Romans 9, he says that nothing can separate us from the love of God and talks of a burden for the lost. There was no doubt I was hurting Tabby, and she had every right on more than one occasion to walk out the door and never to return, but she chose to pray for me. Deep down, she knew she was not going to be the one to share the Gospel with me, but she was praying for a breakthrough. Now I am not saying she just rolled over during my hurtful actions. She may be a little, sweet blonde girl, but she has some fight in her. Even during arguments, hurtful things may have been said, but they would end with me examining myself and realizing she was right and that there was something to her that I could not grasp, an object to her unapologetic faith. At the time, I did not know these prayers were being said on my behalf, and I certainly didn't know conversations were happening behind my back between her and her parents to pray for me. Prayers are one of those ways that people go back and forth and really hang their anger, acceptance, denial on God. People pray for things or situations, and if unanswered, they will respond much as children respond to parents' directions, with either anger or acceptance. In Matthew 6:9–13 (HCSB), Jesus is teaching us how to pray, specifically in verse 10, where it says, "Your kingdom come, your will be done." We are to pray for God's will to be done. It does not say let *my* will be done as I see it should be. People tend to look at God as a genie or Santa Claus, saying, "Here is what I want, therefore deliver on my wish." Jesus says in Matthew 7:10 that if a person asks for a fish, he will not be given a snake. Jesus is telling us that he is going to sort out things that work best for us. When it comes to faith, we typically look at what is right in front of our nose, the situation we are currently in or what we immediately need. God is looking at the whole picture and what is going to work out best for us in the end. This is a hard message for people to accept when you start talking about loved ones taken early through death or horrible accidents or about financial difficulty. When I was a child, my parents did not grant my every wish and desire. They had more wisdom and understanding about what was best for me. Did I get angry or disappointed? Sure. However, I know that they were doing it out of love and protection. Sadly, some have not seen this type of parental interaction, so it is hard to understand an all-loving, all-caring God when our parents were not that. I was fortunate to have parents like that. I did lack that undeniable faith in Jesus Christ and in God. In my disappointment with life, I turned to the god of self and searched out what I could do to make sense of everything. Tabby, on the other hand, was led to a place of prayer in the midst of uncertainty and nervousness. Her and her parents' prayers for me to be found and to meet Jesus would not go unanswered. It just would not happen or be designed the way they envisioned.

The plan was simple: Leave from Waco on a Friday, arrive in Victoria to stay with Travis's parents, and then head over to Del Rio to cross the border to Ciudad Acuña, Mexico. This plan was all thought out on a bar table to first go to Victoria, Texas, where Travis was from and his parents still lived. Stay there a night, then head to Del Rio. From there, we would get a hotel in Ciudad Acuña. You may be asking, "What the heck is there in Ciudad Acuña?" Well, anything and everything a young man would need to totally silence the voice of reason and to crush common sense. Drugs, strip clubs, bars, and in most cases, all three in the same place. Ciudad Acuña is a place where few rules are enforced and most law enforcement can be negotiated with the right amount of cash. One of those types of places that, if your mother knew your involvement, it would blow her mind or result in beet-red cheeks of embarrassment. I had never been to Mexico and certainly never to party. I had heard stories from truck drivers at the oil service company I worked at briefly in my hometown before moving to Waco. As I would wash their trucks, inside and out, I would run across, well, let us say X-rated memorabilia from places visited while working on the Texas-Mexico border. I am not stereotyping truck drivers or the field workers of the oil industry. This is just truth from one man's brief oil career and from knowing a few truck drivers. The large majority of truck drivers I have encountered have no problem sharing their road trip experiences as they take in some of the local entertainment that border towns have to offer. To say the least, I was intrigued and, honestly, a bit disturbed by some of the stories from their road trips. In most cases, these guys had wives and families and went to church. Just another example of churchgoers who said they believe in God, but not one proved that belief by his actions. Empty words backed up with contrary actions. When Travis invited me to go with him and his bipolar friend, Bret, I gave a resounding yes, but, seriously, his friend was bipolar and a bit schizophrenic. I am not sure whether he was clinically diagnosed, but Bret was legitimately crazy. I did not like to be in a room alone with this dude because of some of the crazy stuff that would come out of his mouth. Mix that with a habit of cocaine use, smoking weed, and drinking heavy alcohol, and you have a time bomb, which he was. He was the type of guy who would walk into a bar and purposely start a conversation with a girl who was obviously with someone else, just to start an altercation. Yeah, that really happened. One early morning, Bret, Travis, another guy named Ronnie, and I were hanging in Travis's apartment doing what had become normal. Bret jumped up out of his spot on the couch and left. He got in his car and drove off without saying a thing. He called Travis a few hours later, talking about the government and federal agents following him and that he was headed for Mexico. He showed back up a couple days later.

Bret caused an element of confusion and absolute insanity that would leave you thinking, "This guy is a wildcard." With Bret, you never knew what was going to happen that night. One time, he was running from a local bar hangout, mainly from Baylor University students after somehow managing to infuriate the majority of them at the bar. He was still not sure what happened that night. I was just jerked by Bret, saying, "Let's go!" Other incidents would involve us driving up and down streets in Waco after long nights at the bars or clubs. If there was not an after-party, then we would just trash things. On other nights, as we cruised the I-35 corridor from North Waco to South Waco, we would drive insanely crazy. If in different vehicles, we would drive our pickup trucks as if we were pole positioning in a NASCAR racing event, high on whatever the night had to offer and whatever we could get our hands on. Ronnie, Travis's other friend, was a different breed from the rest of us. I almost think that he and I were in the same boat, trying to figure out how we got here and what we were doing. The only way I can describe Ronnie is to compare him to a cross between the tallest redneck you have ever met and a silent giant. Ronnie never did any drugs but loved his beer and liquor. Once intoxicated, Ronnie turned into a whole other person. This silent giant would transform into something to the likes of the Incredible Hulk's transformation. This became clear one night on our way from Travis's apartment to a strip club. Ronnie had been drinking heavily, and of course, he was driving. Travis was in the passenger's seat, and I was in the backseat. Ronnie asked me to hand him his hunting rifle. A normal person might ask, "Hey, why do you need your rifle as you drive down the interstate?" or "Why are we carrying a loaded weapon?" Nevertheless, I didn't ask. I am not sure what I was thinking at that moment, but what happened next I could not even make out. Ronnie told, not asked, Travis, "Hold the wheel!" As Travis grabbed the wheel, Ronnie rolled the window down, positioned his large frame outside the window, took aim at the overhead interstate sign, fired a shoot, and laughed. What! What just happened? I was in the backseat, sobering up quickly with a sense of fear slipping in. Travis did the same outside the passenger window but, instead, just threw a beer bottle at an upcoming sign; I followed his lead and participated in throwing beer bottles, cheering as each one found its mark, bursting on the side of a highway sign. What does a person do in a moment like this? Nothing. You stay the course, as I was on someone else's turf. I made the decision to get in this truck. I made the decision to spit obscenities, showing my excitement for what just happened while secretly somewhat worried inside about being stopped by the law. These are the moments that built the foundation for my decision to take this trip to Del Rio. To come up with a backstory that would be told to Tabby to lie about my true intentions or whereabouts. These are a collection of bad situations, bad decisions, and bad circumstances that I was now entering into. Why? Why would I go against my core values, ethics of respect, honor, and truth? When we trashed neighborhoods in Waco by throwing trashcans, I would drink more and do more drugs because all I could picture was my father's and mother's disappointment if they knew what I was doing. How they proudly cleaned their yard and house, respecting what they had worked hard for. Picturing the people coming out the following morning to see their yards littered with trash was heartbreaking.

People are quick to judge. Even in the thick of their own sinful lifestyle, people will find someone to lord over in an attempt to feel better about themselves or to relate to in an attempt to feel accepted or purposeful. That is how pockets of people are formed, how communities and 'hoods are developed. Like-minded people celebrating a similar fate. Deep down, it is hard for me to believe that people really believe the words that come out of their mouth when someone is obviously justifying some twisted lifestyle that is like a TV Land repeat of episodes of some demonic comedy. Where the characters change, the storyline changes, but the undercurrents of the same principles of deception are the same every time. I was not a part of some hardcore street gang or some murderous bunch of political militants. I was just a guy seeking purpose and coming up empty. If there was no resurrection of Jesus, no afterlife, no God, then what is the point? To understand why so many people, including myself, enter into a sinful, reckless lifestyle, you must understand that there is not a realization of the Gospel in their lives. There is nothing that resembles the word of God, but this is true with the other side of the cultural spectrum. This is true for those who may not do drugs or participate in malicious activities. This is true for those who seemingly have it all—money, career, or even a part in church leadership who say all the things that point to a faith in God. When people who seemingly have it all, including those who are affiliated with a church or religion, are challenged and faced with adversity, the god they worship will be revealed. John Calvin said,

> When men have repented, and thus give evidence that they are reconciled to God; they are no longer the same persons that they formerly were. But let all fornicators, or unclean or covetous persons, so long as they continue such, be assured that they have no friendship with God, and are deprived of all hope of salvation.

R.C. Sproul dives into John Calvin's commentary of Ephesians 5:3-5 and reveals: "There is a defined difference between those who profess Christ, seeking out to mortify the flesh, occasionally sinning, and those who profess Christ but celebrate their sin." That is what a person really wants—to be different, to be more.

In both his letters to the Corinthians, the apostle Paul takes a stance of correcting and pointing out misunderstanding and outright disrespect and uses Jesus's words to guide and discipline them. It is much easier to take the easy way of life, as he writes, "Let us eat and drink, for tomorrow we die" (1 Corinthians 15:32), if we truly don't believe in the resurrection of Jesus. My life was a reflection of my faith. I did not have any hope of anything after death; therefore, I wanted to enjoy what I could in life because life is short. I did not want to be like this. No one does. I wanted to believe. Deep down, I felt that there had to be something to this life that was not just one big disappointing party, relationship, and hangover one after another. Paul in 1 Corinthians 15:33–34 (HCSB) goes on to say, "Do not be deceived, 'bad company corrupts good morals.' Come to your senses and stop sinning because some people are ignorant about God." Paul was pointing out that the people who were struggling to believe or understand Jesus and his commandments were trusting but with a corrupt and infectious belief system. Ignorance of God has led people to disbelief. My whole life, my whole existence, was built on a belief system that was my own but built on ignorance of God, Jesus Christ, and the Holy Spirit. I had a broken understanding pieced together to form this secondhand, corrupted, evil life of sin, disbelief in God, and a fear of the unknown that drove me to dark places. I wanted to be corrected, as all people want to be corrected or disciplined in a loving, caring way by an unconditional, loving father who desires them. Paul had to reveal truth, love, and compassion for the Corinthians' lives and well-being. My life was full of people who had some opinion on God, faith, or the lack or need of either. I had entrusted my life to so many others, allowing hypocritical testimonies to sway me this way or that. When Travis invited me to Del Rio, I agreed because of the desire and promise of an escape, the opportunity to forget and diminish feelings of being lost, unwanted, and scared. God had something else in mind.

The plan was set. Early in the week, to prep the lie, I would tell Tabby about a camping trip that Travis had invited me on for the weekend. When I asked Tabby about going, she agreed, but it was more of a fearful, unsettling yes. If you ask Tabby today, she says she always knew that there was more to it than I was telling her. She was not oblivious, just uncertain on how to approach the situation. As Friday got closer, I got excited and a bit nervous, and Tabby got more and more anxious about the whole thing. As I was getting my things together, she asked me to do one thing for her: "Please don't do hard drugs." Yes, this is where we were in our relationship, extremely loving, caring for each other, but also realistic about what was going on behind my secretive doors of deception, self-inflicted pain, and fear. When Travis arrived at our apartment, I went downstairs to throw my bag in the back of his truck. Brett was already in the passenger seat with his arm hanging outside the rolled-down window of the truck, looking like an overexcited dog that is going to feel the wind in his face at any minute. As I hugged Tabby and could feel the fear in her embrace, I could also feel the doubt and disbelief of my intentions, or it may have been my guilt slipping out. Either way, this trip was built on a foundation of lies, and we both knew it deep down. As we guys headed out of town, I started to get excited about what was to come—a weekend of drinking and partying and a vacation from the disappointment of myself. It was never about Tabby or escaping her. She was the positive, the one thing that made me feel human, as if I mattered. It was about the demons in my head, the reality I lived with that there really may not be a God and that Jesus may have just been some dude. Referring back to what the Paul said in 1 Corinthians 15 about bad company of ignorant people, I was in the thick of it, and I was indoctrinated with a belief system that made these things acceptable behaviors and outlets.

As we pulled into Victoria, Texas, where Travis's parents lived and where he was from, he immediately started calling friends of his in the area to see if there were any parties or where the hot spots were for that night. Travis's parents were very accommodating and genuinely nice. His mother was a schoolteacher for many years, and his father was a factory worker at one of the local plants. They seemed to be very aware of Travis's party lifestyle. They were not supportive of it, but they were not against it, either. We were all welcomed in their home. We were all encouraged to stay for dinner and not eat out. They seemed to really want that little bit of time with Travis, but the moment was brief—a few hours until we hit the door and jumped in the truck. I was somewhat nervous and a little fearful just because of the unknown of meeting new people and knowing that I was going to be catapulted into situations that involved drugs, alcohol, and sexually charged young adults. We loved the stories that Travis had shared with me about his circle of friends. It was intriguing, but now that I was here, meeting them, I was having a small anxiety attack in my mind. The first place we rolled up to was a house of one of his close high school friends. There were twenty or so people there, music blasting from the living room and a rumble talking. I was immediately offered a beer as I walked in. The aroma of cigarette smoke was trumped by the pungent smell of weed burning. We hung out there for a while, drinking and having superficial conversation until Travis wanted to show us around his hometown. We left, drove around, and saw some of the sights. Travis received a phone call from a friend who had heard he was in town. He immediately invited us to a local hangout. Before we went, Brett really wanted to score some coke and had asked Travis if he knew anyone we could get some from. As Travis called around, he found someone who had some for sale. We pulled up to the house of this low-level drug dealer, and we all walked in. Tabby's words started to ring in my ears about not doing any hard drugs. I was thinking of a plan the entire time of how to get out of this, how I was going to think of an excuse to not snort this stuff. As we shared a beer and talked with this guy, I felt relieved because I wasn't asked to try it there. Travis did not ask for any money and bought the eight ball of coke for us. This is a very important point. When someone buys drugs for you, it is like buying food for you. It is rude not to partake. When we pulled up to the bar, Travis asked us if we wanted to hit this first. Brett gave a resounding yes while I was hesitant, but it did not take a lot of encouraging for me to join in. Travis took the rolled-up baggy in the shape of a small ball of pure white, refined mind-altering substance. My nerves and heart rate registered excitement, not because of the drug, but because I knew I was preparing to break my promise to Tabby. But the other side of me was filled with the giddiness of a child getting a gift.

We searched the truck for something with which to break up and divide the coke into evenly portioned lines for each us. In the movies, they often use a small mirror or countertop, but Bret found a CD case to use in the backseat. I even remember saying at one point, before it was my turn to snort a line, I thought, "I am not sure if I am going to do this tonight." That lasted all of about a minute. As I took the cut-in-half plastic drinking straw and put one end to my nostril and the other at the beginning of line, I was rushed with what I guess was the chemical dopamine in my brain. I was excited and joyful, and it was euphoric. As we sat in the truck, preparing to go into the bar, I sat in a pool of shame and anger deep within myself, realizing that, yet again, I could not control my actions, and the desire had outweighed reason. From that point on, impressions of the whole night were a little sporadic. We stayed at the bar only for a short time because we were all rolling too hard, making a scene, especially Brett, with his hyperactive personality and the combination of drugs, medications, and alcohol. He was a running bull in a china shop. Drugs took me to a place of mental battle torment and reflection on myself that was not constructive but a totally destructive cycle. In 1 Corinthians 10 (HCSB), the apostle Paul warns from Israel's past and their example through their sin. Paul hopes and prays that the Corinthians not desire evil as Israel did: "No temptation has overtaken you except what is common to humanity. God is faithful, and He will not allow you to be tempted beyond what you are able, but with the temptation He will also provide a way of escape so that you are able to bear it" (1 Corinthians 10:13, HCSB). I was wrapped up in sinful, selfish decisions that I could have blamed on the temptations, but I was putting myself into a position to be tempted. I was welcoming and desiring the temptations, but right after a bad decision or horrible night of bad decisions, I would feel the incredible regret and depression of the depraved evil that was present in me. I needed a way out. I needed an "escape" that was not induced by a stimulant, one that would give me more than just an imitation of happiness or acceptance.

Paul's ending of the passage quoted above, "He will provide an escape so that you are able to bear it," meant that God would never let me down, would never let me be pushed past my limit, would always be there to help me come through whatever I was struggling with. It is a nice thought but is it real? I had battled for years, questioning what was the point of struggle and pain. The short answer is that we live in a fallen world where evil is present. The struggle and pain of life reminds us of the need for Jesus, the need for a love that is not conditional or formatted for selfish agendas.

When we got up the following morning to prepare for our trip to Del Rio and Acuña, we got a late start, which was a result of the antics from the night before. As we headed out from Victoria, I had this attitude of, "Oh, well, I already blew it!" When we got to Del Rio, the lies kept spewing out of my mouth when I talked to Tabby over the phone, like a fire hydrant gushing water onto the street. Tabby is a very intuitive person, and when we talked on the phone, her responses would reveal that she knew she was not getting the truth or, at least a stretched, modified truth. When we arrived in Del Rio, we drove straight to the border crossing. It was late in the evening, so the majority of the people in line to go into Mexico were workers going home after a day of labor or groups such as our own contributing to the stereotype of partying on the Mexican border. I have been to Cancún and other tourist spots in Mexico. I went on a senior trip to Cancún and partied there. Even with all the press about the partying that goes on in those tourist places, nothing compares with what goes on in these border towns. The tourist towns are spillage from these border towns. Mexico has become known for lawlessness, but the tourist towns are somewhat protected and Americanized. The border towns essentially have no rules, no limits; what you desire is there, and things that you did not know you desire are there. We went through the whole border check, showing IDs and allowing them to search the vehicle. Travis had gotten a room at a Best Western just a block or so off the main drag of Acuña.

We were settled in, and when Brett woke up from his nap, we proceeded to hit the street. First stop was a restaurant for some dinner to fill our stomachs so that we could drink more. After hanging around the restaurant, we walked the main drag of Acuña, dropping into a bar here and there, just mainly checking out the landscape. At night, this town is flooded with American citizens in search of drugs, sex, and insane drinking without imitations. It seemed that the only Mexican citizens were either working in the establishments or sprinkled in the pools of Americans walking in a zombie state with one carnal objective—getting drunk. As we visited and barhopped, the drinks started to catch up. We settled at one location that was packed from wall to wall. A large group of the patrons in this bar was from a military base just north of San Antonio. They were a mixed group of physically fit men and women spitting Marine mantras, and for some odd reason, I was pulled into this group. Still to this day, I could not tell you what led me to hang out with them. With my insane need to feel wanted and this group of people accepting me into their group, it was probably the feeling of being wanted. Travis and Brett wanted to go to another bar, and I instinctively told them that I was going to stay here and that I would hook up with them later. As I slammed beers and shots of liquor at some point in the night, I was invited back to Del Rio across the border to an after party. I could not tell you what time it was nor where I was at that moment. In my highly drunken state, I agreed. We all stumbled out to a pickup truck and jumped in. A couple of others and I had to jump into the bed of the truck because the cab had overfilled with people. It is a little blurry, but I somehow ended up getting my bag from our room at the Best Western, so I did not intend to come back to the hotel. I did not really put a lot of thought in how I was going to tell Travis where to pick me up the next day, but this was the least of my stupid decisions. I threw my bag in the back of the truck, jumped in, and headed to the Texas border in this truck full of drunken, stupid young people. The wind felt refreshing, and as we sped along the Mexican highway to the border, no one had a care in the world until we had to exit the vehicle at the request of the border patrol. They had us sit on a curb as they went through the truck and our bags with flashlights and dogs. Once back in the truck, we went to a La Quinta Inn in Del Rio, where we migrated between rooms, continuing the drinking. At this point, I blacked out. I can't remember much of anything that happened up until I woke up.

The curtain in the room was ever so slightly cracked to a point where the sunlight broke through like a laser beam that seemed to directly hit my eye. The beam was so intense that it created a warm spot on my face. I rolled around on the seemingly familiar floor, attempting to get comfortable, but when I looked around the room, there were people on both sides passed out. I hastily sat up and realized I was in a hotel room. I sat up and looked around. Fully clothed people lay in the bed with some snoring but most in a comatose state. It looked like everyone had just fell where they stood. I sat there quickly assessing the night, wondering what had led to sitting here in this room. This was not the first time I had woken up in a strange place or had very little to no knowledge of the events leading up to it, but this was the first where I knew absolutely no one in the room. A slight panic started to erupt in my belly as I started to fill in the gaps and tried to figure out where Travis and Brett were. I shouted, with some associated adjectives, "I am in —— Del Rio!" I jumped up in panic, stepping over people, and realized that my bag was by the door with a couple of others. I stepped out the door with my bag in hand and determined quickly that I had no idea where I was or where I was going. I went back in the hotel room, shook the first person I found, and asked, "How do I get back to the border?" Someone mumbled, "Go right." I walked back out of the hotel room, feeling panicked, fearful, and angry with myself, thinking that I had really screwed up this time. Not only was I in Del Rio, I was separated from the only two people who knew I was down here. I attempted to call Travis's cellphone, but it kept going straight to voice mail. I made my way to the end of the parking lot, right on the edge of the road. I looked up at the La Quinta sign and in each direction of the road. I looked with an overemphasizing glare, as a child does before crossing the street, as our parents have taught us hundreds of times. I had no clue where I was or which direction to go. I thought I knew one thing: This road was a loop, and either direction would get me to the border. If I was right, the road would eventually lead back to the road that went to the border crossing, but what I did not know was that by taking a right, it is twenty-three miles to the border and taking a left would have been seven miles. To say that I was lost was an understatement. I was freaking clueless!

I want to paint a picture of my demeanor and appearance. My style in clothing was as confusing as my overall direction in life. Of course, I was wearing what I had on from the night before when the adventure all started. I wore big jeans that were comparable to a Goth-type style with Dr. Martens boots with the big soles. I was wearing a Korn band T-shirt with not one but two choker necklaces, one of which had small spikes. I was dragging a small suitcase behind me on wheels. I was not aware of my smell because I was so engulfed in it that my sense of smell was already hammered into submission, with a vicious case of cotton mouth to accompany it. I had not bushed my teeth. My breath was unimaginably horrible, although my hair was still intact because of a heavy dose of hair gel from the day before. In those days, I went with a 90 percent shaved head, fading from a size 1 to a 2, leaving just enough on the front of my hairline to gel down. Sometimes this is referred to as a Caesar cut. As I shuffled my feet alongside the surprisingly empty road, I thought to myself about the events that had led here, not necessarily just the last twenty-four hours, but the last several years. I thought about Tabby and her role in my life. I thought about the disappointment and sadness that would come over my parents' face if they were to see me now. How was I going to get out of this? Why was Travis not answering his phone? Would they leave me here in Del Rio if they could not find me? It never once crossed my mind to call Tabby because, at this point, I was still trying to protect her. She had given up so much of her life to partner with me. Here I was going out on my own, lying misleading her and damaging our marriage before it had even started. To me, this was a perfect end to a series of crappy decisions. I thought about God. I even cried out in that moment as most people do when in a pinch or pushed up against a life-and-death situation. No matter where we stand in our relationship with Jesus Christ and God or what we know of the Gospel, all the profanities and denouncing who God is or his existence are thrown out of the window. All the faults and disagreements we have placed on God for the way our lives have turned out or what has occurred around us are no longer an issue. In desperate moments, everyone cries out, "God, help me out of this," or "God, if you do this...," pleading and bargaining. Sometimes, I would grow angry and frustrated, saying to God things like, "If you are real, you would...," or other rants of frustrations like an angry teenager yelling at his father for the discipline that has been inflicted because of bad decisions.

In Acts 9 (HCSB), we learn of Saul, who had taken on the task of rounding up the followers of the "Way" of Jesus Christ (Acts 9:2, HCSB). On this particular trip, Saul was headed for another roundup of followers of Christ. As he approached the city of Damascus, he was stopped in his tracks by "light from Heaven" (Acts 9:3, HCSB). He was struck to the ground from an apparent force or out of pure fear, maybe. As he lay there on the ground, he heard a voice asking why he had taken it upon himself to persecute him, Jesus Christ (Acts 9:4-6, HCSB). Here I was making a similar journey, walking along a road, cursing the very God who had brought me into existence, cursing the life I had entered into. I had never been imprisoned for being a believer in Christ, but I certainly did my share of mocking, laughing, and attempting to set up for failure people who believed in Christ. I think of the story of Saul and the apparent force of light that forced him to the ground, which was needed to get his attention and that he could relate to and respect. In our time, if a light came from the sky and forced us down, we would immediately denounce it as a weird weather pattern and move toward safety. As I walked along this road, I rambled not only to myself in anger and confusion, but also to the seemingly empty highway that was usually full of cars, which was eerie, almost like a post-apocalyptic feel. But in Del Rio at around eight in the morning, it can seem that way with the partygoers from the night before, still sleeping, and the devout Catholics already at early Mass. The road was built with two lanes divided by a huge, grassy median from two more lanes in the other direction. I walked on one side, thinking about how to hitchhike properly but realizing that most people don't pick up hitchhikers, especially in a town along the border where people are kidnapped and taken into Mexico. The stories of my mother's overly protective approach to life had impacted me in such a way that I would have these over-the-top fears and concerns. I was somewhat of a hypochondriac with my health and other events. Maybe I could be described more as a pessimist, believing that life's evils and tragedies will overwhelm me someday. Even with this unhealthy fear overcoming me, the truth of the moment was that I was most likely the one who other people feared.

I saw a car speed by in the other direction and then heard it slowing down. I turned around and saw the car come in the direction I was walking. The car slowed as it approached me. It was a four-door sedan creeping up beside me. My heart pumped a bit out of this unhealthy fear as my mom's voice was echoing in my head about murderers, thieves, and rapists, but that was always when referring to picking up hitchhikers. I wasn't sure how this worked when I was the hitchhiker! It was a very confusing moment. Those fears were immediately broken when I saw the face of a twenty-something redhead dressed in her Sunday's best. I guess my years of stereotyping people had allowed people around me to dictate what a murdering person picking up hitchhikers would look like. In my mental database of images of killers, I found no redhead dressed in Sunday's best, but I was so desperate that I would have jumped in the vehicle with almost anyone. She was on her cellphone as she cautiously rolled down the passenger window just enough for sound to carry through, about two inches. She asked, "Where you headed?" I briefly summarized how I was trying to get back to the border to connect back with my friends. I often think about how erratic and confusing the story must had been. After my spiel, she said, "Okay, hang on." She rolled up the window and continued to talk on her cellphone. I waited awkwardly next to the window, debating on my mind what was going on. Who was she talking to? Was there a person on the other side of the phone who was a murdering rapist and I was the target? Those seconds seemed like an eternity, and my mind was racing with what-ifs and scenarios. She rolled down the window and said that she was headed to a Bible study and that she had to go there first to let the band in. From there, someone would take me back across the border to Acuña. She popped the trunk of her car, got out, and asked me to put my lonely piece of luggage in the trunk. I did as she wished, and we both got into the vehicle. There weren't a lot of words exchanged as I sat there fiddling with my cellphone. She drove with her phone still connected to the mystery person.

I wondered and nervously tapped my feet on the floorboard as a child would in anticipation to see Disney World or some other amusement park, although I was a bit fearful and very nervous about the whole situation. I was still redialing Travis's cellphone number every few minutes in hope that he would pick up and end this debacle, but he never did. The location of this Bible study was literally down the road from the La Quinta, maybe a couple of miles at the most. When we turned into this place, the parking lot was gravel and the building did not look like a place where a Bible study or any religious function would be held. It look more like an old auto parts store or some sort of commercial building. It wasn't small, but it wasn't huge either. It was called Club 180. I didn't then get the name of this soul who took a chance on picking up a hitchhiker, but I would learn later that it was Melodee. As Melodee pulled up to the front door of this building, a slender-looking man stood in the doorway waiting as if on a late delivery. I put two and two together pretty quickly and realized that this was the person on the other end of that cellphone. As Melodee drove into the parking lot and up to the front door, this man walked out to the passenger door. I didn't have time to open the door before he reached out to open it. Melodee had exited the car and went into the building. This man reached out his hand to introduce himself, and I sat in the passenger seat of the car, still rambling about my whereabouts. He braced himself between the open door and the frame of the car, almost in an interrogating stance, the type you would see a father present when protecting his daughter. He talked to me directly, attempting to make eye contact. I stared straight ahead, trying to figure out a way out of this mess that seemed to get weirder by the moment.

The grace of God works upon all people even at their worst, even when wholly engaged in the most desperate and sinful of pursuits. The apostle Paul was no different. He was enlightened not in a church or by a preacher or some religious figure. He didn't read some impactful propaganda that changed his way of thinking. He was simply on a journey alone. He was on his way to Damascus with a wicked decree against the Christians there. Also, it is documented in Acts chapter 8 that Saul had overseen the killing of Stephen; therefore, hatred was fresh on his mind. I point this out because there is a growing misconception that God must be met in a certain place, with certain people, and with certain circumstances. Conversion, realization, and/or enlightenment aren't restricted to the church, a building. They are tied to what Paul describes in 1 Corinthians 12 (HCSB). The church is a place of encouragement, teaching, and building one another up in the knowledge and grace of God. In Job 33:15-17 (HCSB), it is written that when we are deep asleep, visions are possible, that God opens our eyes and impresses warnings that could help us turn away from bad plans or reckless decisions. Overall, God speaks all the time. When we are alone, desperate, fearful, and vulnerable, our thoughts seem to be free and not tied up in distraction of everyday events and drama. This freedom of thought provides opportunities of communing with our own hearts; this is where the Spirit of God can to set upon us. There is massive debate among church leaders, church debaters, and nonbelievers what Saul (Paul) actually saw, what he experienced, and what happened overall. Even with the speculation, one truth is abundantly clear—when Saul started his journey to Damascus, he was living evil and selfishly. When he arrived in Damascus, he was now Paul with a newfound view on life. He had an encounter with God, just he and God. No priest, no prayer group, no body, but he, God, and the Holy Spirit. Paul was even confused and blown away about what had happened. When I was picked up off the side of the road by Melodee and taken directly to a Bible study in Del Rio after my drunken, sinfully selfish, self-indulgent night, to be put in front of this man who seemingly was awaiting me, I can relate to what Paul was feeling at the moment he was knocked off his horse, attempting to make sense of what was happening. Just like Paul, my trip to Del Rio was going to rock me and change the course of my life in the matter of a few hours.

13

Allow me to be a bit brash—not offensive, but just to relate my personal observation while working with teenagers, young adults, and men struggling through addictions, not to mention my own personal journey. I can pretty much size up a person's stance and knowledge of God, Jesus Christ, within a few hours of conversation. Not by some mystical power or witchcraft, but by the discernment that has come through similar battles of faith and distinguishing truth from lies I have battled through. Sometimes I can determined this by simply sitting back and watching a person's interactions within a social gathering. Not in a judgmental, biblical Pharisee's way but in more of a cause-and-effect way. Most if not all the teenagers and men I have worked with have learned to fear death and fear a loving and gracious father we call God. All have learned to think of God as the judge, overseer, and the one who disciplines through life events and punishes through our wrongdoings. Most if not all the teenagers and men who have crossed my path have been badly beaten and bruised by legalistic religion that caused them to mistrust God, resulting in mistrusting others and mistrusting themselves. This cause and effect determines what a person truly believes about the Father of our Lord and Savior Jesus Christ—the belief that he is gracious and that he really cares about our own insignificant lives. Does a person believe that God is Love, that God is the unfailing presence and support to be our ultimate companion in life? When the apostle John writes in 1 John 4:18 (HCSB), "There is no fear in love; instead, perfect love drives out fear, because fear involves punishment. So the one who fears has not reached perfection in love." What does that statement stir up in you? Confusion, disbelief, anger, relief, or nothing. Our response to what life throws at us will reflect what a person understands about God's love, t demonstrating the cause and effect. When I hit the scene in Del Rio, if you had read 1 John 4:18 to me, I would have felt angry and frustrated and, most of all, afraid.

Sadly, the circle of people I truly could have trusted as spiritual guides or who were totally transparent was small, people not tarnished with religious rhetoric in the hopes of winning people for a certain religious alliance. I had been extremely damaged by religion and people who are inconsistent either in that religion or some other belief system. I had been saturated by people whom the letter to Laodicea in Revelation 3 speaks of: "I know your works, that you are neither cold nor hot. I wish that you were cold or hot. So, because you are lukewarm, and neither hot nor cold I am going to vomit you out of my mouth" (Rev. 3:15–16, HCSB). There was no consistency in faith, in believing that God was the answer, believing the truths of the Bible. Therefore, my only consistency was inconsistency. This is the major problem that people experience today through their faith walk, vastly inconsistent and the round-and-round crazy cycle of confusion about God and our role in life, which result in a relentless pursuit of whatever is in our view. Not in the unknown or unseen, which therefore creates fear, anxiety, and panic that will result in destructive actions in trying to obtain happiness or find the meaning of life. This destructiveness can act out in many ways, not just the obvious rebellions that occur through drugs, drinking, lewdness, and partying, but also in depression, obsessions, or a consistent need for approval by seeking things that are acceptable within the cultural norm. Possibly, career advancement at the cost of a marriage and family structure, dependence on prescription drugs, or materialism consumes our time and resources and distracts us from God's convictions and disciplines to fulfill his purposes for our lives. Essentially covering up the honesty of our situations with our own constructed image of ourselves, which can be rather impressive but not true. A certain honesty must be realized. True honesty is something few ever search out or receive as constructive, the truthfulness to admit our attachments and addictions that reveal what is controlling our attention. Those lies and distortions dominate our consciousness and function as our false god. This is a powerful tool of the enemy. Saul was called out in Acts 9:4 (HCSB) to realize that he was himself a sinner against Christ. Saul was made to realize and see the evil in himself, which he never saw before. Before any conversion or road to recovery, a person must have a humbling conviction of sin, it is the first step to true change or conversion.

As I sat in Melodee's car with the passenger door open, with this man starting to question me about my whereabouts, what had happened, and why I was trying to get back to the border, I sat there stunned. He introduced himself as Cliff. I was hitting redial on my cellphone constantly in an attempt to locate Travis and trying to make sense of what was happening. Where was I, and why was this happening? I am sure similar thoughts ran through the apostle Paul's mind as he encountered God on his journey to Damascus. Cliff continued to talk to me. His attempt to gather information turned into an attempt to get me in the building. As he invited me, I shot him down each time, but then he mentioned that their projector inside was not working, and he asked me if I had any experience with working with computers. Dang! Yes, I did. I told him that I did have some experience, and my instilled helpfulness traits kicked in, which had been modeled by my parents while I was growing up. I got out of the car, not realizing what I was about to walk into. As he walked me to the door, I entered and heard the sounds of instruments playing, not in song, but more of a warm-up, testing sound. The projector was in the center of the room on a small table. I tried several things. I looked at the connected laptop but couldn't get anything to work. This may have been due to the incredible nervousness I was feeling or the overwhelming hangover I had, or a combination of both. I explained to Cliff that I was unable to get the projector working. He invited me to have some donuts and juice or coffee. I explained to him that I really needed to get back to the border, back to Acuña, and to be reunited with Travis, but he insisted that I stay until the service was over. Melodee was on the stage, warming up with the band, and Cliff said that someone would take me as soon as it was over. I would like to say that I stayed because I wanted to, but sometimes situations have to be forced. My bag was locked in the trunk of Melodee's car. She was singing on stage. I was screwed. I was totally out of my element. What made it worse was that I wasn't sure what I was. As people showed up and started to find their seats, I sat in the back, attempting to blend in to the decor to not be noticed; however, that was not possible. As I previously described my attire, my outer appearance, along with my demeanor, was not the most inviting, but, lo and behold, it seemed that each person who entered the building would come and introduce himself or herself, which is particularly annoying when you want to be unnoticed.

I remember one particular guy introducing himself. He was about my age and engaged. He asked a few questions, and I seemed to vomit my story out to him in a most truthful way, telling how I had lied to Tabby about this whole weekend and some of the events that had led up to this moment. I remember his saying, "Wow, she is going to be upset." Yeah, that was an understatement. I remember saying that I was preparing myself for her to leave me. Each person who came into this small building introduced himself or herself and welcomed me. As the place filled up and the music started, it was nothing special, just a group of individuals singing some church songs. It was very uncomfortable for me because I had never been exposed to a church where people raised hands, clapped, or looked excited about church. I had been warned about these types of churches. They weren't a religion, and you have to be careful with these type of churches. They were crooks or cults trying to convert you. The whole time I was at this service, I thought I was in a church, or my definition of a church at the time. There was music and what I would refer to as a sermon that Cliff presented. The subject for that day was what hell is like. It was part of a series. Yes, a whole series on hell. When Cliff started the opening monologue, he quickly recapped the series, and then said, "Today, we are going to talk about what hell is like." I really thought that I was maybe in a cult.

When Cliff started talking, it was as if he was speaking directly into my soul, like he had torn my chest open, revealing the truth in my heart. Like an extract was made of the thoughts and fears I had deeply hidden in my psyche, the late-night nightmares and fears of being dragged to hell. The fear of the great unknown of death and fear that, if there was a God, then I was going to hell. Cliff covered the attributes of hell. The weeping and gnashing of teeth described in Matthew 8:12 (NIV) and Luke 13:28 (NIV). He referenced a song by Billy Joel called "Only the Good Die Young," and its lyric "And they say there's a Heaven for those who will wait. Some say it's better, but I say it ain't! I'd rather laugh with the sinners than cry with the saints. The sinners are much more fun." I was familiar with this song from years past, when the oldies station would blare from my parents' radio. Cliff also referenced the smell of hell, described in the in the book of Revelation as an unbearable, sulfurous stench. Cliff equated the smell with one he had experienced, of pig's guts being discarded at a dump, symbolizing the Dung Gate that is mentioned in the book of Nehemiah. Here's a little quick history: Ancient Israel had no sewer system, no means of moving the actual dung from the city. Human or animal wastes or whatever was unwanted went to the Dung Gate. You can imagine the smell and multiply that by a million, and we might be close to the smell of hell as described in the Bible. Overall, Cliff explained hell in a way I had never heard before, but that was not what captivated me. It was the way he delivered the message with confidence and conviction. When he took a turn in the message and started to pose questions to the crowd that had gathered, it started to stir something in me. He made statements about living in sin, recognizing sin, and pursuing God, Jesus Christ as being the way, the truth, and the light (John 14:6, NIV). The room seemingly became empty except for Cliff on the small, lighted stage. I was sitting in the back in a foldout metal chair with my arms crossed and body slouched in such a way that sends a message that I disagreed with and disrespected Cliff's message. At that moment, listening to the very bold, invasive questions and what I considered accusations, my outer appearance held true to my rough, jagged presence. But inside, in my mind and spirit, my world felt like it was becoming unraveled. This stranger, this message of conviction, truth, and the way to restoration was challenging me, stirring up a rage and anger that I had never felt before. The rage and anger wasn't directed at Cliff or his message but at all the so-called Christians who held these truths away from me. On the other hand, I had probably been shown truths of sin and the Gospel before but had been so distracted by my busy, self-destructive lifestyle that I couldn't hear. Well, my attention was solely on this message and on Cliff. A moment of utter displacement had led me to a total reliance on strangers, but were these really strangers?

I had claimed in the past to be an atheist, but I never stopped believing in God. I just stopped trusting God. Why? Up to this moment, this encounter initiated by Melodee's leap of faith to pick up a wayward stranger and Cliff's message of truth, I had been impacted by surface-level Christianity. No substance, nothing past the empty words that fell from people's tongues in an effort to pump themselves up with some sort of false sense of religious protection or superiority. My experience with religion left me empty, and the followers of those religions seemed empty as the words they recited seemed powerless. That may sound offensive, but you have to see it from the standpoint of someone who has only a surface-level understanding who God is, what the Bible is, and how the Holy Spirit plays a part in this journey. Remember, Jesus to me was nothing more than a painting that my parents hung on the wall and our mascot for Christmas and Easter. Well, alongside Santa and the Easter Bunny. Hearing a message of truth, expectations of God, experiencing God, confessing and making a decision to follow God were foreign concepts. I was baptized as a Catholic, so in my mind, in the way that I understood, I was baptized in the "super" Roman Catholic Church. I am going to heaven regardless, I thought. Catholics didn't carry Bibles around and definitely not to church. There was no need to because the congregation depended on the priest and layreaders to read the Bible. This is true of most religions; no one carries Bibles and is certainly not challenged to discover God or challenge the truth in an effort to know God. This group that attended Club 180 to listen to different people share their experiences, interpretations, and truths of the Bible was foreign to me. Everyone who walked into this building that morning carried their Bibles, and it really blew my mind that this was a kind of preservice, because they would then disband and go to their respective churches. I had never seen anything like this and certainly would not have experienced it if not for this most peculiar situation. In a situation where I had no choice but to experience this, to be at the total mercy of strangers and this odd setting. As Cliff closed his message and the band began to play, they sang a closing song. I stood to my feet and shook hands with people, and it seemed that everyone in the place wanted to personally tell me goodbye. Cliff came over and asked if I was ready. I certainly was.

I went over to Melodee's car, and she allowed me to get my bag out of the trunk. I thanked her for the ride and made my way over to Cliff's truck. I threw my bag in the back of the pickup and jumped into the passenger seat. Cliff started some surface-level questions about how long I had been engaged, where I was from, and what I did for a living until I finally came out and asked him, "What are you, a preacher or something?" The question was a bit rude and brash, but my feelings were all over the place at this moment and, damn it, I wanted answers. He explained the dynamic of this group that meets before church services to go deeper with God and to know him better and pray. He explained that he wasn't a preacher, that he was actually a pilot who loved Jesus. This day was getting weirder by the moment. Not only was I lost without a ride home, but I was also in a car with a Jesus freak. I started to remember the warnings that I was given about crazy people who took faith and religion too far. Living in Waco, I had heard lots of David Koresh and Branch Davidians stories, which were now going through my mind. Koresh claimed to be the second coming and encompassed all that was defined as a cult leader. Ultimately, Koresh and the Branch Davidians burned to death in their compound outside of Waco. I am glad to announce that neither Cliff nor the people who attended Club 180 were any crazed cult. They really did love God, trusted God, and desired more. Cliff said a lot of things during that twenty- to thirty-minute drive to the border, but the most impactful was his explanation of the Gospel. Also explaining that God gives us chances and opportunities to decide to follow him. I had to agree with Cliff that when I had traveled to Del Rio the previous Friday, I did not expect to be at church the following Sunday morning, that talking about Jesus was not in my plans. Cliff explained the Gospel to me in a real way. A transparence about him opened up my mind to think that I may have just been given bad information, or corrupted data, if you will. I was flooded with thoughts of what if I had been wrong this whole time, and also the feeling that I had finally been shown a desire hidden deep in my heart. A higher purpose that Tabby had such an unwavering love and trust in. Cliff dissected my life. This experience, in a way, intrigued me. I opened up to him in a way that, when the words fell out of my mouth, I was surprised and shocked by them. This was the first moment in my life I had thought that God was taking an interest in me in my twisted, corrupted life. The whole experience was overwhelming. I was shocked with an emotion that was past tears or any other physical representation. I felt a level of confusion and disbelief that I had never felt. It was the fear or anger that I had felt before when I would have my bouts with nightmares and evil presences. It was a feeling that I needed more.

When we got to the line of cars to cross the border to go back into Mexico in an attempt to find Travis, I spotted Travis's truck in the other line coming back crossing back into Texas. I told Cliff, "Hey, there is Travis, the guys I rode here with. Hang on, I will be right back." I got out of the vehicle and ran over to Travis's truck. Before he could get a sentence out, I told him to meet us over in the parking area. Travis asked, "Why? Just get in the truck now." I told him that I was having a conversation. As his frustrated facial expression turned into a blank stare, along with Brett's profanity-filled remark to get into the truck, I ran back over to Cliff's pickup, and the conversation continued. As we proceeded through the line to

Mexico then back to the other side of the border, crossing to go back into Texas, Cliff asked if my hungover friends and I were to get into a car accident and die, would I be positive of the outcome? I had heard this question several times before, but here was a regular guy, not a pastor, asking it. It was the first time I answered the question truthfully. I said, "No, and probably hell." Cliff then did something that had never happened to me before. He prayed. Yes, prayed out loud right there in the truck. He didn't say, "I am going to put you on my prayer list," or "I will be praying for you." He just said, "I am going to pray," and he did it. It was the first time in years I had closed my eyes and acknowledged a prayer. I didn't feel physically different, but I felt more enlightened by the truth. Travis was parked at the parking area, waiting for Cliff and me. We pulled up beside Travis, and I jumped out, grabbed my bag from the back of Cliff's truck, and threw it in Travis's. Cliff got out and introduced himself to Travis and Brett. Travis and Brett cracked some jokes at our expense, but then Cliff did something that blew me away again. He prayed! He simply said, "Let me pray for your trip home." Cliff gave me a handshake accompanied with a bro hug, and I jumped in the back seat of Travis's truck. When Cliff got back into his truck, before Travis put the truck into gear, Travis turned around and asked, "Where the —— were you?" As I looked out the side window, I responded, "I think I was in church!" As Brett laughed and Travis gave me a look of disbelief, I started to feel the weight of what had just occurred.

Back to Saul in Acts 9:7 (HCSB) (before he was known as the apostle Paul): "The men who were traveling with him stood speechless, hearing the voice but seeing no one." Later, in

Acts 22:9 (HCSB) Paul explains, "Now those who were with me saw the light, but did not hear the voice of the One who was speaking to me." The men saw the "light" but didn't understand and were speechless, but in Acts 9 (HCSB), these men were needed. They were used by God to deliver Saul to Damascus. We never learn the story of these guys who were accompanying Saul on this journey, but we can safely assume by their association with him that they were most likely not too kind to Christians either. Nonetheless, they were used by God. I have grown to believe as I read through the Bible and take the Bible as what it was intended for, a document of historical events, that the overall encounters with God are the same. There is a stepping away into a sinful, selfish lifestyle filled with greed, lust, and pride followed by difficulty filled with death and pain, followed by an encounter with God. It's why the Bible is such an impactful piece of who we are. It is why it is called the living word. Paul, who wrote much of the New Testament, says in Hebrews 4:12 (HCSB) that "For the word of God is living and active and sharper than any two-edged sword, and piercing as far as the division of soul and spirit, of both joints and marrow, and able to judge the thoughts and intentions of the heart." Travis and Brett were like the men mentioned in Acts 9:7 who were accompanying Saul. God was using Travis as a vessel for the truth without Travis's even realizing it. When Travis asked me to go to Del Rio-Ciudad Acuña, this was not some wild, spontaneous plan that he had come up with. He was driven by discernment and the Holy Spirit to want to go to Ciudad Acuña and to ask me to come along. Some might still believe that God works in people sitting in pews and church buildings only and not in those whom society has turned a blind eye to or written off as heathens, but the truth is that God works in all people, all situations. Our culture has lost touch with the reality of what we are in an attempt to become religious. We forget that Saul was a murderous, evil-driven, prideful, angry man whom God used. God used the men who were along for the ride when they walked with Saul to Damascus. God used David, who was a murderer; Noah, who was a drunk; Jacob, who was a cheater; and Peter, who outright denied Christ to his face! As Joseph comes to the end of his horrible journey in in Genesis 50:20 (ESV), he is enlightened with the truth that God was with him through it all for his good. As Joseph's brothers were trying to make sense of everything that had occurred, Joseph tells them, "As for you, you meant evil against me, but God meant it for good, to bring it about that many people should be kept alive, as they are today."

When I sat in the back seat of Travis's truck headed back to Waco in a somewhat shocked, somber mentality, disbelief was already attempting to set in. What I kept coming back to was that Travis and Brett had witnessed this event. They heard Cliff tell them I had been with him and even heard Cliff pray over us. I like to think that I have an insight on that moment when God came upon Saul as he went to Damascus and the men with him stood there with a priceless look on their faces, not understanding what was happening. I still grin when I think about the look on Travis's and Brett's faces when Cliff started to pray over them and, especially, when I told them I was in church that morning. As I sat there in the truck, I reeled over the events, as my mind was in overhaul. I was trying to process in my mind what had just happened, what was truth and lie, and what was real and what was fake. I started to wonder if it really did happen. Also, how was I going to explain this to Tabby? She was under the impression that I was camping. Now I was going to come back and tell her that, "Hey, babe, I wasn't actually camping. I went to Acuña to party, got tore up from the floor up, and ended up with a group of strangers in a La Quinta. Oh, and I also did coke this weekend. You know, the one thing you asked me not to do. But hey, it's okay, because I went to church!" Yeah, this was going to go over really well. The men accompanying Saul had to physically lead him to Damascus because he could not see. Here I was in a similar situation. Travis and Brett leading me back to Waco because I was surely in no shape to drive and some blindness was occurring in my mind. I couldn't see past the events of the last four hours.

When we hit the line for McLennan County, where Waco is located, a bit of anxiety rushed over me because I knew this was going to be a crazy night filled with tears, anger, and disappointments. I was hopeful, though. I had this sense of discernment, if you will, to just be brutally honest and truthful. That might come easy to most, but this was not my strong suit. I wasn't an outright liar, but I would hold back pieces of the story to prevent people's feelings from getting hurt. I learned this technique early in my life. Our culture is full of half-truths and white lies. Up-front honesty hurts and can slap us in the face, but sideways truth cushions that blow for all parties. This was not right, but growing up, we were always careful to pick and choose what to tell so that the blowback wasn't fierce or painful. I am not sure where this all started, maybe from my parents' early days of their marriage or something else deeper. Either way, this was my approach to the situation. Again, it wasn't right, and I highly recommend the whole truth and nothing else, but sadly, I didn't share the whole story up front. What I found was a common trait in so many of the situations that I put Tabby through. This particular moment was when I would start something new, telling the whole truth or what I could at least recall after a series of intoxicated events that resulted in waking up on a hotel floor sandwiched between complete strangers. I felt deep in my mind that I was supposed to just be open and honest. Let the results be the results. Part of me was like, *Hey, she is a Christian, so this will be okay*; then the reality of what I was going to tell her would overtake my mind. *She is going to freak. Well, nice knowing her. Guess it is better for her to move on with her life.* Either way, I knew what I was about to unload on her was going to hurt.

It usually feels like forever to get to Waco when you hit the county line just after the small community of Marlin, but on this particular trip, it was incredibly fast, and the usually tight-knit Sunday traffic along Texas Highway 6 between Bryan–College Station and Waco was unusually nonexistent, or, at least, it seemed that way. Travis pulled up to the apartments where we stayed, and I jumped out of the truck and grabbed my bag from the bed of the pickup. As I stood there, I told Travis and Brett goodbye. I then took a deep breath and walked down the sidewalk to the door leading to our apartment. I opened the door to the foyer of the building and took a left while staring at our apartment door. I hesitated, then knocked. Tabby answered the door with a look of mixed emotions, but she was already primed with frustration and anger about my being out of town for the entire weekend, seldom calling her and leaving early Friday and getting back late on Sunday. Let's just say the foundation was not built for a joyful reunion. As we hugged and slightly pecked each other on the cheek, I laid my bags on the ground and went right into it. I asked her to sit down because I had something to tell her. I started with, "First, I didn't go camping. We went to Del Rio and partied in Acuña." Before she could get out a word, I quickly went to the positive part of the story, explaining to her that I had gone to a church service this morning and that I met a man who shared the Gospel with me and prayed for me and our marriage. As her eyes and facial expression remained unchanged, I was surprised that she didn't rejoice right then, but she knew my half-truth stories and explanations of events, so she was waiting for the other half of the story. I could tell she didn't believe me. I remembered that Cliff had given me his card and wrote his name and cellphone on the back. I said, "See, his name is Cliff Wilson. I have his card!" Thinking that I had immediately eradicated any doubt, she responded with, "Really?" I said, "Yes, really; there is his card." She responded with, "You expected me to believe that you met a man named Cliff Wilson? The same name you used to prank call me at work?" Okay, let me back up a moment. Tabby worked at an insurance firm, and I would occasionally prank call her, attempting to throw her or her co-workers off. The name I used numerous times was Cliff Wilson. Yes, the name that I had made up in my comical acts in an attempt to get a laugh had just been thrown back in my face by God, putting an actual man in my life with that same exact name to share the Gospel.

We went back and forth for several minutes as I explained the whole trip, what we did, and what I couldn't really remember, and that I had done drugs over the weekend as well. The most glaring and overwhelming thing that threw her over the edge was that I stayed true to the fact that I met a man named Cliff Wilson and that I went to church. After the argument had escalated to a point where neither of us was getting anywhere, Tabby took her engagement ring off her finger and slammed it down, grabbing her purse and storming out. I proceeded to the shower where I let the water pour over my body in an attempt to wash myself inside and out. Trying to make sense of everything, I started to question whether I had interacted with a ghost or a figment of my imagination. I mean, the same name that I came up with for prank calls was being used on me now. With my history of playing with cultish activities of Ouija boards and tarot cards, did I somehow create some sort of figment of my imagination? But Travis and Brett were there as well. So this would mean it was a mass hallucination. I had hallucinated before while experimenting with some drugs, but was this a flashback? I stayed in the shower, going over every aspect of the last several hours but came up with the same conclusion. This really happened. I had accepted the fact that Tabby may not walk back in the door and that I may have destroyed my engagement, but I was strangely okay. I was sad and disappointed in myself, but I was okay with whatever happened. What I didn't know was that, as I was showering and going through this event over and over, Tabby had left and taken the card that I laid on the table with Cliff's contact information on it. She took a bold step out of desperation and in an attempt to believe what she had prayed for since she learned of my issues with God and faith.

Tabby called the number written on the card. "You don't know me, but my fiancé is Gerald, and he just told me that he met you. Are you real?" Cliff responded, "I am real," and went into the story to reinforce what I had told her. Cliff even prayed with her. When I got out of the shower, I went into the bedroom to dress. I was surprised to hear the door open. Tabby came back home, and we discussed the events a little more in detail. Of course, she wasn't happy that I lied and that I had done all the horrible things throughout the weekend, but she was happy to hear that God had intervened in a big way. She was excited and called her mom and dad to tell them what happened, that that I met a guy who shared the Gospel. I remember actually getting on the phone to tell part of the story. Bruce and Kathryn were ecstatic. They were living in Bay City, Texas, at the time and took it upon themselves to contact Cliff and arrange some time to meet. For several days, I relived this event and tried to make sense of it, but not really changing my habits or actions. Cliff and I followed up a few times after that encounter but eventually stopped connecting. After a couple of weeks, I was back in the bars and visiting strip clubs on certain drink special nights. Tabby and I were still proceeding with our marriage, and as far as our relationship went, we had more good times than bad. With my job at the banking center becoming more and more demanding, my responsibility traits kicked in where I would manage my nights out and drinking so that I could perform well at work. I stopped doing any type of drug that I categorized as a hard drug. I smoked weed off and on and drank consistently at social events or nights out at clubs. I had started doing prescription drugs, using uppers and downers to help with the lifestyle of staying up late, waking up early, and paying attention at work. The Del Rio experience was quickly becoming a distant memory, almost like it didn't happen or was a dream.

The sense of failure and anger with myself was building up to an unhealthy level. Each night I went out to drink or visit a strip club and tell my wife otherwise about where I was, I was reminded briefly of Del Rio and Cliff's message. I had started to feel like a complete failure in the eyes of God. I was expecting some magical change by which God would just make all my situations, actions, and evil desires go away, but that wasn't the case. Before Del Rio, I was a mess. I was depressed, angry, and frustrated with life. I was fearful of the future and fearful of death. After Del Rio, I was overwhelmed with the experience of meeting Cliff and wished it never had happened because I couldn't forget it. I couldn't deny that something really mysterious happened to me. That all my secret prayers filled with vulgar and obscene rants to a God had actually been heard. Whether I believed it, didn't care nor wanted to care that God was actually a listen. I had a desire to find people who were truly living a life that God desired for his people. We are exposed to things that we never forget, and a certain amount of responsibility goes with that exposure, whether for evil, truth, or good. The letter of 2 Peter warns against false prophets and teachers among us, that a large responsibility goes along with the revelation of truth. Peter says in 2 Peter 2:21 (HCSB), "For it would have been better for them not to have known the way of righteousness than, after knowing it, to turn back from the holy command delivered to them." When I was rocked with this truth about God, I was changed forever. Saul in Acts 9 knew the stories of the disciples and about Jesus

Christ. We don't know why he hated Christians so terribly or what fueled his rage. Maybe it was some encounter with a Christian, maybe it was a misrepresentation of God. Maybe, just maybe, Saul was surrounded by hypocritical testimonies of those who claimed to be Christians, yet their words and prayers were nothing more than just that. Maybe Saul yearned for something more in life and had those rage fits of prayers of desperation just to feel something.

Even before I started this journey, before I went to Del Rio, before I met Tabby or anything, I had heard the man who was knocked down and had an encounter with God. This is a story I remember because we all want that intimate encounter, that in-your-face-for-sure experience that rocks the foundation of all we believe in. That's what Del Rio was for me. It was my road to Damascus. Christ is no longer visibly moving among us. It's the Holy Spirit who resides in brothers and sisters among us. Therefore, encounters with the living God come through people who are obedient and willing to serve God. Cliff is not God and is nowhere near perfect; he is flawed like the rest of us, with doubts, fears, and failures, but he also knows God on an intimate level. God meets you where you need to be met, where it will be the most impactful. Timing is everything. I went to Del Rio on this mysterious journey in February 2003, three months before I was going to be married. Sure, people were praying on my behalf before this trip occurred, and Tabby was hoping that the good would soon outweigh the evil in me, but it had to be on God's timing. My life experiences, my background, my family structure, my developing anger and disgust with religion and church, and my experiences with the occult or demonic dreams all came together in several hours on a Sunday morning in February. The fear of death that gripped me as a preteen throughout my early twenties and the religious split-tongue approach to life and acceptance of low expectations were all blown out of the water when I stepped out of that La Quinta in Del Rio to find myself completely lost and not knowing which direction to go. God uses encounters, utilizing brothers and sisters as enlisted soldiers in his army for souls. Melodee followed her discernment. For her to take a chance and pick up a hitchhiker, for Cliff to have developed a series of sermons in between raising a family and working as a commercial pilot, and that I would sit in on just the right day, hearing from Cliff the exact content I was having nightmares about—that's the work of the Holy Spirit. Each encounter with a man or woman is a mysterious encounter with Jesus himself.

God blessed me with Tabby. A grace-filled woman with an joyful heart for those hurting, in pain, or just plain sad. Since meeting Tabby, I have desired to be a better man. She was the first woman to really bring that out in me, but I always felt I was missing the mark. I know now that God was making me a better man. He knew the desire of my heart and what I needed: a radical, overwhelming experience to generate real change. I had never gone to church camps or sat through youth events. I had been allowed to quit or move on to something else. The expectation was that I would at least try. If I didn't like it, I could quit, but I really never wanted that. I wanted more and not merely the status quo or to achieve the low expectation placed on me. Overall, I wanted more out of life and more out of God. This encounter in Del Rio with Cliff and Melodee was a personal encounter tailored to me. It wasn't some intellectual experience, but rather, for the first time in my life, I had an awareness of the love of God. It propelled a glimmer of faith and a spark of trust. God knew that it wasn't just books, evidence, or even the Bible that was going to get my attention. God made me. He knew what I was drawn to. I needed to know not just that God existed or that some cosmic intelligence was beyond the stars, but that God was right there with me in my day-to-day life, attempting to get messages through my blindness as I moved around waist-deep in the crap that I had gotten myself into. It was not proof of God's existence I wanted. I wanted much more. I wanted to experience God's presence. I wanted God's expectations placed on my life to give me meaning and drive me in ways that I would never be able to go without the knowing his presence.

In May 2003 Tabby and I got married. I wish I could say that I was this perfect husband and that I showered her with love, affection, and encouragement. While there were times of those, there was also drinking behind her back, popping pills, and a secretive porn addiction that was growing more and more disturbing by each porn website visited. After the Del Rio experience, the message and encounter with Cliff, my life was considerably different. I had become aware of my evil, my sin, and my filth. Instead of attempting to clean up my act, I decided to hide it or, at least, that which was not so acceptable within a church crowd. I wanted Tabby to believe I had changed, that I really was the best husband for her, but in my mind, the comparisons and overwhelming task of trying to flip my life around into a different direction was exhausting. Therefore, I went out sparingly. Travis and I started to limit our visits, and I tried to be a better man at least on the outside. Tabby and I went to church only when we visited her parents. I had adopted the very selfish and prideful notation that I didn't need a church to worship God. This mindset was more inherited from my family's outlook and my limited and recycled comments from other misguided people. I was alone. I had Tabby and hung out here and there, but I had no one to really work with these feelings and work through this disappointment in my actions. The apostle Paul writes this in Romans 7:14–25 (NIV):

> We know that the law is spiritual; but I am unspiritual, sold as a slave to sin. I do not understand what I do. For what I want to do I do not do, but what I hate I do. And if I do what I do not want to do, I agree that the law is good. As it is, it is no longer I myself who do it, but it is sin living in me. For I know that good itself does not dwell in me, that is, in my sinful nature. For I have the desire to do what is good, but I cannot carry it out. For I do not do the good I want to do, but the evil I do not want to do—this I keep on doing. Now if I do what I do not want to do, it is no longer I who do it, but it is sin living in me that does it.

Paul understood sin and the desire to overcome because he was not always a Christian. He was converted later in life, after life experiences. He pinpoints sin that has taken over his actions but in the same breath agrees with the law. The things I did before I went to Del Rio never really hit me as sin. They were more something I did as part of my identity. The things I was a part of didn't become sin till I had an encounter with

God in Del Rio. I wanted to do well, but I would just find myself knee-deep in sin and in my own shame.

Pornography was there from a young age and was accepted socially, culturally, and for the most part by the mass of male peers around me. I was somewhat open with Tabby about my desire and justification for porn to be a part of my routine, but once I came back from Del Rio, I was filled with shame and the need to hide my actions. I drank and did drugs casually, but porn was different. It was easy, accepting, and I always felt wanted, but those rushes of hormones and chemical reactions in my mind and body would quickly be replaced with shame, anger, and guilt. Why was I struggling with this so badly? Why was my life turning into even more loneliness? Paul finishes up in Romans 7:24-25 (HCSB) by saying that he is a wrecked man and asking who is going to save him. He states that through Jesus Christ we are delivered. In Acts 9 (HCSB), Paul, then as Saul, was struck with blindness and sat on the street with no food or water. A local prophet named Ananias was told through a vision to find Saul and pray over him (Acts 9:10-19, HCSB). The problem was that I had not made an actual decision. I had not professed my faith in Jesus Christ and God; therefore, I was getting dry. I was reeling from one experience and hadn't built from it or sought more such experiences; therefore, it was becoming out of touch and distant. I was dying of spiritual thirst. The further that Del Rio experience became, the more I discredited it. In my eyes, I had become what I despised, a hypocrite. Not so much in the eyes of my family, friends, or co-workers, but in the eyes of my wife and, most of all, in the eyes of God. The problem is, or I should say the x-factor is, that God's grace is made sufficient in my weakness, and he wasn't finished turning my weaknesses into opportunities to reveal his grace (2 Corinthians 12:9, HCSB).

14

In May 2003 I married the woman I would spend the rest of my life with after what I believed to be a very real encounter with God in Del Rio just a couple of months before. Many changes occurred as our wedding approached. These changes were not noticeable or even realized by others and sometimes caught even me off guard. They were subtle at first and then became more intense as time passed. A few weeks after coming back from Del Rio, I was overflowed with excitement and clarity mixed with confusion and joy about the future, but I soon felt my same old self after a few days. This happens many times with people who have had a spiritual experience, often referred to as a mountaintop experience. This is a state of extreme well-being and happiness, or comfort that is brought on by the Lord through the power of the Holy Spirit. Modern-day culture or the emerging pop-Christian culture has somewhat corrupted the purity and authenticity of this experience by an emotional response brought on by light shows, music, and intense speakers. These things are not necessarily bad, but when an experience driven by the Holy Spirit is replaced with music and speaking, then the mountaintop experience loses its impact. Not all will agree with that, but it can be so for a man who sees many surface believers in God and his Word being discredited by their actions and false convictions. When the experiences are founded on biblical truths, they are authentic and last throughout the individual's life. Mountaintop experiences can be described as places or states that God allows us to be in for a few hours, days, or months when we are euphoric about the truth or revelation revealed to us. But a person cannot stay there because faith in God will not grow or be sustained if it is not exercised. During these close spiritual encounters, we are charged, rejuvenated, and made aware of truths that pushed us into a place of reliance on God, only to then hike down the mountain through the valley of life, where our alliance is tested.

When Moses came down the mountain after visiting with God in Exodus 32—he had left the people at the foot of the mountain to await his further direction—he found the people singing and dancing not for God but for a golden calf they had crafted to be their god. Moses didn't try to reason, understand, or join in for fear of being considered different, misunderstood, or weird, but rather, he crushed the golden calf. I imagined this moment as like when a parent comes into a room to reward his or her child only to find that the child has done the one thing he or she was told not to. Moses's anger was righteous, and he did not sway or tremble at the sight of the crowds turning from the one true God. He simply set a standard. Later, in Exodus 32:21-29 (HCSB), he did something that causes people today to question the Bible; he basically said, "Who's with God?" Those who weren't for the Lord were put to death. However you read this and whatever you think about it, it doesn't change the events. Moses was setting a clear alliance, stating his intent. The corruption in the camp—those who had provoked the masses to join into crafting a golden calf, sacrificing and worshiping it—had to be eliminated. They had an intense journey ahead of them and needed to eliminate the corruption that would just hinder this journey and not point to God. When I came back from Del Rio and told this amazing story about how God met me in the most unlikely of places, that's all it was at the time—a story. Tabby elected to stay with me after confirming the circumstances and validity of my meeting with Cliff in Del Rio. The problem was that I continued to live the same life, or at least to try to. Just a couple of weeks after this interaction with Cliff and Melodee in Del Rio, I was in a strip club on a Monday night, drinking one-dollar beers and getting ten-dollar lap dances. The problem was that it felt almost forced like I was making myself go. It is hard to explain the feeling that I had. One night at a bar that I frequently went to, I sat there, and the thought really hit me for the first time, *I don't want to do this anymore.*

This feeling sometimes would cause me to dig my figurative heels in the ground by putting more and more rebellious actions into my diet. I attempted to make the feelings and thoughts of shame, guilt, and anger go away by piling on more and more rebellious acts. This played out in many ways, whether with drinking, popping pills, or partying till the morning hours. All the while, I was slowly pushing my relationship with Tabby into a tale of two lives: the man who loved her, adored her, and would die for her, versus the man who was self-indulgent, corrupt, and animalistic, chasing desires of the flesh like a dog after a car. She was hurting. Tabby was tasked with leading our household in all aspects—financially, spiritually, and romantically. Overall, I was only holding it together. I had grown to resent Cliff and the whole experience in Del Rio because it seemed to always be right there to remind me of my failures, actions, and empty promises. God had made a big statement about my decisions and confirmed my fears of hell and the promises of the cross. He had answered prayers I had prayed in some of my darkest and most desperate moments. When I went to strip clubs or bars before the Del Rio experience, I didn't really feel anything but guilt and maybe some shame, but that was mostly resting in my feelings with Tabby because I wanted to be a better man for her. Now I was feeling this not only with Tabby but also with God. Even with all of the drama, my selfishness, and questionable actions that most Christian people would shun, Tabby stayed right there by my side. We moved forward with planning a beautiful wedding with all of our close friends. My groomsmen consisted of Travis, Patrick, and my childhood friends whom I had kept in close contact with. Like most groomsmen and stereotyped wedding parties involving several guys in their mid-twenties, there was that moment before the wedding when one of those groomsmen broke out liquor. Okay, maybe not all wedding parties, but the ones that I had been a part of. While we were dressing in one of the rooms, Patrick busted out a huge bottle of Crown Royal. Someone quickly found some cups, and we poured drinks all around, taking a few shots to loosen us up for the evening. As a cup was handed to me, I looked out of the corner of my eye to see my father standing there with a face of disappointment. This was another moment where time seemed to slow down, allowing me to take in each detail of the moment.

In that moment, as our eyes connected, the years of addiction he had dealt with and its pain, hurt, and sadness poured into my spirit. I saw God as massively disappointed in me. Before I visited Del Rio and experienced God, I saw God more as angry and distant. Now God was just another disappointed being in my life. My dad never said anything about that moment, but I know he remembers it just as vividly as I do. For once, I didn't try to conceal my shameful actions.. No other word can describe the shame I felt at that moment, but I was more concerned about being publicly accepted than honoring my father. This was true with my relationship with God as well. My doubt of God and his presence was replaced with fear that I had lost salvation because of my repeated failures. I felt unworthy and would go in cycles of self-punishment that felt more appropriate to my sinful nature. Self-punishment plays out in numerous ways, usually built out of a place of disgust for what a person sees in the mirror. I didn't like what I saw looking back at me in the mirror; therefore, I would hurt myself either physically or mentally in the seclusion of my sins that were secret but still known to God. In Hebrews 10:26 (ESV), "For if we go on sinning deliberately after receiving the knowledge of the truth, there no longer remains a sacrifice for sins..." Paul is warning those who have been given convincing evidence but were sinning willfully against that truth. Deliberately sinning against God despite an active knowledge of his laws was just like my deliberate act of drinking alcohol in front of my father, who had tried to hedge us from that destructive addiction. It was as if I had spat in the face of my father and of God.

Overall, our wedding was beautiful. I never imagined my wedding being so beautiful and certainly never envisioned that God would place a beautiful woman beside me. There were a few hiccups here and there, but I can't really remember the details — that tells me there wasn't much to them. Directly after the wedding and reception, Tabby and I got prepared to go on our honeymoon, which was a cruise that her grandfather purchased for us. It was a great gift and blessing. We headed out the morning after our wedding with excitement and a little nervousness of being on a boat for seven days. This would be the first time that Tabby and I would spend a week alone. No friends, no family, just the two of us. We headed to Galveston and started our check-in for the cruise line. Some people go on cruises as an excuse to spend massive amounts of money getting wasted. We have been on two cruises during our marriage. On this one, I was the guy intending to get wasted. You know, the "you only live once" mentality. I wasn't on the ship five minutes before I had a drink in my hand. Sadly, it was the first of many. The cruise was an up-and-down event with some good times, fun times, and disappointing times. Overall, it was a good experience. Well, until the sixth day of the cruise. This is when guests get the bill for all their credit purchases. It was said that the sixth night of a seven-day cruise is the loudest with the arguments of couples and families as they receive their bills. When we received our bill, beverage charges exceeded $700. All beverages are free except alcoholic drinks. Tabby didn't drink, and I was embarrassed and ashamed but covered it up, angrily pointing at everyone and everything besides me. When our honeymoon was over and we had to get back to regular, everyday life, the problems from before our wedding were awaiting us.

In the first months of our marriage, there were major ups and some major downs. Tabby always defined those first couple of years of marriage as "When it was good, it was good, and when it was bad, it was really bad." She was right. Some moments stood out as special and on others I was totally off the reservation with my decision making. I was trying to hang on to my childish ways. Paul says it in 1 Corinthians 13:11 (AKJV), "When I was a child, I spoke like a child, I thought like a child, I reasoned like a child.: When I became a man, I put aside childish things." The issue in our marriage was that I was acting as a child, not feeding my marriage and definitely not leading my marriage as a man should. I was holding on to this wacked-out imagination of what a man is supposed to be. As my experience in Del Rio started to become a distant memory, I would recall that time wistfully, wanting God to meet me like that again and reveal something to me. I knew that I wasn't leading my wife or serving this marriage as I should.

My Del Rio story was just a story at this point because I didn't have anyone to help make the connections. Well, let's just say I wasn't paying attention. Janice was working with me at the banking center. As I mentioned in the early chapters, she was an unapologetic follower of Christ, unwavering in her faith. She was a rock, and I was a leaf going wherever the wind blew. Janice become my Ananias, helping me make sense of daily life and the valleys of life that can be lonely and confusing. No matter what I told her or expressed to her, she would rapidly fire back with joy and encouragement and with the love of God. The entire year of 2004 was a year of confusion, education, and revelation. Each day, as I went to work with the problems of either my own complaints or issues with my marriage, she would give smooth insight that seemed to hit me as I walked away. Janice caused me to second-guess my decisions when I would tell her about some drinking binge I had been on or some club that I had gone to. She never judged, never condemned, but she also never condoned or agreed with all that came out of my mouth. She offered or led me to a conviction that was welcoming and freeing in some ways. As Ananias laid hands on Saul to help him see, Janice was allowing my blindness of God's daily interaction to guide me right to the doorstep of his truth. Those days working at the banking center were some of the most intense, not for the work, but for the education and example set in front of me in the form of God's disciple Janice.

Late in 2004 my role in the banking center had become more involved. I was now managing the banking data center, but my success didn't come without Janice's coaching throughout my immature, erratic approach to management. I always say that those few years at the banking data center were hell. I never wanted to be a desk jockey and certainly didn't want to be a slave to a paycheck, but that is exactly what I was becoming. In hindsight, this was God's provision and protection for my life. The level of responsibility I was assigned to was frustrating, but it kept me halfway straight because of the fear of losing my job and, most important, disappointing the handful of people I fully respected in the organization. There was also a bit of pride that I received from my parents. I would explain my job with excitement and joy of just having gotten a good job. I have always respected my parents' opinion and have always battled somewhat with approval. Overall, I just wanted to make them proud. I think that some of that came from the guilt of my lifestyle that they had suspicions about but were more or less unaware of. With any management role in a large organization, there is always some corporate initiative or attempt to get the team of employees to be active in their community by way of donations and volunteerism. At the time, I was nowhere near a volunteer mindset and certainly wasn't donating any money to any organization working to better the community. I was dumping my cash into activities that were contrary to the mission of most nonprofit groups. When I was tasked with getting the Waco branch involved in the community and creating some sort of presence there, I thought to myself that nothing says volunteer like being mandated to do something. As I brainstormed to think of a way to simply satisfy my bosses, I thought of only two organizations: United Way and the Salvation Army. United Way had all the commercials with athletes, and Salvation Army had all the bell ringers in front of businesses.

When I called up the organizations, United Way offered a pledge program in which they would come out and do some presentations and work with human resources to set up a payroll deduction to make donating easy. I worked with United Way and set up some lunches and breakfasts and even was asked to be the local representative for my business at the monthly executive meetings. This was my first experience working with an organization outside of my workplace for no pay. I got to know one of the top women in United Way in Waco, and I was really drawn to her display of compassion and desire. She really helped those in need, those who have been dealt a crappy start to their existence or just lack a support system to recover from a bad season of life. For the first time, I started to look outside the selfishness of my own heart, if only for a few moments. I would experience peace about just being around people who had dedicated their lives to helping others. Over time, after my experience with God in Del Rio, things were definitely different. Nothing overwhelming and nothing anyone could point out—just an internal torment of right and wrong. For the first time in my life, something I had not sought was almost placed in my mind and right in front of me. Seeing people laying their lives down for the good of those in need stirred me. This led me to pursue some sort of Christmas outreach in Waco for my team of employees at work. What started as a mandated effort had turned into something that I took up and ran with. This created excitement and something to look forward to. It was more of a break from myself. When I was more concerned for others, even if only for moments, life seemed more meaningful. Like something was connecting us all as humans, something bigger than the internal battle of my own shame and guilt. It was the feeling that I had while gardening alongside my father as he taught me how to tend plants, prepare soil, water, and harvest. It was a feeling of peace and meaning. Watching in amazement a tiny seed grow into food was similar to watching a person's life blossom into something that produced so much joy. Just like seeds, the ones that don't germinate or don't have the right care will produce little to no fruit. In some cases, that plant will produce distorted, premature fruit because of too much or too little of the essentials like water, sun, and pruning. The plant will grow crooked and the expected size will be affected. In some cases, the roots don't develop fully because the plant is just trying to survive. That same plant can be cared for, giving it more attention and resources, but will always be a little different. Not bad. It can still produce the same delicious fruit. It just has a different appearance and shape. This is what I saw when working with the volunteers, learning about people that lived their lives to serve others. The people they served were like underdeveloped, neglected, and forgotten plants that were just trying to survive. Not worried about producing any type of fruit, just worried about the essentials to just live. Just observing and learning about this whole subculture of people who took time to help other people unapologetically with grace and mercy while maintaining discernment to protect themselves led me to search out the Salvation Army.

I called up the Salvation Army because I had learned that they needed volunteers each year to help with their Toys for Tots program that helps families provide for their children. Along with food, the families in need could get Christmas gifts for their children. The program is super successful each year, and lots of business and organizations participated by donating items to the Salvation Army from late October until the week before Christmas. However, few people gave their time to help process the donations. In Waco, the staff consisted of a few dozen people to organize and prepare age-appropriate toys and clothing for thousands of residents who would flood the tiny Salvation Army building off Interstate 35. Also, this same staff would prepare a meals at Thanksgiving and Christmas that would feed hundreds of families. I really didn't know what to expect when I called up the Salvation Army and asked for some volunteer opportunities. All I knew of the Salvation Army was that they ring the bell at Christmas and that a line of homeless people would be lined up at the downtown Waco shelter. I called the main number, and when I mentioned volunteer opportunities for a team, I was instantly forwarded to a different number. I dialed the number, and a woman picked up the phone, introducing herself as Jessica. She had a slang-type accent and was very direct and to the point. She was not rude but more or less conversed like a New Yorker. When I mentioned that I was looking to bring a group to help out during the Toys for Tots program, she agreed with excitement but asked that I come down first to check out the operation. I worked in downtown Waco, and the Salvation Army was only maybe a mile from my office, so I took a brief moment and shot down there.

When I entered the small double doors at the entrance to the foyer of the building, I looked to the left and saw church service bulletins and a board with all sorts of groups, meetings, and other events on a tack board. Kind of like a college dorm entrance with all the different clubs and awareness groups. I thought to myself, *Is this a church?* Thinking that I might be in the wrong place, I cautiously walked to the hallway to find a lady in her mid-fifties dressed in what looked like a type of military uniform. I asked for Jessica, and she immediately said, "Follow me." She led me down a short hallway that opened up into a large room with tables and chairs stacked along the walls. A set of doors was on the west wall of the room. One set looked like the swinging kitchen doors in a diner, and the others looked like generic office doors. This very serious, stoic woman with her well-pressed military-type uniform led me to an office, saying, "Jessica, someone is here to see you." As I stood outside the door just barely peeking into the office, I saw a large Hispanic woman in her late twenties wearing glasses and sitting behind a desk that looked like a filing cabinet had thrown up and an old outdated computer. I went into her tiny office after I was invited. I shook Jessica's hand, and she wasted no time asking me what I had in mind for volunteers, how many people, and what type of schedule. She was obviously a woman with a lot on her plate and had little time for chitchat. After a brief intro and asking what my expectations were, she wanted to give me a tour of the building and introduce me to some people. I was thinking to myself, *Why?* But she had this manner of inviting you into her world. She took me to every room in the building. The building was very small for the type of operation they were responsible for. She took me to the chapel of the building. I commented that I didn't know that the Salvation Army was a church, and she very subtly said yes, as if everyone knew it. We talked throughout the walkthrough of the facility, and she said, "You're in banking. We need more professionals in business. Would you be interested in helping with the interview process?" The look on my face must have given away that I had no idea what she was talking about. She went into detail how each family served by the Toys for Tots program is required to apply first, and the staff have to review the family's finances to determine whether they qualify. I agreed. Why? I have no clue. Maybe it was the fact that someone wanted me to join their team. Maybe it was a manly pride thing of, "Yes, I can do it!" Or simply perhaps I was intrigued. I was not sure, but I agreed, and before I left, I had a schedule in hand for my team to fill out and for me personally to donate a couple of evenings and Saturdays working at the Salvation Army. This was going to be interesting.

In 1852 William Booth embarked upon a journey that would start a movement that we are still experiencing the ripple effect of today. Booth took the Gospel of Jesus Christ and exited the conventional church concept and stepped away from the pulpit to hit the streets of London with a desire to win the lost multitudes of England. Unlike any well-established church leadership built on rules and regulations, Booth took nothing more than the Bible and a burning passion. Booth and his wife, Catherine, became the founders of the Salvation Army because of their invading approach to the war for souls. This rocked the current church foundation at the time, resulting in his withdrawing from the church, and Booth and his wife traveled throughout England, conducting evangelistic meetings.

Booth didn't come up with some master plan that was new or intend to create a religion. He took what Jesus taught and didn't dissect it, manipulate it, or interpret it. He simply saw a problem with the way the church was seeking the lost—those wandering around aimlessly who would not even step into a church, much less sit with a priest or preacher for help. The Booths took the Great Commission of God, spoken through Jesus Christ, at face value.

> All authority in heaven and on earth has been given to me. Go therefore and make disciples of all nations, baptizing them in the name of the Father and of the Son and of the Holy Spirit, teaching them to observe all that I have commanded you. And behold I am with you always, to the end of the age (Matthew 28:18–20, ESV).

Now I was standing in the building and looking at a handful of people who had bought into this vision set in motion over 150 years ago, this approach to serving people unconditionally and unapologetically. Since leaving Del Rio and experiencing what I believed to be God, my actions had not changed all that much. Sadly, I was still putting my wife through some pretty tough situations as I justified my need for clubbing, strip clubs, and pornography. I was still popping pills when I got my hand on something whether it be Valium, Xanax, codeine, or a bag of candy, which was a mixed bag of whatever. These first few years of marriage were the darkest and most confusing for both of us. Obviously, our experiences were different, but we were both going through some major changes in our lives. Growing tried, weary, and frustrated. For me, I started to ask deep questions of God. My prayer life was evolving right in front of my eyes. I prayed before I went to Del Rio, but it was more as an insurance policy or desperation. Now I was praying because I knew there was something way bigger and deeper than my mind could fathom. I was praying prayers that were more of a plea to understand why so much pain happens, why kids die terrible deaths, why people starve to death each day, why we pray to take desires away that were hurting me and Tabby, or to change me. Have you ever prayed those prayers? If you have, I am sure that you have seen the results of those prayers. If you are in the middle of those prayers, watch out and be ready. If you have not started, well, don't let fear or disbelief stop you. I tell people this: if you pray, pray to God for thirty days—heck, even a week—each morning, during the day and at night while journaling your thoughts and prayer highlights, you will see something happen. I am not promising some bolt of lightning to affect your life or your financial issues to be solved with a check in the mail and certainly not saying that your lustful desires will simply dissipate. But you will become more enlightened, aware of what you are, who you are, and what you need to do. You will become aware of the opportunities that God has provided in the past, but you were so blinded by yourself that they went unnoticed. What I experienced was simply looking in the mirror and saying the things I saw in myself—failure, nasty, liar, cheat, disgusting, etc. Sometimes I would asked God, "If you are so amazing and so awesome, why would you make me this way, to make me desire destruction and to make it feel so good?"

About this time, when I reached out to the Salvation Army out of a corporate mandate to be more involved in volunteerism, Tabby had started massage therapy school on the weekends. The school was held in a hotel conference room at a local hotel in Waco. These were long weekends because she would be at school all day. They were long for me because I was off work on the weekends, and I had grown to really yearn for those moments with Tabby on the weekends. Now I was forced to be alone. Being alone was not good for me because the longer I was alone, the more my sense of failure and disappointment with who I was would weigh heavier and heavier. This would usually lead to a binge of pornography and video games until Tabby got home. This type of drug would prove to be the hardest to extract from my psyche. The feeling of acceptance mixed with the lack of any expectations from the eyes looking back from the computer screen was welcoming and calming. A few hours of surfing porn was followed by a flood of shame and disgust. So when I was only at home, I was just beating myself up for everything I was not and everything I was. The first Saturday I stepped into the Salvation Army with a team of employees from my workplace, we worked hundreds of large garage bags, boxes, and bins of donated toys, clothes, books, food, and anything else people donated at Christmas during these massive pushes for Toys for Tots. It was mind-blowing, but when I was there, I felt needed, purposeful. The job at the banking center as the manager never gave me a sense of confidence or that silent peace about what I was doing. It was more of a "what have you done for me lately" feeling, as most jobs and careers demand. I hated that feeling of being a battery, a source of power just to generate work for a certain sector of commerce, ultimately being a resource until the company decided you were no longer needed. I hated that feeling of conditional value. You have to understand that I watched this play out with my father, who has been in the oil industry for over thirty-five years. When I was about fifteen to sixteen years old, the company he worked for was sold, and he was left without a job. As my mom, sister, I all sat in the bedroom, talking, my dad was in the bathroom for an extended time, praying and gathering his thoughts and next steps. Now, married and with my own children, I can respect and understand the anxiety and fear he felt in that moment. We sat there waiting for what our fearless leader was going to come out and reveal. My mom, being the comforter and the person who believed unwaveringly in God's plan, hugged us and told us everything was going to be all right. Everything has always been all right, and this approach to difficult situations has rung true with my sister and me as we have grown up. No matter what life threw at us, it will be okay. When dad lost his job, I could see the incredible level of stress he was feeling while staring at us, probably thinking of the mortgage and his own self-worth. At that moment, a thought was created in me. It was just a small thought then, but now it has grown into something fierce. From that day on, I looked at work and job as something to not have faith in because it could be ripped away in a matter of seconds. I guess you could say I was somewhat sour at how my dad and my mom immersed themselves into dad's profession, only to be treated like a replaceable part or used battery by the industry. I stepped into the Salvation Army and started to meet people who had given their lives not to a corporate agenda but to a bigger, more overwhelming position that invested in people. There was a need to make money, obviously, but it was not the main goal because God would provide a way. Meeting these people with their unwavering faith in this radical mission to serve people blew me away and drew me in.

I had already started down a road of materialism, searching for what represented success or made me look important. I had piled up a good amount of debt on myself but didn't think of it as a bad thing at the time. I had accumulated this debt only for selfish reasons, and I had nothing to show for it. Children hadn't even hit the picture yet, but I was already becoming a slave to my paycheck. I had fallen into what I considered a trap. Get a job, buy a car, clothes, house, travel, and go out to eat, blah, blah, blah, chasing the American dream of comfort and security but not God's dream. To have all that this country can offer you, freedom to be whom you want and to do what you want—that is the American dream in a nutshell, or at least, the more modern version. I hated what the American dream had become for me: just a debt snowball and pressure to perform to a standard set by my peers and the culture around me, better known as "keeping up with the Joneses." This pressure to perform and to be a certain way drives a man mad. It is impossible to fulfill the desires of the world and what others expect of us and to seek God at the same time. This is the great hypocrisy and worldliness- in choosing whom and what we will serve. Matthew 6:24 (HCSB) goes straight to the point when Jesus states that no man can serve two masters. I was trying to divide myself between God and the world, to have my treasure on earth and in heaven, too, and to please God and *people* at the same time. When I landed in a Bible study at Club 180 in Del Rio, I was awakened to this truth. More awareness had sprung up in me about what I was doing with my life. I started to see things for what they really were and what my role was. I didn't know what to do with this newfound awareness because it made me feel uncomfortable and overwhelmed, as if I was on an island by myself. I had Tabby and her parents who were believers, but no one could relate to what I was going through. I was afraid to disappoint my own parents with the truth of my life and my thinking process. I felt like a freak, almost as if I had two personalities. On one hand was the Gerald who loved his wife, went to work, paid his bills, and tried to be a good son and brother. Another side of Gerald self-medicated with drugs and alcohol, utilized porn and clubs for acceptance, and looked at himself in the mirror with great disgust. Then throw in this torment of truth: I believed God is real but doubted that he cared. And then there was Del Rio.

Del Rio became my point of reference, the crossing point or time when God radically met me in a special way in the most unlikely of circumstances. I could not ignore or discredit it. Just as Cliff said as he drove me back to the border that day in Del Rio, "You have to question whether this is an accident or not that God placed you in my truck today." This incredible truth that God intended that encounter was starting to develop in me, an awareness that maybe my life was not a waste. Maybe we all really have a calling or a special path that God requires of us, but we choose whether to walk it. I wasn't reading the Bible or going to church and certainly wasn't reaching out to people whom I considered Christians to help with these questions. I consider Christians weird, like those late-night, low-budget, screaming Christian TV hosts, or the one-eyed nun on TV who spoke in the middle of the morning from a regional Catholic church. Christians were badly misrepresented in my experience from an early age. Those Christians just wanted money. People who spoke in tongues, talked about spiritual meditation, prayed aloud in public, or talked about God openly were just weirdoes to me. I was told more than once while I was growing up by those closest to me to beware of those weirdoes; that they are just trying to change or convert you. Walls were built up emotionally and mentally. Tabby knew firsthand about my approach to those who would try to share. I would shoot something back at them like, "I am Catholic!" or just tell them what they wanted to hear or respectively decline. Think about it this way: If I were in a burning building, everything around me is burning and being consumed by fire. Yet when someone comes to save me, I tell them, "No, I am good. I work in the banking industry." Or I just acknowledge the fact that there is a fire and the need to be saved but then just wander around. Or better yet, I acknowledge the fire consuming everything around me and calmly walk off because I do not want some weirdo stepping into my life and trying to change me. This is essentially, what I was telling people and had adopted as my overall mindset to those approaches. The apostle Paul wrecks those notions in Romans 12 because he realized that the people had made a huge mistake and taken religion as a system of notions and a guide to speculation, essentially becoming a fan of God, Jesus

Christ, but not followers. Maybe not even a fan, but someone who just gives props to the work that God has done. The mark of a Christian is genuine love. Genuine love for Christ is not fake; it is authentic and recoils from evil. It is full of a joy that is not seated in some odd emotion but deeply rooted in faith. In the face of hard times, Christians press forward while praying harder and helping fellow Christians in need. They have a high level of hospitality. Christians also do not curse their enemies, they laugh with happy friends and share tears with sad friends. They are not stuck-up but make friends with nobodies. These are the marks of a Christian as the apostle Paul tells us in Romans 12:9–21 (NIV).

When I reported to the Salvation Army for our first official serving day on a Saturday morning, a couple of others and I showed up early to do our time. We sorted out bags upon bags of toys and clothes into age groups and sexes. The bags were stacked to the ceiling. The small building seemed to bust out at the seams, with classrooms and meeting rooms serving as storage rooms for all of these future Christmas gifts. It was humbling to be a part of something that I had taken for granted for so long. My parents always got everything we wanted, within reason, and we definitely didn't go hungry. The following several days, I would serve periodically as an interviewer for the families who were filling out applications to be recipients of the Toys for Tots program. Jessica had scheduled me to work with her. She was to train and walk me through anything that might come up, since this was my first time. I arrived to find a line of people wrapped around the building. I was a little afraid at what I had just agreed to do. I had been around some pretty questionable and dangerous characters and in some rough places, but these people were different. They were lined up in need, because this was the best option in their current circumstances for providing for their children. As I came in the front entrance, I had to break the line of people to get to the front door. I reported to Jessica, and we settled into our stations, which were a big row of folding tables. I was part of the section reviewing applicants' level of need, required examining their expenses and income. It sounds harsh, but with so many people with only so many items to go around, some people are turned away, although very few. It seemed like the moment when Jesus takes the few loaves of bread and fish and feeds thousands (Matthew 14:13–21, NIV). As I sat there asking the applicants what I considered very invasive questions , hearing one heartbreaking story after another, I was overwhelmed with emotion. This was the first moment a seed was planted about fatherless homes or the lack of an intentional father. One after another, single mothers came in dragging their kids, to sit in the fluorescent-lit fellowship hall. Judgment swept over my mind as I saw their expenses on expensive vehicles and the latest fashions. It is easy to judge and discredit people from afar, dehumanizing them because of stereotypes, deep-seated racism that comes out in innuendo or sideways comments. For me, that all flew out the window. My heart melted, not in a way of giving them all they wanted or to even particularly to help their situation, but I related to that feeling of, "I am doing best with what I have and what I have been shown."

Jessica knew I was in over my head as my questions became more and more trivial. During downtime or lunch break, she talked about her life and where she came from, not believing in God, having a much-distorted view, and mentioning being saved. Jessica was also raised in a Catholic home, more so than mine because she was from a rich Mexican culture where being Catholic was more of a people group than a religion. I listened as she explained her story and her heartache with life. Something was happening as she spoke. She connected with me in such a way. She was one of the few people since Janice and Cliff who were not family to reach out and share personal life events. I started a dialogue with her about my struggles in life and with God. She never flinched, even when I tried to shock her with some of my actions. She just listened almost in a way where it was nothing. Not in a rude way, but as if this struggle and questioning were perfectly normal. As we worked throughout the day and got to know each other, she popped the dreaded invitation, "You should come to our church tomorrow." Instead of denying and coming up with an excuse, I told her that I would be there. *What!* I thought to myself. I had just agreed to go to church. Jessica had built a level of trust and credibility within those several hours we spent working. I felt somewhat connected to the Salvation Army in a weird way, as if I belonged. And not only Jessica, but all the workers and staff at the Salvation Army did something in me, like I had tapped into some part of me that wanted more. More of what? I wasn't not sure, but I knew that I desired the feeling, emotion, and sense of purpose and direction within these people. Cliff's words in Del Rio had echoed in my head about God, Jesus, and the Holy Spirit. I sometimes asked the question to myself, "Am I here by accident or something more?"

The most overwhelming thought and, depending on what side of God you stand, the most fearful, is that your life is not an accident, that this life has a purpose, and we have a choice whether to fulfill that purpose. So much blame is placed on our circumstances, the people around us, our parents (or lack of them), money—and the list goes on— but God's word is very clear that you assume your role in life in a particular time and place. The prophet Ezekiel reminds us that God holds individual generations responsible for their sin. Yes, sins are passed down, and, yes, there are terrible situations, but someone has to break that sinful nature. People hate to be judged, but when you understand who God is and what judgment truly is, then judgment is welcome discipline to help us reach our purposes in life. Ezekiel writes in Ezekiel 18:30–31 (ESV), "Repent and turn from all your transgressions, lest iniquity be your ruin. Cast away from you all the transgressions that you have committed, and make yourselves a new heart and new spirit!" He ends this chapter in verse 32 by saying that God has no pleasure in the death of anyone. God does not desire to discipline us for our sins, but it must be done. Sounds like a caring father wanting to correct his children, but if your view of discipline is distorted or warped from that which is biblical, then a negative emotion can be tied to discipline. My view of correction was based on making the authority figures in my life happy and comfortable, whether my parents, bosses, or others. I have realized that my life of rebellion was the only freedom I knew from the rules and regulations people had put on me. I was in a place of trying to make everyone happy with me because I had been disciplined with conditional constraints, following rules and laws more for the comfort of others and disregarding my own needs. Tabby offered unconditional encouragement and support, and her family had attempted that approach as well, but it is hard not to walk among the comfort that I had built. Ezekiel uses the symbol of being lost in the wilderness in chapter 20, where God says to those lost in the wilderness to not walk in the statutes of their fathers, nor to keep their rules or defile themselves with their idols (Ezekiel 20:18, NIV). I had hung tight to the idols of my generations' past of vices and addictions and rules based in comfort, versus what God desires. In Ezekiel 20:16-17 (NIV), God says that Israel rejected his rules, walking among idols and profaning his Sabbaths, but that he spared them. With Cliff's words persisting in my mind, Janice's gentle direction and encouragement as we worked at the banking center, and now Jessica sharing her life and encouraging me in my life challenges—those were three people not associated with me or my family who were reaching out, taking time to encourage and to really care about me. Was this just an accident?

When I agreed to go to church after Jessica's invitation, my response was so quick—shockingly quick—that it felt like the right decision. It was the first time ever that I was somewhat excited about going to church, but I wasn't doing it for God or some great spiritual realization. I was doing it out of obligation to Jessica. She had respected me and encouraged me and shared her story; I felt somewhat indebted to her. Plus, I had still a couple of more weeks ahead of working at the Salvation Army; therefore, I didn't want to create any static, and I didn't want to lie to her since I felt she had been truthful to me. When I came home that evening, I didn't mention anything to Tabby about my agreeing to go to church the following Sunday.

She had been at massage therapy school all day and would be the following morning as well. Both her Saturday and Sunday classes were from 8:00 a.m. to 5:00 p.m. As she got home that Saturday evening, we chatted about the day briefly until working on something for dinner. I didn't mention the church invitation because I was somewhat embarrassed and really just didn't want to talk about it. I didn't really think too much of it, but I knew that if Tabby and her mom caught ahold of just a snippet that I was going to church, I wouldn't hear the end of it. Not in a bad way, but I was so against what I considered weirdos in church that I didn't want to be associated with it. So Sunday came, and Tabby got ready to head out the door for massage therapy school. When she left, I got up out of bed, played some video games, looked at some porn, and got ready to go to church. Yes, that is what happened that morning. The fear, anxiety, and stress about going to this church service got more and more overwhelming as the time got closer. Therefore, I was medicating my feelings in any way possible.

You may have heard people say that they haven't been to church in a while or have fallen into a lifestyle that is, let's say, so undesirable that they fear they might burst into flames upon entering. I didn't think that, but I did joke about it. My fear was more elementary, in that I worried about my interaction with people. In the tiny parking lot at the Salvation Army building, I sat in my truck until right close to 9:00. That way, I wouldn't have to talk to anyone—or so I hoped. Sneak in and hurry out. Still a tactic I use today when I am in a high-stress situation. It takes all I have, praying and going over who I am in God to walk into a social event with a lot of conversation. I have a fear of sinking into the room, not being noticed, a feeling that it wouldn't matter if I weren't there. I have worked on this and have my wins, but if I am honest, I still struggle. So, obviously, in those days, walking into a church building full of strangers, I was a bit overwhelmed. When I entered the double glass doors into the chapel part of the Salvation Army, I encountered a couple of people handing out bulletins. They welcomed me as if I were a long-lost member. Jessica sat close to the front but made a point of welcoming me. The tiny church had red carpet, vintage hanging light fixtures, and the classic pew-style seating. People were scattered throughout the empty pews. As I went to the middle of the church and put my hand on the pew, it felt like the little church where my dad and I served all those family funerals at back home. As I sat there, I looked around at the types of people. Some were noticeably off the streets. Some smelled of alcohol and some drugs. Small families were sprinkled in among the band of misfits. People came up to me and welcomed me. I had this feeling of normality for once. I music struck up, we sang a few songs, and then Captain Gilliam stepped up to the podium. Captain Gilliam wasn't a captain by military standards but by the rank structure of the Salvation Army. I can't remember one word he spoke that day, and I can't remember one song that was sung. I also can't remember any verses or even the theme of the sermon. You know what I remember clearly? Acceptance.

I felt something very similar to what I had felt in Del Rio, but without all the drama of waking up in a strange room and hitchhiking—it was just a feeling of acceptance. Jessica's past was spotted with her own bad decisions and sins. She opened up about that with me. The people in this church didn't look me up and down or ask those cliché questions like, "So what do you do for a living?" or "Good morning, nice weather"—you know, those comments that are space fillers. I was welcomed with genuine conversation that really showed they were interested in who I was. As I started to head out to my truck, I turned around to meet Captain Gilliam and his wife. We had a small talk, and then I remembered that I had been there for an extended time. My whole plan to get in and out failed because I was connecting with people in the church. Something about the Salvation Army church rocked me. It stirred back up those feelings I had coming back from Del Rio a year or so before. The following Sunday, I went to church again at the Salvation Army, again without Tabby's knowledge. I decided to tell her that Sunday when she got out of massage therapy school. When she got home, we had dinner, talked about the day, and I went into my secret of going to church the past two Sundays. Her face was priceless, a mix of joy and confusion about why I lied about that, of all things. But after explaining and asking her not to make too big a deal about it, I asked her to come the following Sunday, since she would be out of school. She agreed.

Tabby got dressed for church that morning. She was anxious with anticipation. I warned her this would not be the type of church like the Episcopal churches she was accustomed to. She didn't bat an eye. She was just Tabby being Tabby, supportive and encouraging. As we drove up and made our way in, I was excited to introduce her to the people I had met, and they were equally excited. To this day, I love introducing Tabby as my wife and getting the response, "I have heard so much about you!" She lights up like a Christmas tree! That first time we sat together in a church was a split feeling, partly that I was doing the right thing, and partly that I had sold out. I had become a hypocrite, those I hated and on whom I put so much blame for why I didn't like church.

I fought these feelings like a wrestling match of good and evil in my head, a very real and intense battle. I believe this is our spirit. We hear our inner voice, and we hear those whom we often have a hard time identifying—the same experience the apostle Paul had when he was tormented by his past sinful desires. I am sure someone can attest to these types of emotional battles fought all alone in our inner spirit. Ezekiel wrote about how, after all the sinful, selfish, and dishonoring ways Israel had acted out, God promises them a new spirit. Ezekiel 36:26 (ESV) states, "And I will give you a new heart and a new spirit I will put with you. And I will remove the heart of stone from your flesh and give you a heart of flesh." God promises in this passage that he will work a good work in them that will qualify them for good works in the future. God will change the people from the inside out and give them a new heart. My heart, my mind before I went to Del Rio was insensible and inflexible, unapt to receive any divine impressions. The vulnerability, the circumstances of how I encountered God in Del Rio softened up my heart. If only for a few moments, my spiritual senses were birthed. I was conscious of a living God and the very real spiritual pains and pleasures, but it was more like watching a newborn calf attempting to walk when birthed, stumbling and falling everywhere. This is what William Booth set out to do in 1852, reach those who were struggling to know God, struggling to build a relationship with God, struggling in life, while trying to point people's attention away from the world's comfort and to God for comfort. God was working in me. I can now say that looking back, but I continued in reckless and rebellious actions privately. I started to lie more and more about how much I drank, whether I smoked weed, and whether I was at a strip club. This was happening while I had started to go to this church. My lifestyle didn't change, but the moments in which I could indulge were limited because of my marriage, my work, and my responsibility mounting up. Tabby had put her foot down on my seeing Travis, and he had moved to Dallas for a short time to finish up some schooling. So it was easy. It felt like the walls were caving in on me—no friends, a marriage, and now this newfound awareness that God had a purpose for my life. It would drive me mad. My late-night questions to God or about God would generate an unhealthy fear of death that I hadn't felt in a couple of years. So when Travis invited me to meet him in San Antonio for a weekend party fest, I jumped at the opportunity. I felt like I needed to escape and to get some relief. My decision to go to San Antonio against my wife's wishes would prove to be the final straw for me and Tabby and a "line in the sand" moment between me and God—I on one side with my idols, sins, destructive lies, secrets, and lifestyle and God on the other. As Moses stood at the gate of the camp, which was the only way out, he said, "Who is on the Lord's side? Come to me" (Exodus 32:26, ESV). This decision to go to San Antonio with Travis and spend the weekend doing things that I knew deep down were not good for me put me in a position of standing in this camp and making a choice to stay and die or to go with God.

15

Spending time as a child and teenager raising farm animals, I have seen my fair share of disgusting things and experienced some firsthand. Nothing compares to the time when I was bottle-feeding a calf that my parents had recently purchased. For those who don't know, when calves are weaned off their mother, they must be bottle-fed to bridge the gap between a liquid diet and feed and grass. One day, my sister and I were feeding the three or so calves we had. We used these huge bottles that looked essentially like a baby bottle but ten times bigger. One calf was not moving out of the way to allow the next one to eat. I reached to the rear of the calf and placed my hands on either side of the tailbone and attempted to push the calf. You can see where this is going. The calf instinctively raised its tail and projected a fluid from its anus that I can only describe as the most vile, hot, brown fluid that covered me like chocolate milk that had sat out in a one-hundred-degree Texas summer day. As I stood there in disbelief, staring at my mom, there was a brief moment of shock and then an explosion of laughter, followed by my being on the verge of tears, mostly from the smell. My sister, of course, laughed uncontrollably, as I had to be sprayed off by the garden hose. Do not worry, I would have my time of laughter at my sister's expense as she came running from the chicken coop one evening in full sprint with an extremely infuriated rooster chasing very close behind her. That scene still makes me laugh aloud. My sister running with her hair flailing around from side to side, arms waving, with a rooster attempting to spur her, leaping every few steps to gain ground. Sadly (or fortunately), that rooster was laid to rest by my father, who ended up making an extremely good pot of chicken and dumplings! The most disgusting thing that I have ever seen is an animal eating its own vomit or feces. Most animals will instinctively vomit if their food has not been digested properly, then as soon as they vomit, they will turn to sift through the vomit for any remains of food. Chickens and hogs will do the same with their feces. Disgusting, yes, but very much a part of the animal kingdom.

A reference to Proverbs 26:11 in 2 Peter 2:22 (ESV) says, "The dog returns to its own vomit, and the sow, after washing herself, returns to wallow in the mire." Peter says this after pointing out some harsh truths about false teachers and leaders; saying in 2 Peter 2:21 (ESV), "For it would have been better for them never to have known the way of righteousness than after knowing it to turn back from the holy commandments delivered to them." After Cliff shared the truth about Jesus, God, and hell on that fateful day in Del Rio and Jessica's unapologetic attempt at getting me to church services at the Salvation Army, I had built some knowledge of Christ through teachings and the testimony of others. At this point, my faith, if that is what you want to call it, was built on others' perspectives and experiences by way of sermons or testimonies. My battle with my own fear, guilt, doubt, past experiences, and feelings of unworthiness was really where my faith lay. As Peter compared people acknowledging a truth but then returning to their original ways to a dog returning to its vomit, it is abundantly clear why I was struggling. I was becoming overwhelmed by the performance and requirements of becoming a Christian. The desires of my heart would be outweighed by the past experiences or expectations that I was yoked with. Jesus states that the gate that leads to life is narrow, but the gate that leads to destruction is broad, and many will enter through it (Matthew 7:13–14, NIV). Why? Why do so many people openly choose a road of destruction and live in some type of ignorant bliss? Marriages, relationships, health, finances, and everything about us is affected by the decisions we make each moment of each day, but the awareness of these decisions is vastly different for each person because of their level of fear, guilt, doubt, past experiences, knowledge, exposure, and feelings of unworthiness or worthiness. Since Del Rio and a handful of church services at the Salvation Army, in addition to watching Tabby's unwavering faith in God and her parents navigating their faith in God in their everyday lives, things were getting very confusing and scary. We fear what we do not understand. The depression, drugs, alcohol, anger, bars, strip clubs, and pornography were safe for me to accept. They were what I knew, like an old friend.

When Travis called to catch up and reconnect, I wish I could say that it was entirely his idea to go to San Antonio for the weekend, but it wasn't. If I remember right, he just wanted to connect in Waco, but I was the one who pushed the issue of needing to get out of town. This was one of those moments when I used Travis; I knew what to say to intrigue and entice him. I mentioned to him that another friend of mine and I wanted to get together in San Antonio, and since Travis was going to be going to Victoria anyway, which was only an hour from San Antonio, the logistics worked out. The plan was laid out very similarly to the trip to Del Rio: leave on a Friday and return on Sunday. That weekend would be a complete disconnect from reality. Just the thought of it relieved, settled, and excited me. When I told Tabby about the planned weekend trip to San Antonio, she looked at me with disappointment, like the wind had just been taken out of her sails. I intentionally did not tell her that Travis was coming. If you ask her, she will tell you that it was surprising because I had been to church a handful of times and developed some surface-level relationships with the church leaders. She saw this trip as my taking a step backward. She knew that I was occasionally drinking and smoking, but she didn't know that I was still having extremely dark moments of torment from the question, "There is a God; now what?" It's a fair question, one asked by anyone with any sort of tie to or closets full of darkness, deceit, secrets, guilt, and shame. From my experience, people who haven't walked with God or experienced what an ongoing, everyday relationship looks like ask these questions because we are giving up a life we know, a life that, in our reality, is working. There is a great disconnect between what the church teaches, which is to turn your life over to God and to accept Jesus Christ as your savior and to leave the sin in your life. This raises a couple of issues. First off, how can you turn your life over to someone you don't know? I had an experience with God in Del Rio, and I had several experiences with what I believe to be God's counterpart, the devil, Satan, or demonic presences. I had met the expectations of evil, and I was good at it and getting better. I have never been a person to blindly follow anything or anybody. It's not in my DNA, and if you read the Gospels closely, the disciples didn't blindly follow either. They walked with Jesus, watched him work, listened to his words, and allowed him to train them—except for the apostle Paul. He had to battle his own emotional and physical challenges with disconnecting from the world and connecting to the source, which is God. Paul's struggles are well-documented throughout his letters, speaking from a place of credibility about how hard the choice is to follow Christ versus the world or our flesh desires.

It is a travesty that some Christians have mocked, distorted, and discouraged so many people from ever entering a community of believers because of their reckless and judgmental approach to issues of the heart. I had grown to despise those individuals. Every time I would see a picketing group, whether taking a stance against homosexuality or abortion or some other target group, I would be infuriated with a rage that came from a place of defense. Don't get me wrong; those things in themselves are sins, but attacking an individual for a decision eliminates opportunity for the love of Christ to shine through. How will people know the love of God if we are consistently judging and attacking and debating theology? Theology will always be trumped by the truth that there is a God and he loves and cares for us and that he has a purpose for our lives. Theology is there to support and teach but not take the place of God. No one, and I mean no one, can force another person into a relationship with God by spitting hate slogans and damning another person to hell. The bottom line is that when Jesus said to worry about the plank in your own eye before you judge a speck in your brother's eye, it was to approach your brother with a clean and pure heart. I felt outnumbered and overwhelmed by the number of people I knew who were Christians, yet nothing about their life, dependence, or purpose screamed out, "I love God!" First John

2:9-11 (HCSB) says that anyone who claims to be "in the light" and hates his brother is, in fact, still in complete darkness. Dallas Willard, a Christian philosopher, said: "Almost all evil deeds and intents are begun with the thought that they can be hidden by deceit" (*The Spirit of the Disciplines: Understanding How God Changes Lives*, HarperCollins, 1991). My attempts at church had just further confused and frustrated me, but the conviction was overwhelming, and I had mistaken this conviction about my thoughts, the lies I carried around, the deceit and the darkness that I hid, for condemnation. Actually going to church forced me into a place of a rigorist approach to hide my actual thoughts and feelings, attempting to be seen as changed. This was my attempt to wash the vile filth I called life off with a water hose by sitting in a few services, like my mom sprayed me down with that water hose as a kid after being covered with fecal matter by that calf. From the outside, I looked cleaner and more presentable, but it was still the old me underneath, and the same issues still lay right below the surface. The time between Del Rio and right before I left for San Antonio for another weekend-binging party trip, I felt more like God had hindered or infected me. I didn't want to believe that God wanted me, and I certainly didn't want to believe that all the years of bad decisions, rants, and my perspective were wrong.

There is some twisted comfort in those places we hate the most or do not even realize that what we turn to is twisted, because it has become our reality. The Allegory of the Cave by the Greek philosopher Plato in his work *The Republic* describes people imprisoned, chained to a wall in a cave for a long period. The people grow to choose the cave and chains when offered freedom. Why? The prisoners see shadows portrayed on the wall but never see what is making the shadows; therefore, they draw fear and discomfort from the shadows, but when taken out of the cave, they find peace in returning to bondage rather than reality. Someone forced out of the cave cries and, in a rage, fights the process because their reality is being ripped from them. There is comfort in bondage and sin, and life is easy when a person lives with low goals and expectations. A demonic mantra and desire spoken over us ever so lightly says, "This is who you are; you are not like them." This consistently puts us in a state of comparison to others and measuring up to those who seem to have it figured out or have something we desire. Addiction is strange; the brain is rewired to desire a certain type of feeling by doing certain actions to have the chemical release that is referred to as the reward system. This is a good thing that God has given us, but like most things, we, as humans, find ways to distort that which is given. Church, religion, God, and the Bible stirred up many feelings of anger and rejection. It was not that Jessica at the Salvation Army ever said or did anything to made me feel rejected; I actually liked going there. It was God. It was the expectations. It all seemed too legalistic. It took me back to when I was a teenager in middle school, not being accepted for who I was and what I looked like. When I feel rejected, my defense has always been to push those away who are rejecting me. This defense is learned from years of feeling rejected by God and accepted by those who opposed God. I had decided long before as I sat in that bathtub as a child in fear of the coming death sentence we all are given that I would do anything I could not to feel that way. This feeling created a huge gaping hole of darkness and fear that had to be filled with something. Operating on the information I had at the time, which was hearsay, I had unknowingly created my own gospel to live by. I knew that I would never measure up or even come close to those Christians who lived in a cloud of blind faith with no concern about the coming day or the what-ifs of what could go wrong. Growing up and seeing my parents toil through life and knowing their individual stories of struggle of losing their parents at an early age and the pain that was inflicted on them by a family who supposedly loved them soured my approach from an early age. In Marilyn Manson's book *The Long Hard Road Out of Hell* (HarperCollins, 1998), he ends with a chapter called "Fifty Million Screaming Christians Can't Be Wrong." The entire chapter consists of court cases and letters from mayors, Christian groups, and activist groups meant to notify Marilyn Manson of how horrible, disgusting, and evil he is. Attempting to blame him for and outright convict him of all sorts of cultural challenges and events. These letters are from groups of individuals who act, look, and believe differently than him. Some would go as far as blaming their children's mishaps on his music and influence. Of course, what they do not realize is that, for the finger they wave in disgust and blame, three more are pointing back at them, confirming his rants and mocking of the Christian faith with each word on each document demonizing him and his life. This is what Christianity and followers of a loving God resort to when there is a lack of understanding or an extreme curve to the legalism like hate and conditional love, basically a Pharisee approach, but for the sake of what? Wining souls? Doing God's work? Or is it pushing a personal agenda or blame for their own convictions in the name of God?

It is really hard to pinpoint the moments when I grew so far away from God, but in all honesty, I never was close to God. My mom and dad had their own personal relationship that they would share to a certain point, but their opinion of the church, the church members, and how people's belief in God was between them and God haunted me as I sat in those pews at the Salvation Army, like I was doing something wrong. I was mistrusting, on guard, and standoffish at times, believing that they wouldn't be talking to me unless they wanted something from me. I believe that my desire to go out of town, to get away, and to escape my mind that was questioning everything I believed about God was an attempt to return to the figurative safety of a prison cell. Life is easy when you don't rock the boat or change, but as a child, I always believed there was more than what was visually presented. I had accepted it but never let go of those dreams that there was more to life than just working, paying taxes, and dying. In my mind, I had refused that long ago, and that refusal had played out in a rebellious state that I used to go on a journey. That rebellion had led me into destructive relationships, which led me to moving to Waco and making a friend who was a bartender, which led to my meeting Tabby. Rebellion led me to Del Rio, making a rash of terrible decisions and a series of lies to eventually meet up with Cliff in Del Rio talking about hell, Jesus, and God. Rebellion had paid such a big part of my life. I can stand here now and say God was in every situation of my life because he knew that I wanted more out of a faith in Jesus Christ. More than merely a cheap painting of Jesus praying on a rock, hanging in the dining room of my parents' home. More than just a half-naked man hanging from a cross that people wore around their neck as they party, drink, and do the same drugs I did. When I read the Bible and heard the stories, I wanted to know those people. I wanted to be a part of something bigger than myself; we all do. No one wakes up and says, "Hey, I think that I will go to a strip club or buy a hooker or do a line of coke." It is a process of disappointment and living up to the low expectations placed on us or people expecting us to meet unrealistic expectations without a foundation of truth and grace in our lives. More times than not, my prayers were insurance policies just in case I died, but those prayers have always been answered in some sort of way. My prayer to experience purpose, find truth and have meaning was never answered though. Perhaps it was answer but not in a way I could understand, perhaps I was not ready yet. Perhaps my intentions were not in the right place for the prayer I was praying. Sure I would tell people differently, but honestly, my prayers were super private and super intense, and sometimes had some of the most vulgar language, followed by a disrespectful rant. I knew God as I knew some famous athlete or political figure. Sure, they are good at what they do, but what does that have to do with me?

When I was preparing to go to San Antonio, something was different. Sure, I was feeling guilty and shameful because I was giving Tabby half-truths about what we would be doing in San Antonio, but this was different. It was a force or something like a pressure of some type over or against me. Like a spirit of discernment, saying, "Are you sure about this?" I knew I was walking into a bad situation. The stop signs and warnings were there, but I was in a place neither to listen nor give them much thought. I fought through it by prepping my clothes and getting my bags packed. I packed my truck and planned to leave early from work and head straight to San Antonio. Waco to San Antonio was usually a three- to three-and-a-half-hour drive, but with Friday traffic, it would be more like four to four and a half hours. Tabby had planned to have some friends over that weekend as well for a sleepover, watching movies and catching up. The fact that Tabby wasn't going to be home alone helped soften the blow of guilt for my not being there for the weekend. Somehow justifying my actions was a common thread in my decision-making by comparing myself to others around me in an attempt to help me feel better about myself. In retrospect, the half-truths and outright lies I used to tell myself to protect Tabby were actually doing more harm and pushing me into a place of more deceit. Not to Tabby, but to myself, denying myself and my identity. Going to San Antonio, I knew what I was agreeing to, and it was a direct contradiction of the knowledge and conviction that I had experienced (Hebrews 10:26 (HCSB)); therefore, I was accepting my role as the presumptuous sinner. In all honesty, church and testimony took me to a place where I had a fleeting idea and thought that I needed to change, but then this massive, overwhelming feeling of rebellion swept over me, and it was comfortable. Rebellion was who I was. I followed the rules because I had to and not because I wanted to. I went to work, paid bills, and now attempted to attend church and stomach the testimonies of others out of obligation. The rebellion, the chemical reaction that happened in my brain when I just thought about acting out was so addictive. Lying, acting out, going to strip clubs and dance clubs, doing drugs, popping pills, cursing, and sometimes denying God altogether was what I ran to when things got weird or too demanding. Sure, I love Tabby and had wanted to marry her, but the pressures of being the husband that she and what her parents expected and what was being preached from the pulpit sent me spiraling. I was being confirmed about who I was when no one was watching. I had built an excellent talent of being a do-gooder when the right people were around and being the opposite when others were around. Who I was and who I wanted to be was getting massively confusing and tormenting.

People can spew suicide in times of need, to be noticed or to directly call attention to themselves in a highly charged moment in which they are just attempting to manipulate a situation. At times in my life I have shouted, "I will just kill myself!" Then there were the times when I would really lay out the pros and cons about suicide alone, nothing more than my thoughts and the internal voices that I can only equate to demonic and heavenly attacks fighting for attention. Those moments when I would wake up in the middle of the night and either sit in the bathroom or jump online and look at porn became stronger and more intense after Del Rio. The more and more I rebelled, the more fear would come over me and the more that questions of who and what I was would rip at my psyche. The apostle Paul says in Hebrews 10:27 (NIV) that those under the Gospel who will not accept Christ—those who do not accept they may be saved by Him—have no refuge left. I knew enough of the truth of Jesus Christ and God. I even had some impactful experiences, yet I was still turning away. Why? Why would a person just turn away from such a profound truth and escape from torment? Fear. Fear of the unknown. To attempt to mesh everything into one transparent, vulnerable, and obedient life is one of the most freaking fearful things that can be imagined by a person who brings a lot of baggage into that scenario. It is easier in a way to train and teach someone a new skill when they have no experience, versus someone who has prior knowledge and experience whose skill you are trying to help perfect. I was highly experienced at a life built around low expectations, judgment, hypocrites, and fakes. I had created this whole habitual lifestyle of rebellion that from the outside was judged, mocked, and criticized. I never had instilled enough confidence in who I was to just not care what people thought; therefore, I felt the need to hide and to share only with those I could trust. I trusted Travis with the rebellion.

Before you smirk at my next statement, please hear me out; I admire those like Marilyn Manson, Maynard Keenan of Tool, Eminem, Jonathan Davis of Korn, Snoop Dogg, and Corey Taylor of Slipknot, and I now realized why I was so drawn to them. They had the confidence and courage to say, "This is who I am, like it or not." Let the critics come and attempt to destroy me. I never did have that confidence, but I wanted to be able to stand in front of everyone I knew and say this is who I am; disgusting as it may be, this is who I am. Like it or not. Tabby and her family were slowly breaking the fear and filth I felt, through unconditional love that I was given only by grace, because I certainly didn't deserve it. I knew I was changing, and I knew something was going on with my feelings because I started to hide things extremely well in an attempt to earn some type of approval. When I said my goodbyes to Tabby for the weekend and got in my truck, relief overcame me because I could just medicate all weekend, veg out, and put little effort in what I was about to do. But the closer I got to San Antonio, the more anxiety built up. Why was I nervous? Why was I feeling guilty? I had never felt this level of guilt and anxiety before. I was having a hard time keeping everything separate. Usually, I would just shut off my emotions; that way, I wouldn't feel guilt or shame for what I was doing. I would just deal with the repercussions later. I wouldn't think about the people I could be hurting, and I wouldn't have to think of my purposeless life. I would just have moments of total disconnection, but this was different. Everything was running together. When I met up with Travis and my other friend from San Antonio, I was primed and ready to get as drunk and as messed up as I possibly could, to escape what was going on with me. It is what I called "blown out of my mind." We had dinner and started drinking immediately. I felt like a consumed person, a motivated person, wanting to get as far as I could from the emotional turmoil I was experiencing. That night, we hit a couple of clubs and bars, arriving back at the house sometime in the early hours of Saturday. We didn't waste any time as we awoke from our drunken state from the night before to have a group lunch at a local Mexican food place. We got up and got ready, and then I decided to take off my wedding ring and put it in my bathroom bag. We started drinking early in the day followed by a little drugging, and hit the late-night scene again on Saturday. By the time we hit the club, I was essentially in a mode in which all my inhibitions were gone. I was operating at such a level of intoxication and disconnection from reality that I was fully that person whom I had hidden from so many others, moving a hundred miles an hour like I was running from something. That night, I crossed boundaries and lines that I hadn't crossed before. The night is a flood of blurry images and missing moments because of the amount of intoxication I had experienced. Very similar to the events that led up to Del Rio, but this time, no church service or friendly faces awaited to help guide me.

As I awoke early that Sunday at around six or seven in the morning, I gasped for air and grabbed my chest as if I were rocketing out of the water after almost drowning. I'm not sure if you have ever felt this, but I have, too many times—that feeling of waking up relieved that you are alive but then a little disappointed that you are, because now the reality of life has just hit you. When I woke up, this overwhelmingly loud, screaming internal voice said, *Go home and come clean with your wife about everything.* I jumped up, grabbed my bag, put on my wedding ring, and jumped in my truck. I was still half-drunk and the stench of the night before lingered. As I made my way down the road and onto I-35 back to Waco, the reality of what this internal voice was telling me was hitting me. I started to say that this was crazy. I cannot go home and confess to this weekend's events and betrayal, along with the years of lying and betrayal that she knows nothing about. This will crush her. This will just be a repeat of what her biological father put her through as a child before her stepdad, Bruce, came into the picture to pick up the pieces. I didn't want to be another part of hurting this incredible woman and violating her trust, but as I was reminded that morning, I am a part of that. I am a part of the hurt and pain. I have taken advantage of her unconditional love and grace and used it to further my selfish agenda. Then the thought entered. It would be better to die than to see the look on her face. A community right before you get to Austin is called Buda. Every time I pass through Buda, I am reminded of my decision that Sunday morning coming back from San Antonio to not kill myself. How history has a twisted sense of humor. My dad's crossroads in life were either changing his ways or ending his life, with his failed suicide attempt, and here I was debating the same. An overpass in Buda perfectly presents a concrete column without any obstructions. I decided to kill myself. But I wasn't alone in that truck that day. I believe a battle for my soul was going on right there. As I accelerated the truck, banging the steering wheel, pumping myself up to run directly into the concrete column, with tears and uncontrollable weeping, the voice within said, *You must go through this. This is the easy way out and you have always taken the easy way out. It is time to make a decision. You will break Tabby's heart, you will violate her trust, and you will cause a great deal of pain, but it is time for you to face it.* As I reached ninety miles per hour and looked at the column coming closer, I slammed on the brakes and slid onto the side of the road. Grasping the steering wheel, staring forward, and then looking to the passenger side of my truck, I simply said, "Okay, okay, I am going to do this."

This incredible peace came over me as I entered the Waco city limits. It was a peace that I have heard described best only by death row inmates when they accept their fate. As I pulled into the driveway, I simply got out of the truck and went through the garage, coming through the door to the kitchen. When I walked in, Tabby and her friends were all sitting in the living room, talking. No words were spoken as Tabby's eyes and mine connected. What seemed to be minutes passing by was only a second at the most. I said, "I need to talk to you, Tabby." Tabby's friends seemed to know something was up and instantly started to gather their things and say their goodbyes. When they left, I told Tabby I needed to tell her several things. As I laid out the hard truths and betrayal of the past couple of days, she listened, and her eyes slowly glazed over stoically. She asked me several questions, to which I answered honestly. One question caught me off : "Did you wear your wedding ring this weekend?" It was as if she already knew that I hadn't. I was honest and told her no. That I had taken it off and left it in my bathroom bag. She says that my taking my wedding ring off and going out as a single guy hurt her the most. She said it made her feel like I went out as if she never existed. That was hard for me to hear because that is the last thing I wanted her to feel. But her statement was true. I did go out as if she didn't exist because if I had left my wedding ring on, it would have been like taking her with me and reminding me of all the ways I have failed her. She retreated to the bedroom, sobbing with deep hurt. I wish that had been the last of my confessions, but it wasn't. I followed her into the bedroom to continue to confess and lay out the issues I had since we had been together. I had to confess everything. The drugs and alcohol, my late-night socializing at bars and clubs, the pills I still took occasionally throughout the week—everything. It was understandably overwhelming for her to hear. One confession after the other left her feeling shocked and numbed. Then something happened in that moment when I looked into her eyes. The look of hurt and pain that I had just inflicted on her was familiar. I have seen this look before. I remember seeing my mom with this same look years ago. Remembering my mom with those same tears in her eyes and with the same look of deep hurt and pain, I then realized that I had just become what my parents warned me of and what I said I would never be. I ended my confession with a promise to never touch alcohol or drugs again, to drop everything and make a choice to start my journey with God. Tabby very patiently got up and grabbed her keys. There were tears in her eyes, but she was so overwhelmed and numbed that she seemed eerily calm. For the first time, I didn't try to stop her from leaving, and I didn't attempt to talk my way out of it. I was already convinced that this is what I needed to do, for better or worse. Whatever came of this would be for the best. I was at peace, a peace that only God could give. I noticed that wherever she went, it was on foot because her car remained in the driveway. I later found out that as she was putting the keys in the ignition, she abruptly stopped. She knew she shouldn't drive because she was afraid she might do something crazy like drive her car off a bridge.

Tabby returned a couple of hours later. She told me that she went to a vacant house across the street that was still being built. She could actually see our house from one of the front windows and could see me searching for her and crying in the driveway. In that house, she screamed and shouted and cried harder than she ever had. She questioned God and why he would let her marry a liar, a cheat, and an addicted man, someone she promised herself she would never marry. She felt angry and betrayed, and she questioned the entire marriage. She felt humiliated and very naïve. She also thought about having to file for divorce after only being married a little over a year and the embarrassment that would follow. She cried hard over that thought, as she took marriage very seriously. Those vows of forever—she really meant that. She told me that "for better or worse" kept ringing in her head over and over. She told me her conversation with God was full of questioning and seeking guidance. It went something like this: "For better or worse? But this is way worse. Why would you allow me to marry this man? Why did you pick me to be his wife? I don't think I can handle this. How can I ever trust or believe him again? What do I do? How do I overcome this? I don't know that I can. My marriage just started and now it's over." She immediately heard, "No, it's not. It is just beginning." She looked up and around, looking for the voice she had just heard and then quickly realized God was speaking to her. Her first reaction was to question, but then she immediately felt the most amazing sense of peace she had ever felt. Sitting there in that peace was when God told her that I was telling her the truth. I would never drink or do drugs again. That she could go back and that this marriage would be saved, and not only would it survive, but it would flourish. So Tabby and her rock-solid faith in God returned home. When she walked in the door, she found me sitting on our bedroom floor with bloodshot eyes fresh out of tears. I started to speak to her, but she told me to be quiet and let her speak. She said, "As crazy as this sounds, I believe you." I sat there shocked. She then explained to me her whole experience and talk with God. I sat there in awe that God had confirmed through my hurting wife exactly what he had told me on the way home, that it would all be okay. On that day, God saved my marriage. He took my wife aside and spent precious time with her, confirming that this time was different, that this time I was telling the truth. This was the second time God interacted with me in a most violent way, in a very real way. The first time, he gently brought me to a place to hear a message, but this time, it was a direct slap in the face. A final straw. It was time for me to put up or shut up. I had leaned into my-selfishness and affected the relationships around me by pushing away when it got too difficult. I could have taken the easy way out that day on the interstate right before I entered Austin. I would once again have taken the easy way, the more comfortable way. Life is hard. Living is harder than death. What had feared death all along, but I actually feared living. Tabby and I started living that day. It didn't seem like it and certainly didn't feel like it, but we started to pick up the pieces of a broken, weather-beaten marriage and started to restore it.

Waking up the following Monday after the most impactful and insanely intense weekend of my life, in which I went completely from one side of the spectrum of deception, lies, and addictions to scream over to the other side, where I was completely blown open. This felt more like a beating. The emotional bruises and damage I felt was almost crippling, but I can only imagine what my wife was feeling as she woke up to head out to work herself. Those first several days after the disclosure of who I was when she wasn't around was similar to those feelings after a funeral of a loved one when everyone is shuffling their feet in disbelief and pain over the loss and attempting to get on with life. It's hard to pick up the pieces and move forward. It is so much easier to walk away, give up, and restart in a new place, but that is not what God calls us to. He calls us to stand up and work and face challenges. The way people look at marriage is discouraging. I think a drastic disconnection is occurring in why marriage was given to us by God. Man is to sacrifice his selfishness, his selfish desires, and leave his parents and become one with his wife, symbolizing the unity of God with his people. This beautiful thing we have distorted terribly with our selfishness and cultural pressures. I had badly beaten our marriage, not to mention emotionally wrecked my wife, whom God had placed in my life, with selfishness and the lie I bought into from the world of what a man is supposed to be. My foundational issue had been rocked in the past two years, from the day I stepped into Club 180 in Del Rio to this intense battle I had with myself, both good and evil, on my way back from San Antonio. My skepticism and lack of knowledge of Jesus Christ had led me to this moment. In Genesis, after the story of the first marriage, people skim over a verse as if it were a side note: "And the man and his wife were both naked and were not ashamed" (Genesis 2:25, NASB). Can you imagine standing in front of your wife or husband completely naked physically with the lights on? Most of us feel weird even thinking about that. Now take it a step further, standing in front of your spouse with everything you struggle with in secret, your fears, your worries, down to the most intimate details about yourself when you are alone with your thoughts or what you hold back—the truth. Yikes! What got us to a point where we are ashamed in front of the one person we have chosen to spend a large portion of our lives with? Sin, selfishness, and allowing the changing culture of corruption, compromise, distortion, and absence of God's truths to dictate how we should live. A foundation built on shifting sand will always be shifting—and will eventually collapse under the pressure of life (Matthew 7:26-27, NIV). A massive number of us are buying into the message and being taught to trust in ourselves. I have seen where trusting in myself gets me. My life was built on shifting sand; heck, it was more like mud. Trying to build on some sort of foundation, but as soon as I would get some sort of direction or some sort of grasp of life, it would all come crashing down over and over. What was missing? Here I stood with a wife in pain, trying to figure out what I could do to fix this, to take charge, and to make this marriage work.

When I returned to work that following Monday, Janice came up very quickly and told me that something was wrong. She said some kind words and I shared with her a brief summary of what had occurred, without all the gory details. As usual, she encouraged me. I had just made a decision to drop everything that had caused my wife pain and led me down a destructive path; however, those things were who I was, they were my identity. This is the hard part about changing one's life for the good. The things that screwed up that life or resulted in a lot of hurt and pain are part of who that person is. For me, drinking and smoking cigarettes were easy because I could just avoid those things. Tabby supported everything I chose to do by giving up those things as well. She did not have an issue with those things, but the simple fact that she was willing to give up those things for life because of me spoke volumes. What I had a hard time dealing with was my emotions—how to move forward. What was the purpose of changing my life, and how was I supposed to change, really change? My whole life, I have felt more like an unmanned boat being blown and carried by the wind and current wherever, sometimes hitting the shore head-on and sometimes being blown back out to sea, just moving here and there with no rhyme or reason. My convictions on issues were surface-level, with no depth to them. I could be swayed by a quick breeze of words out of either fear or acceptance. I was living in fear more during these first days after my proclamation of sobriety and being a changed man. The fear was of screwing up or breaking a promise to Tabby yet again. I was accepted for who

I was at the Salvation Army; therefore, I felt motivated to continue to attend church there, plus a dozen people there were worse than I was, or so I thought.

A week after I returned from San Antonio, we went to church service at the Salvation Army. I couldn't tell you what the sermons were all about, but I do remember feeling that Captain Gilliam and his wife really cared for the people in that church. I was drawn to them because they had dropped a "normal" American life to live a life dedicated to serving the people. This held a high level of credibility with me because they lived this life out; they actually walked with God no matter what. Nothing you could say nor do to them would shake their faith. It was encouraging to meet a couple who seemed to encompass what I knew of the radical people who walked with Jesus. I wanted conviction like that. I wanted purpose and direction that wasn't my own, that was part of something bigger. As we drew into the church and got to know some people, I felt safe, but with my social life and friendships failing fast, I was alone outside the church. I cut off contact with Travis altogether. I simply just quit calling him and didn't answer his calls. This wasn't the right way to handle this, but it was the best I could come up with at the time. I felt like I needed to hide, needed to sever any relationship, activity, or habit that caused me to sink into my selfishness. Making a choice to just not drink alcohol throws people in a defensive mode by defending why they drink; this is usually out of some deep-seated guilt they feel because they know ultimately that they may not need to engage in that particular activity. I felt like I was a kid again, hanging on the monkey bars and attempting to hang on as long as I could before I lost my grip, white-knuckling each day and growing exhausted and frustrated. Needless to say, after a few weeks, everyone who had been in our circle of friends had become distant and estranged in some cases. We didn't care, though, because we were no longer going to put others ahead of this marriage. I had officially hit rock bottom when I was sitting at work in my office and started to be flooded with all that had occurred since meeting Tabby, since Del Rio, and since San Antonio. Something was missing, something I wasn't getting. The next Sunday, Tabby and I returned to church, and Captain Gilliam had a guest speaker who was going to be leading a week of camp meetings. I had heard of camp meetings before, from secondhand, off-color comments, that this was a bunch of weirdoes and that I needed to steer clear of them. I was on guard for sure now, but I was willing to give it a shot. Honestly, this church, these people were the first outside my family and Tabby to show me some type of unconditional love. They knew more than my own parents did about my life and seemed to embrace me more and seemed to really care about me, Tabby, and our marriage. Tabby and I agreed to attend. I made special arrangements to attend each night of church and leave work right at 5:00 p.m. each day.

The week was full of teaching, music, and what people refer to as altar calls, where the speaker will end on a message and if someone wanted to respond to the message by getting prayed for. Also, some were "turning their life over to Jesus" and "reaffirming the faith." At the time, these terms meant nothing to me. As I sat in the pews each night and listened to the teachings and watched people worship with their hands in the air, dancing, and some of the church leaders praying for those who would go up to the front, I was obviously out of my element. Even though I felt more and more uncomfortable with each passing night, I still went with Tabby by my side. She never forced me to go; she never questioned. She simply supported and encouraged me. Tabby has a unique spirit, one not seen a lot. Even with all the pain and distress I had caused her, she knew something was going on in me far greater and out of the realm of her understanding. She had her moments of sadness and anger, I am sure, but as we went to these services, she would gently walk in with me, holding my hand like a child going into a dental appointment. I held her hand tightly just to remind myself that I needed to step up and be the best man I could for this woman. As the camp meeting came to a close on Saturday, there was a final push for those who didn't know Jesus to take the first step to being introduced by raising their hand. As everyone sat in the pews, looking around, a person raised their hand. The person stood up, got prayed over, and sat back down. The music started to play, and we all stood up to start singing the closing song for the evening. As I stood up, I got this huge knot in my stomach, and as everyone sang, I closed my eyes and told God that if I needed to raise my hand, then he would have the speaker ask again. As the knot in my stomach got more and more intense, as my skin started to burn, I stood there having a conversation with God. I told him something that I had never acknowledged that was the focal point for the entire week—that I needed him, that I couldn't do it any longer by myself, that I had made a mess of my life and almost pushed all that was good out of my life. I stood there with the closing song playing, just praying. As the song ended, Captain Gilliam went to grab the microphone to announce the after-service meal, but the speaker got up and made a beeline to the microphone.

He said, "I get the feeling that God is telling me there is one more person in this room who is ready to give their life to Jesus Christ." I stood there like a statue, starting to get weak in the knees and breathing harder as everyone looked around. He said it again, "There is one more in this room." In that moment, those seconds that seemed to pass by ever so slowly, I was flooded with thoughts, memories, and events that I had experienced. Had my life been an accident? Was there some point to all this? I thought about those times in Catholic Church, the stories of valor and courage by the apostles that went across the crowd. While I sat there I was stirred and festered in frustration driving by a desire for more, driving me to places that I am not proud of but were very much a part of the journey. The dysfunctional and demonizing relationship I shared with Maggie had been built from deception and lies, but now a woman of great conviction and faith stood next to me who believed in me when I didn't. Why? Cliff sharing the Gospel with me in Del Rio in his truck after the most bizarre sequence of events; Janice encouraging and unconditionally loving a stranger in a workplace; Jessica accepting and pursuing me in the hopes of simply coming to church; Tabby's parents, Bruce and Kathryn, seeing something in me that I certainly never saw when I looked in the mirror; and, finally, praying Jesus, the portrait that I have looked at more than any other portrait; take away the Americanized aspects of this portrait and focusing on the meaning of the photo itself. Jesus on his knees, looking up to the sky, with his hands clasped together in prayer. The portrait I tried to outrun and hide from but was always confronted with when I walked into the dining room of my parents' home as a child and am still to this day. Praying Jesus was there when I was a child, reminding me, but I was too diluted with fear, anger, pride, and disgust for what I had allowed others to dictate about my faith. The posture of Jesus praying and looking to God—here I was, looking to God. Thinking about the decision I made on the way back from San Antonio to live. To start the journey of uncovering who I was made to be, my purpose versus what I had allowed others to inflict on me as my identity. Everything had failed. Nothing I had put faith into lasted, and the foundations I attempted to build on top of—more and more rubble and sand was failing. In that moment, standing with the weight of my body being held up by my hand braced on the pew in front of me, I didn't hear or see anything. I felt an overwhelming emotion. I was feeling relief, emotional bliss. It was as if everything that had crashed around me for so many years in my failed or halfhearted attempts to build my purpose or be accepted was wiped away. A quiet realization swept over me.

I needed God. I needed to know Jesus Christ. My hand rose, shaking and seemingly weighed down by some unseen pressure. My eyes were still staring at the floor, not realizing what I was just agreeing to. As the speaker said, "Amen," he asked several questions and said a prayer that I repeated, which I can't remember to this day because of the emotionally charged moment. The feeling was overwhelming. I fell to the pew, sitting there with my hands on my face in tears, realizing that God had been reaching out to me my whole life. I just hadn't been listening. Starting with my father's making a decision to stop his addiction, with my mother to support and weather the marriage as a protective lion charging at anything that would come to hurt her children or her marriage. With the praying Jesus portrait that hung in our home, that many would have overlooked as Catholic rhetoric or hocus-pocus religion. Then the handful of people who had been placed in my path, giving me words of wisdom. In those moments alone, sobbing, praying in some drunken state, attempting to beg my way into faith and into a relationship, God was there. He was there all the time. I was flooded with emotions—some sad, some happy. Parts of me felt as if I had missed so much and hurt so many, and for the sake of what? Nothing but the pure evil that rests in all of us, which is confirmed by the Holy Spirit. Happy, because for once in my life, I felt I had a purpose, that I was a part of something bigger than just my small, meaningless life. My life had importance. Jesus Christ, the Holy Spirit, had been working in me for a long time, even in the most depraved moments. As I looked at Tabby, she had a look of utter shock and amazement but covered with a confirming smile that only Tabby could offer. Even to this day, if I look in a crowded room and see her, even if we are not by each other's side, I look for that face—the face of the woman whom God literally placed right in my path as she tripped on that ottoman into my lap when we first met. As I stood to my feet and looked around, the moment was surreal. As people started to exit the church into the fellowship hall for dinner, a few stood around wanting to congratulate me. They hugged me. Captain Gilliam peered at me from across the room with a smile of pure joy. Jessica hugged me, but it wasn't one of those hugs that was overwhelming. It was more like a "you finally figured it out" hug. Tabby and I embraced each other, and like the old cartoon movie *The Grinch*, I felt my heart grow that day. In February 2005 I accepted Jesus Christ as my Lord and Savior.

One of my favorite men in the Bible is Nehemiah. His claim to glory is rebuilding the walls of Jerusalem. After being deeply moved and rocked by God to go on this journey to rebuild Jerusalem's walls, he did something that many of us bypass when faced with difficult situations—assess the damage. He took time to walk around the walls and survey the damage, taking note that the city had been vastly beaten and distorted. The fountain gate where the city received fresh water had been destroyed in such a way that he couldn't even get there and had to turn around. The city's waste was kept outside the dung gate, which was exactly what you would imagine with a word like "dung." That gate was destroyed, and the city was exposed to the trash and waste. After his assessment, Nehemiah simply said, "Let's start rebuilding!" This is where I stood, assessing the damage and attempting to figure out what had been destroyed and beaten. The bruises and lacerations of a life lived without God had to be rebuilt, but without knowing exactly what those areas were, it would take time. There were surface-level issues like the alcohol and drugs, but those are just by-products of deeper issues. To this day, I haven't picked up a drink or ingested any type of drug. I wish I could say the same for the pornography addiction, but I held onto that addiction for several more years after making the choice to radically change my life. Yes, this may seem contradictory, but remember, this is a journey. It is important to recognize that it is everyone's choice to enter into a journey and how far they go with it. For me, I would battle those same emotional battles as I did before I accepted Jesus Christ, but what was different? Instead of me pouring into myself, I would look to God in the Bible, through prayer, debating, arguing or just talking. I begin to reach out to people of faith whose actions matched their words and convictions. To this day, as my faith matures, I seek out those who are more mature to disciple, mentor and train me.

That day in Del Rio was a special day in my journey with God. This was the moment God stepped in and directed me and put me in front of his willing disciple to share the Gospel of Jesus Christ with me. Without Del Rio, I am not sure where I would be. Without Tabby, I am not sure where I would be. Without the grounding of basic truths of life from parents who valued hard work and commitment, I am not sure if I would be sitting here with over 14 years of marriage under my belt and a beautiful family built from adoption. I am able to testify that since that day at the Salvation Army, our marriage has been increasingly better year after year. Have we had issues? Yes. But the real reward is to bring God into those issues and welcome his convictions to help us curb our selfishness in such a way that we are pursuing each other over self. The bottom line is that everyone is on a journey. Even if you didn't grow up with any recognition of Jesus Christ or God, or the very mention of the Holy Spirit causes all kinds of weird feelings, you're on the journey. Even if you grew up with a religion shoved down your throat to the point that you get nauseated at the mention of church or God, or if you are late in life to know that there is a God, you are on a journey—your journey. Everyone's journey looks different because God has specific purposes for your life. He is always refining us like silver. A couple of years ago, I hit rock bottom again. I had held on to a secret pornography addiction that I was reverting to and using as the drug that it is, to medicate myself from those same feelings I had before I rose my hand in that Salvation Army church.

Why? Why was I battling and struggling with this luring drug of pornography while confessing a relationship with God? Why was I a failure deep down? The truth is that if struggling with something personal that you have been convicted about, whether a drug addiction, pornography, financial irresponsibility, self-image issues, sexually identity— the lie is that you are a failure. The truth is that we are a work in progress, and God desires a relationship with us, not a mandate to follow. A relationship takes time to form, trust has to be built, love has to evolve, and we have to be refined. We are always being refined and molded regardless of whether we want to admit it, disbelieve in God, or simply think that we are going our own way. The Holy Spirit will always trump the lies spoken over us each day and slowly eradicate our selfish desires that pull us away from God. I am a walking evidence of Zechariah 13:9 (KJB): "And I will bring the third part through the fire, and will refine them as silver is refined, and will try them as gold is tried: they shall call on my name, and I will hear them: I will say, It is my people: and they shall say, the Lord is my God."

The journey is about walking with Jesus just as the disciples did. I don't have blind faith; I have extraordinary faith. My faith is built on confidence and a progression to walk in relationship with Jesus and attempting every day to be obedient to His word. I accepted the free grace that is offered to each one of us to be sufficient in him because I know that his power is perfected in weakness. "Therefore, I will most gladly boast all the more about my weaknesses, so that Christ's power may reside in me" (2 Corinthians 12:9, HCSB). What does this look like, really look like—boasting in my weaknesses so that Christ's power can reside in me? It sounds like the talk of a lunatic or someone delusional, right? Someone who has lost all hope or come to the end of themselves? That's exactly what it is. The diminishing selfish desires being replaced with Christ's call for a relationship and his desires for you and the people around you.

God is taking each individual on a journey. Each person has different hurts, pains, brokenness and experiences that dictate that journey, but regardless of what this world has thrown at the person or inflicted on them, a relationship is still being formed. For me, this looks like a scene from Genesis 50 (HCSB) when Joseph looks at his brothers who sold him into slavery, ultimately leading to one hardship after another and directly setting him up for his God-given purpose. As he stood looking at his brothers, he tells them, "As for you, you meant evil against me, but God meant it for good in order to bring about this present result." God has shown me an abundance of grace in my weaknesses. He has allowed me to use my weaknesses and testimony to further his Kingdom. What does "using my weaknesses and testimony" look like practically? Let's refer back to two men of the Bible briefly for some insight. The Apostle Paul and Joseph of the book of Genesis had dealt with some intensely difficult situations. Each of their situations, while unique and incredibly challenging in itself, empowered them to be great leaders by being open, transparent, and obedient to God's two greatest commandments: "Love the Lord your God. ... Love your neighbor as yourself" (Mark 12:30–31 (NIV)). For me, practically, this meant to love God and find ways to love others. My wife and I were leading a biblically based *gathering* out of our home for young adults and teenagers in a small town outside Waco a few years back. Most of the teens and young adults were from some type of broken home or just couldn't find acceptance in a local traditional church. My wife worked at a high school and got to know a lot of the kids, which grew into her building trust and, before long, knowing all the issues going on. One particular day we were thrust into this unseen ministry because of a teenage couple who had gotten pregnant and needed help. My wife and I were placed into the teenagers' lives, and the rest is history. Over a five-year period, over fifty teenagers spent time in our home or around us in some capacity while we unapologetically presented the Gospel as we provided meals at our home and went to sporting events, graduations, theater performances, and on camping trips. We also dealt with the pregnancies, abuses, illnesses, sexual orientations, addictions, tutoring through classes, the death of family members or classmates, arrest, and racism that these young people were experiencing and needed the love of God interjected into.

The bottom line is that you must learn to love yourself to love God; you must love God to truly love others. Obviously, all kinds of debates surround that statement, I am sure, but this is my experience, compiled with others' experiences. We currently have an organization with the focus of pornography and sexual stronghold awareness and recovery. This organization is called Hangover to Jesus (www.hangovertojesus.com). Our focus with Hangover to Jesus is to share hope, our story of continual restoration and the process of recovering from porn addiction. With God and through his unconditional love and grace, my wife and I were able to walk together through nine years of painful infertility. We sought God, and he laid adoption on our hearts instead of fertility treatments. We were led to domestic infant adoption and called to have an open relationship with our son's birth mother and grandmother. We are a transracial family, and have the most loving and beautiful, open relationship with them. We adopted our second child, a daughter, and have the same open relationship with her birth mother and birth father, experiencing a similar beautiful, open relationship with her birth parents. I know that my journey, just as yours, is specially designed for you, no matter where you are today, no matter what you believe, and no matter what you have done or are doing. Bottom line: God loves you and wants to meet you where you are. He wants a relationship. That is where we find peace, unconditional love, and grace. That is where we experience the Holy Spirit—in a relationship.

Made in the USA
San Bernardino, CA
03 September 2019